THE THINKIN
10 SUBJECT P(

NAME:

ADDRESS:

AGE:

Grade Level:

Phone Number:

Date:

Table of Contents

4...... Science

66.... History

106... Geography and Travel

138... Mathematics

182... Business and Technology

216... Language Arts, Literature & Copywork

274... The Arts

310... Social Studies

352... Films and Tutorials

386... Home Economics

412... Projects

The Thinking Tree
Publishing Company

Sarah Janisse Brown

THE THINKING TREE
10 SUBJECT PORTFOLIO

PARENT & TEACHER INSTRUCTIONS:

This 10 Subject Edition includes interesting illustrations, maps and educational
coloring pages. Use the handbook with a variety of books and videos to learn more about each topic.

1. This Curriculum Handbook makes record keeping easy and stress free! It can be used for all ages but is designed for Upper Elementary & Middle School Students.
2. You can keep learning fun, while never missing a required subject.
3. Every book, project, game and video can be counted as schoolwork.
4. You can keep your homeschooler's learning journey all in one place.
5. This Portfolio gives your student freedom and structure to use a variety of learning tools and resources!
6. Your student can learn with library books, movies, online games, tutorials, formal classes, unit studies, life experience and textbooks.

The Student can use 2 to 5 pages each day. And should showcase all their best work in this Portfolio. Parents must ensure that the Portfolio is used for record keeping for all books, films, and programs used for research and educational purposes. The student will use a certain number of Informational books, films and tutorials on each subject from the internet, family bookshelf or local library.

This Portfolio can be used for Organized Unschooling, Fun-Schooling, Charlotte Mason, Delight Directed Learning, Eclectic Learning, Notebooking, Unit Studies, and Traditional Learning.

Photography of your child's projects can be added to the portfolio.

Science

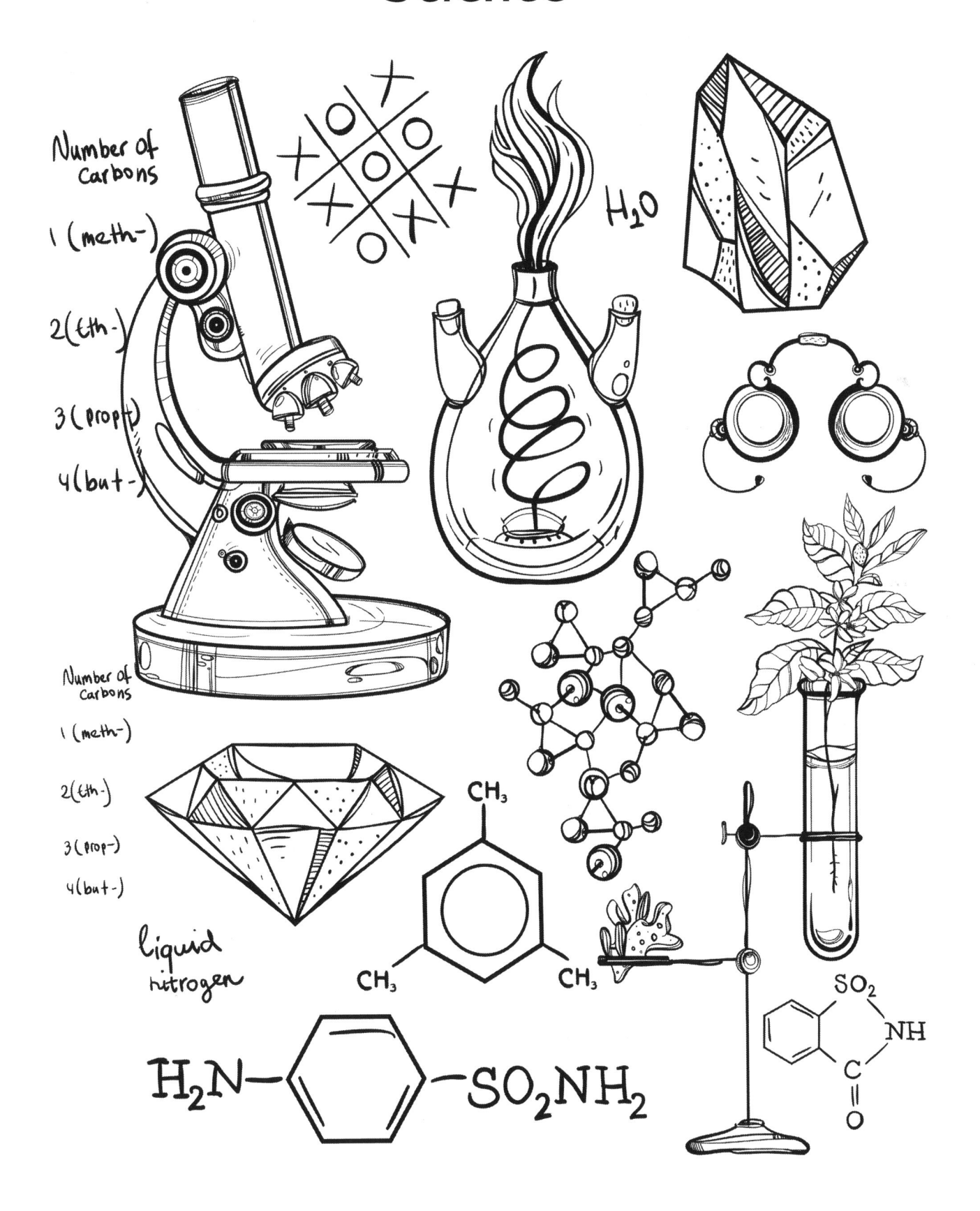

Number of Carbons

1 (meth-)

2 (eth-)

3 (prop-)

4 (but-)

H_2O

Number of Carbons

1 (meth-)

2 (eth-)

3 (prop-)

4 (but-)

liquid nitrogen

$H_2N--SO_2NH_2$

Science

What do you want to learn about science?

1.

2.

3.

4.

5.

Action Steps:

1. Go to the library or bookstore.

2. Bring home a stack of at least FOUR interesting books about science. Choose some that have diagrams, instructions and illustrations.

3. Plan to watch science tutorials and do your own research and experiments.

Supplies Needed:

You will need pencils, black drawing pens, colored pencils, gel pens and markers.

Projects and Experiment List:

Choose FOUR Books About Science
To Use As School Books!

1. Write down the titles on each cover below.
2. You may also choose Videos, Tutorials and Documenteries to help you learn about these topics.

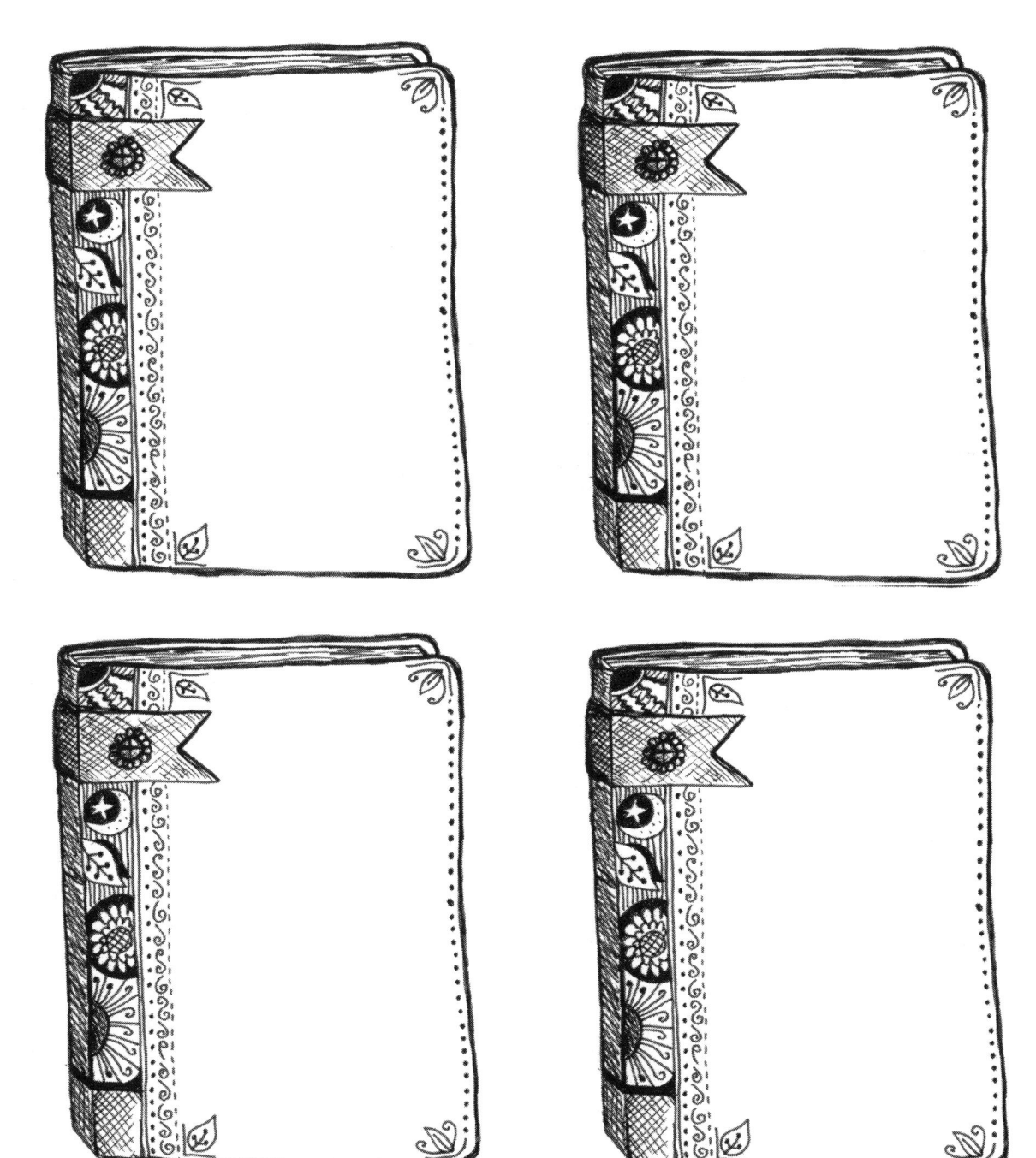

Projects, Observations & Experiments

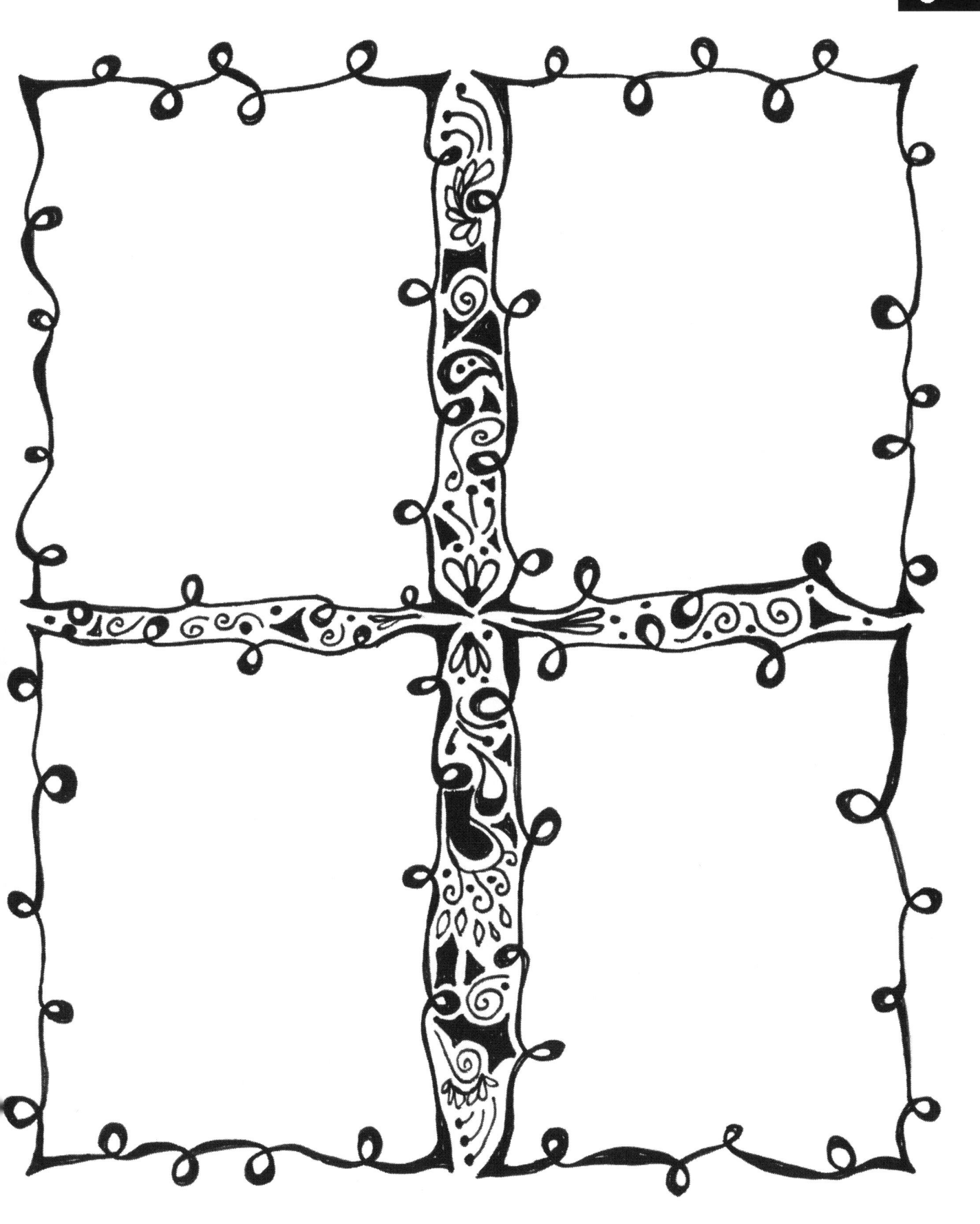

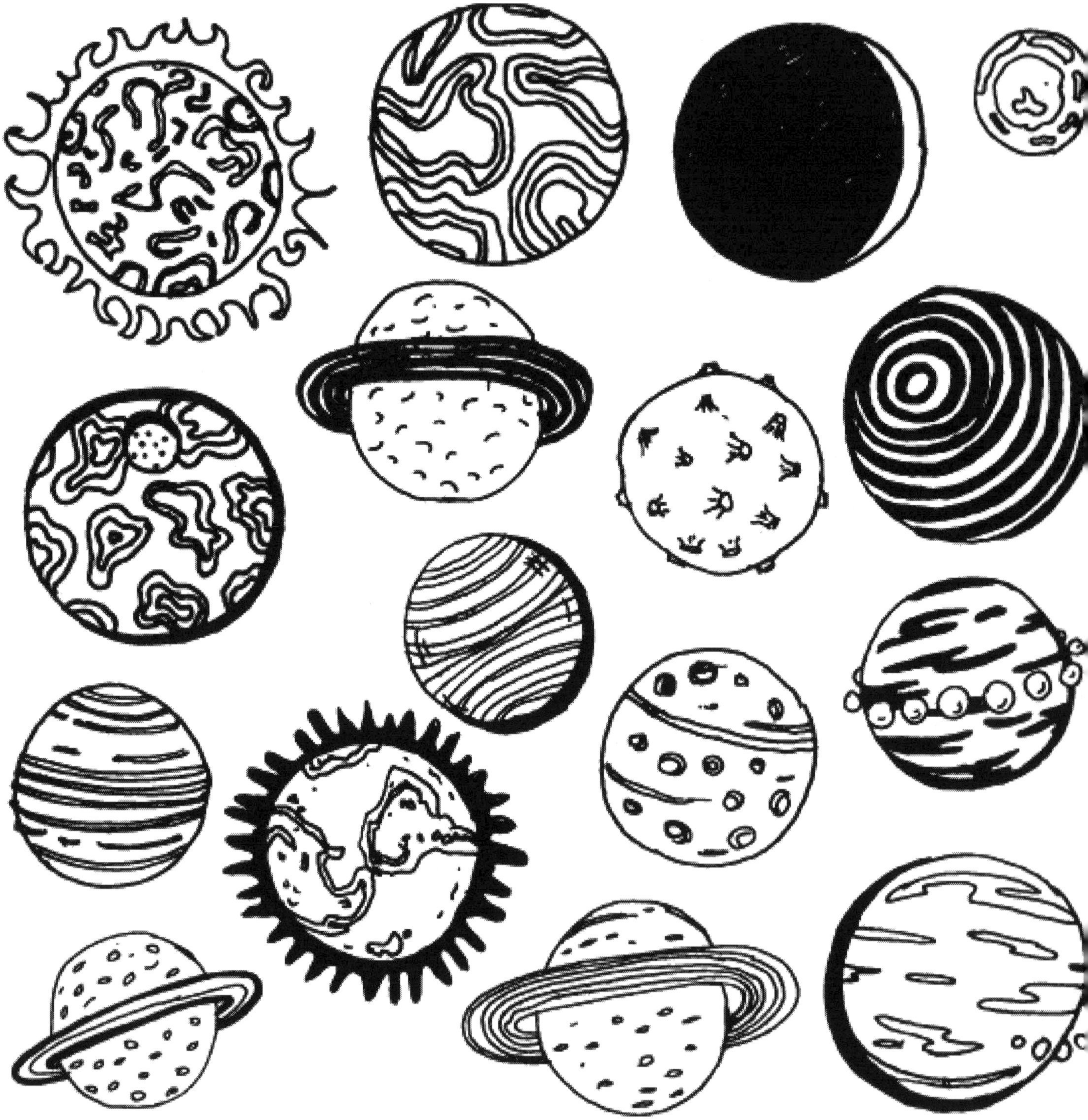

S

Projects, Observations & Experiments

Projects, Observations & Experiments

TOPIC:_____
DATE:_____TITLE:
_____

S

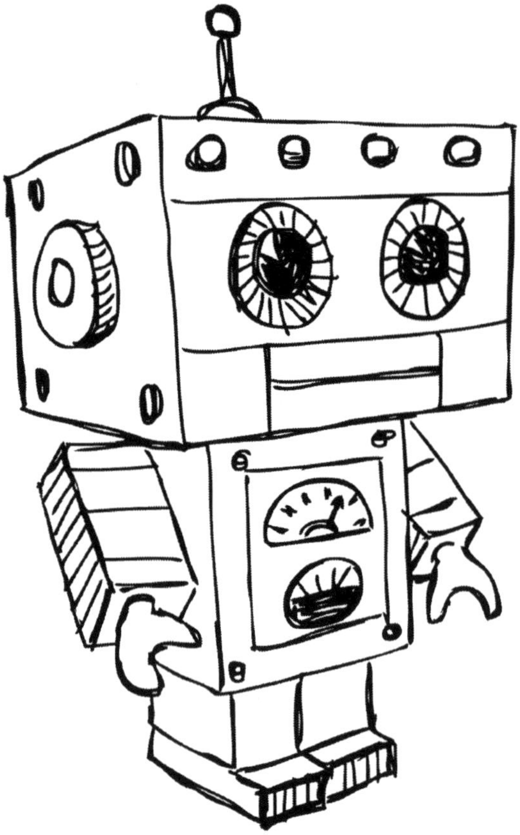
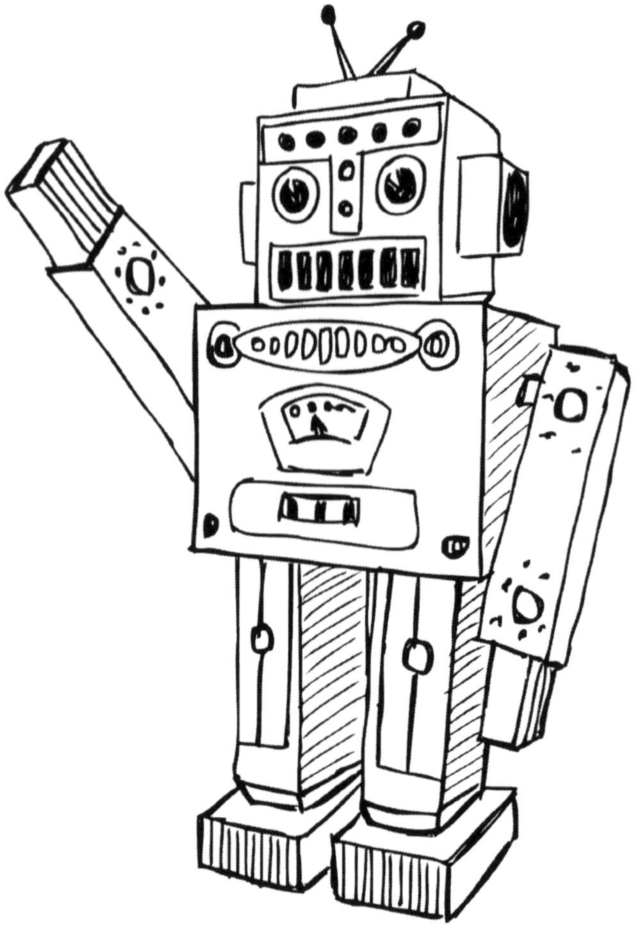
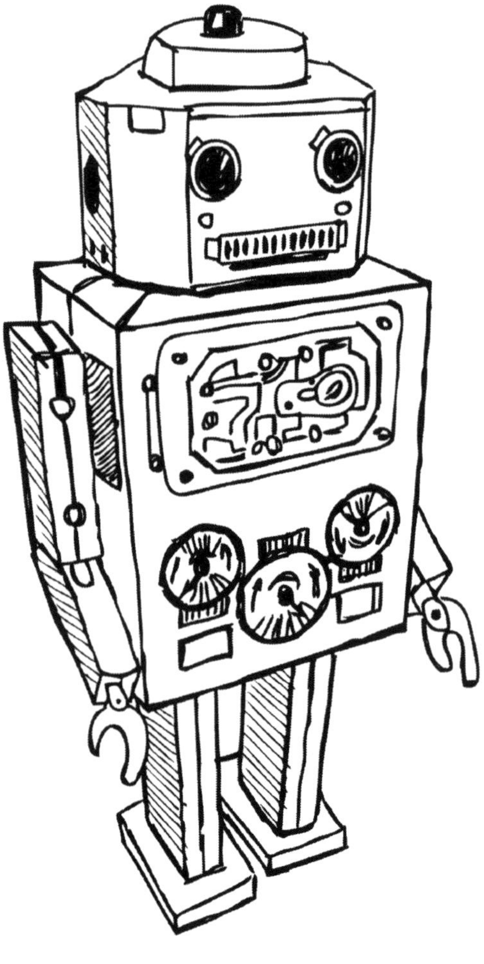
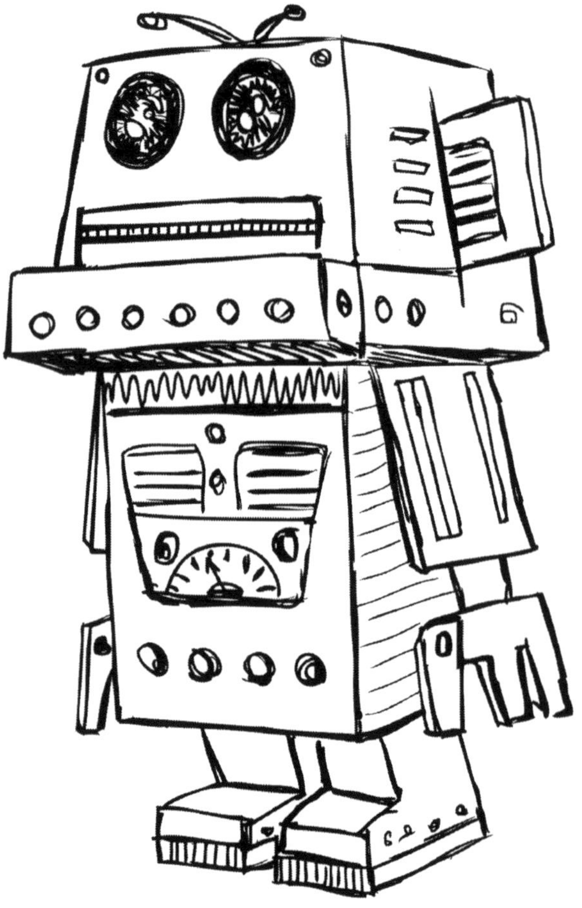

Projects, Observations & Experiments

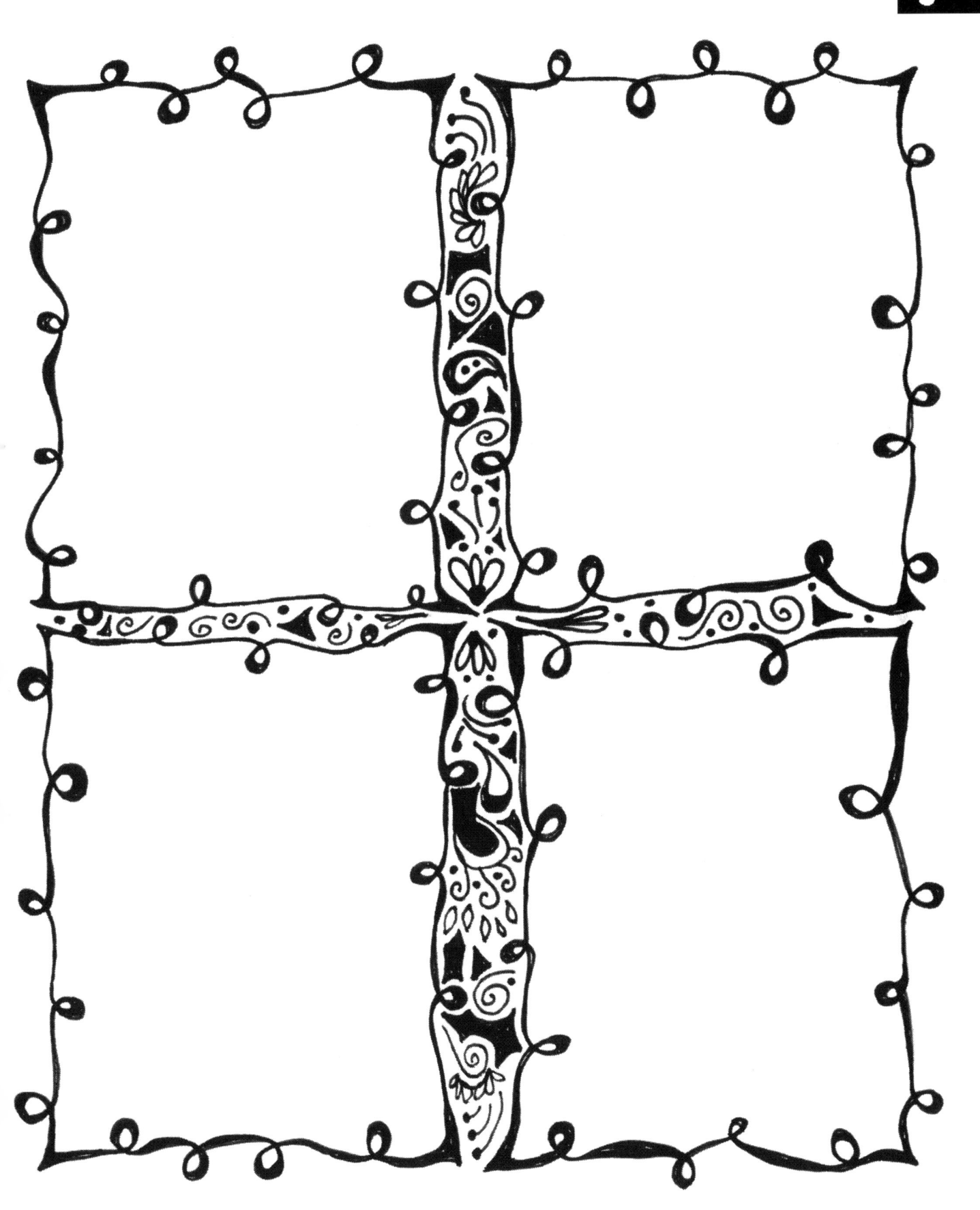

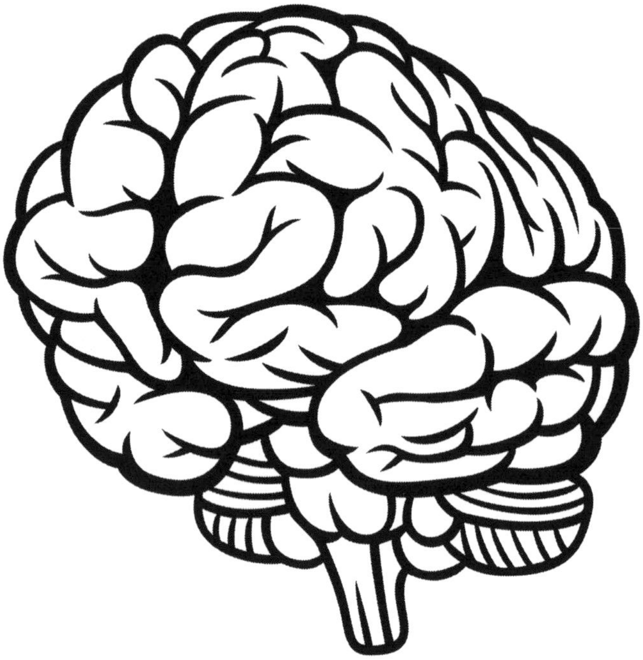
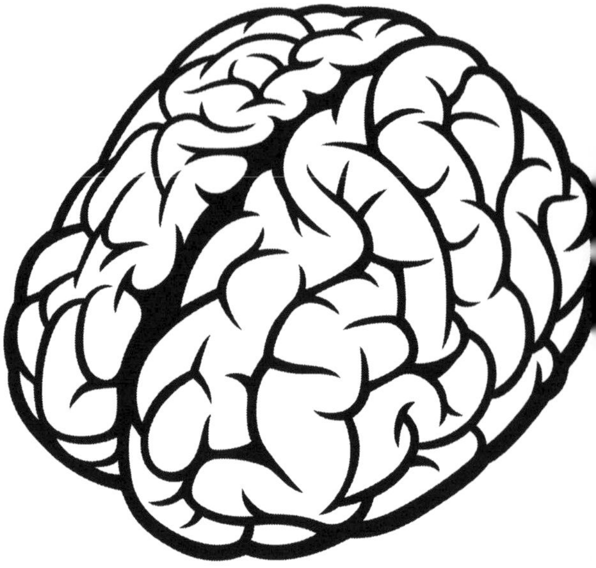
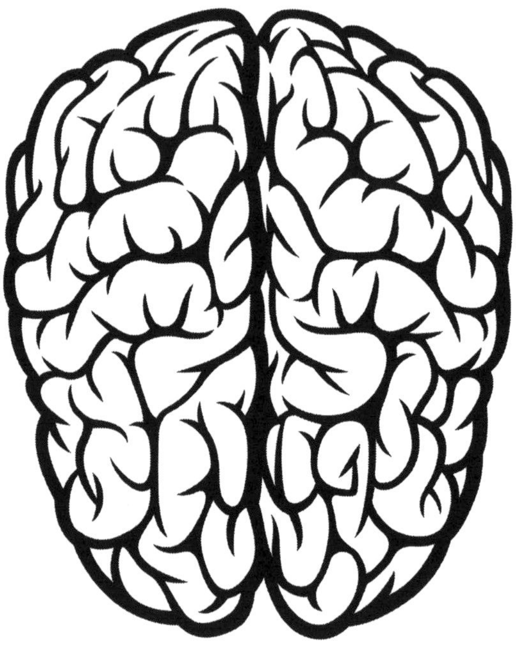
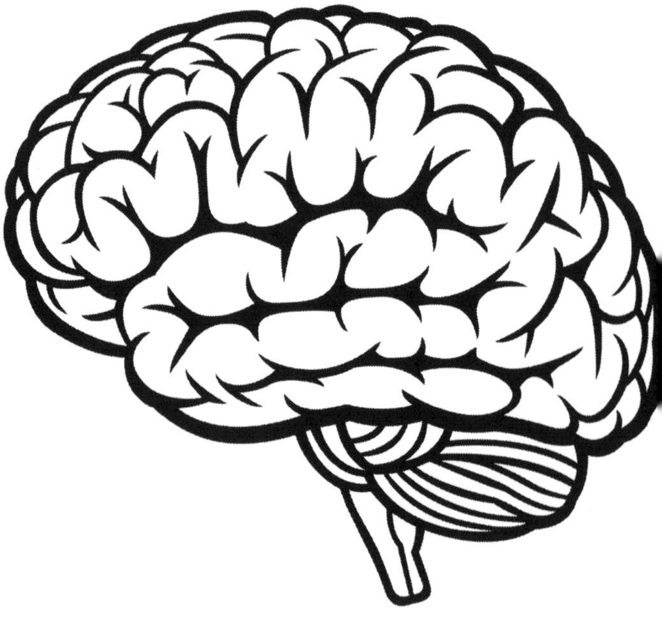

S

Projects, Observations & Experiments

S

Projects, Observations & Experiments

Projects, Observations & Experiments

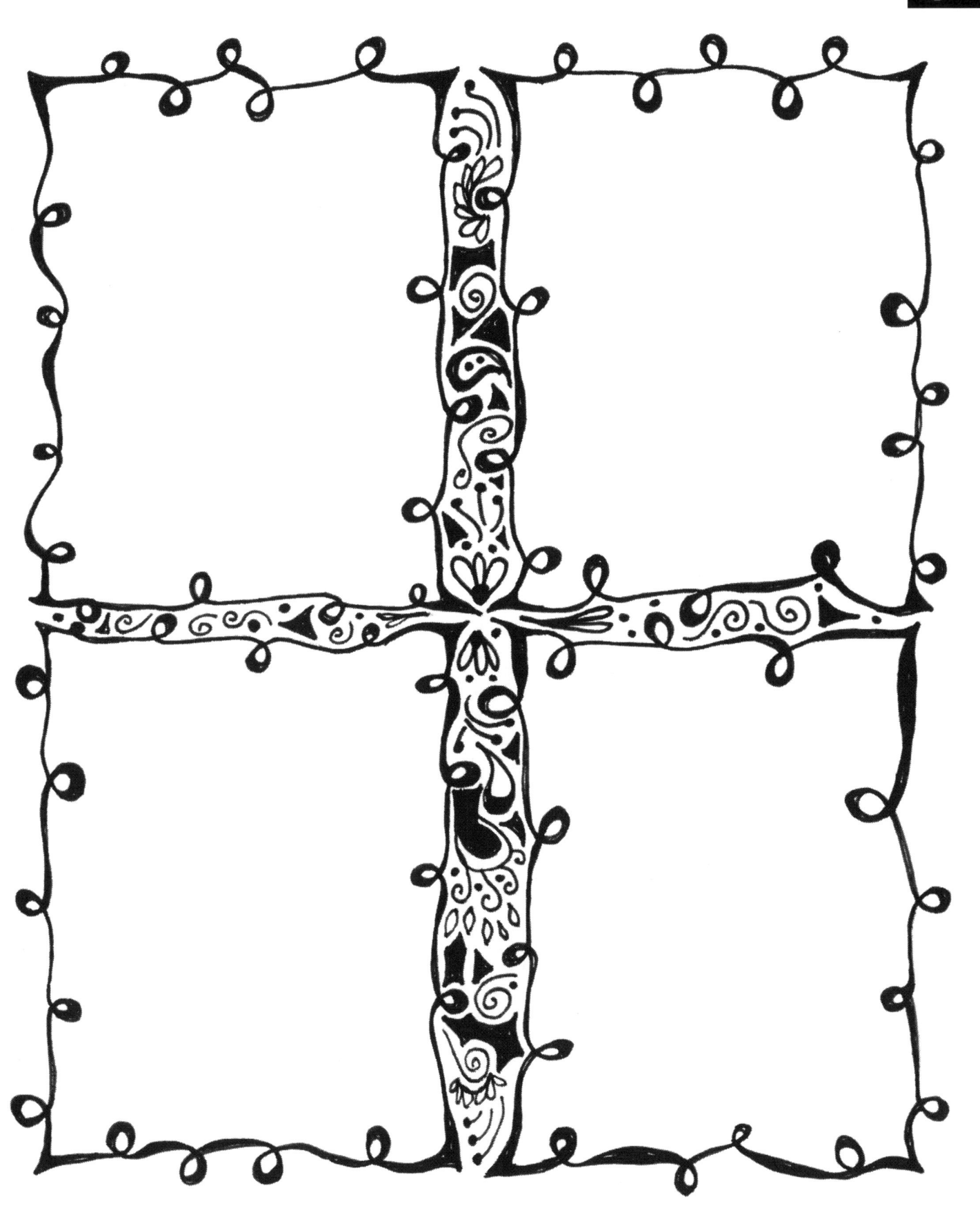

CHLORID

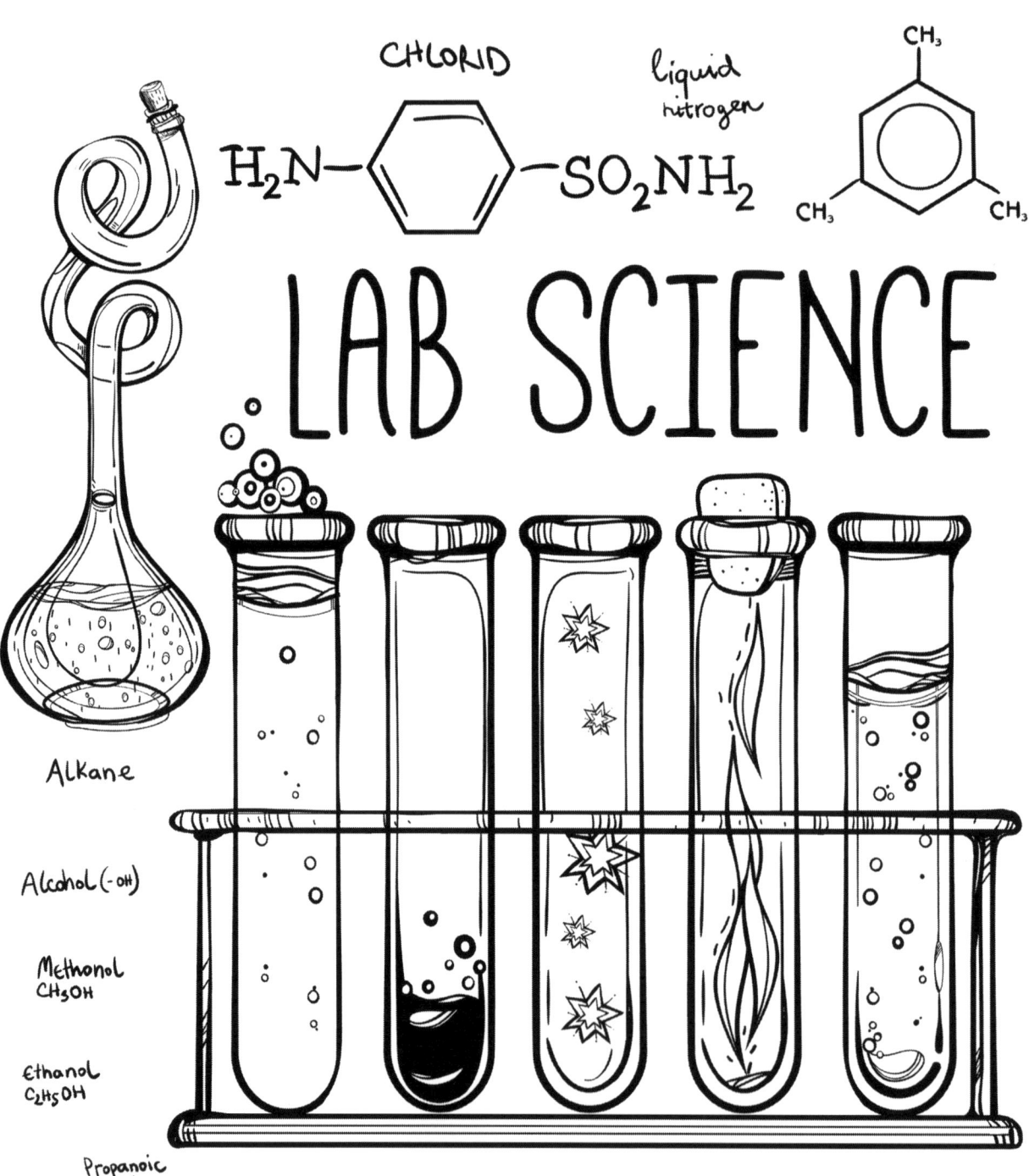

$H_2N-\text{[benzene]}-SO_2NH_2$

liquid nitrogen

CH_3 / CH_3 / CH_3 (trimethylbenzene)

LAB SCIENCE

Alkane

Alcohol (-OH)

Methanol CH_3OH

Ethanol C_2H_5OH

Propanoic Acid

S

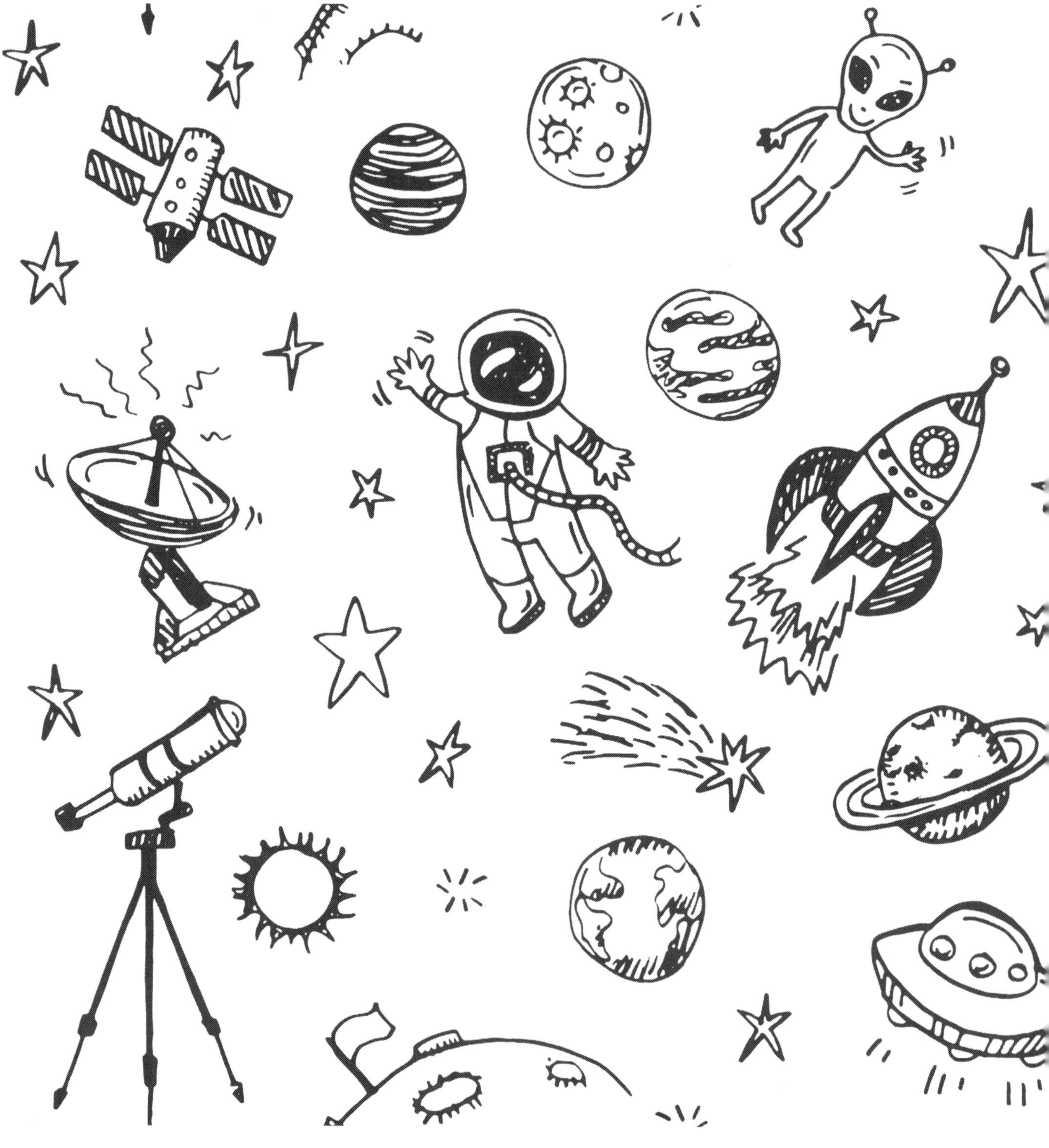

S

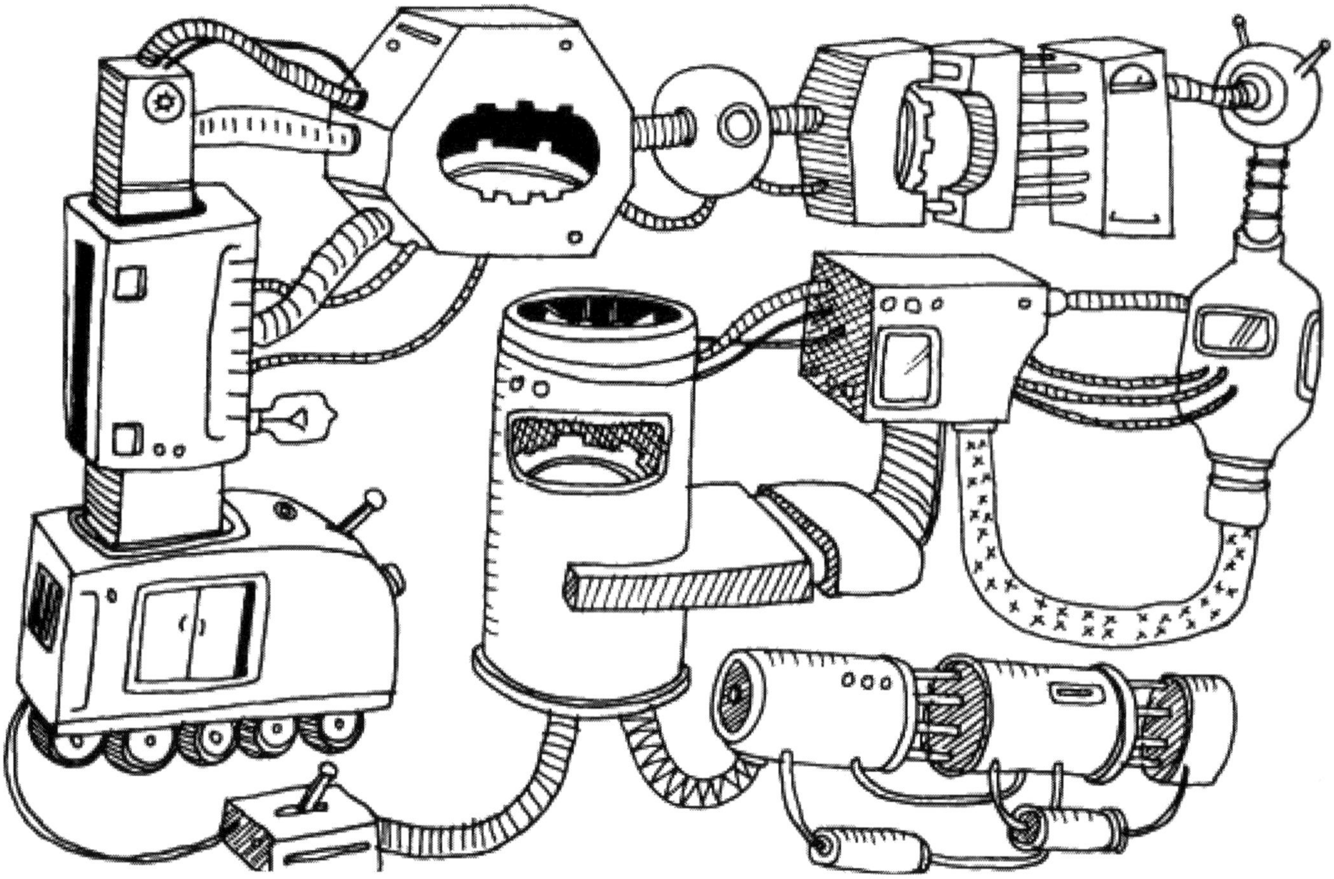

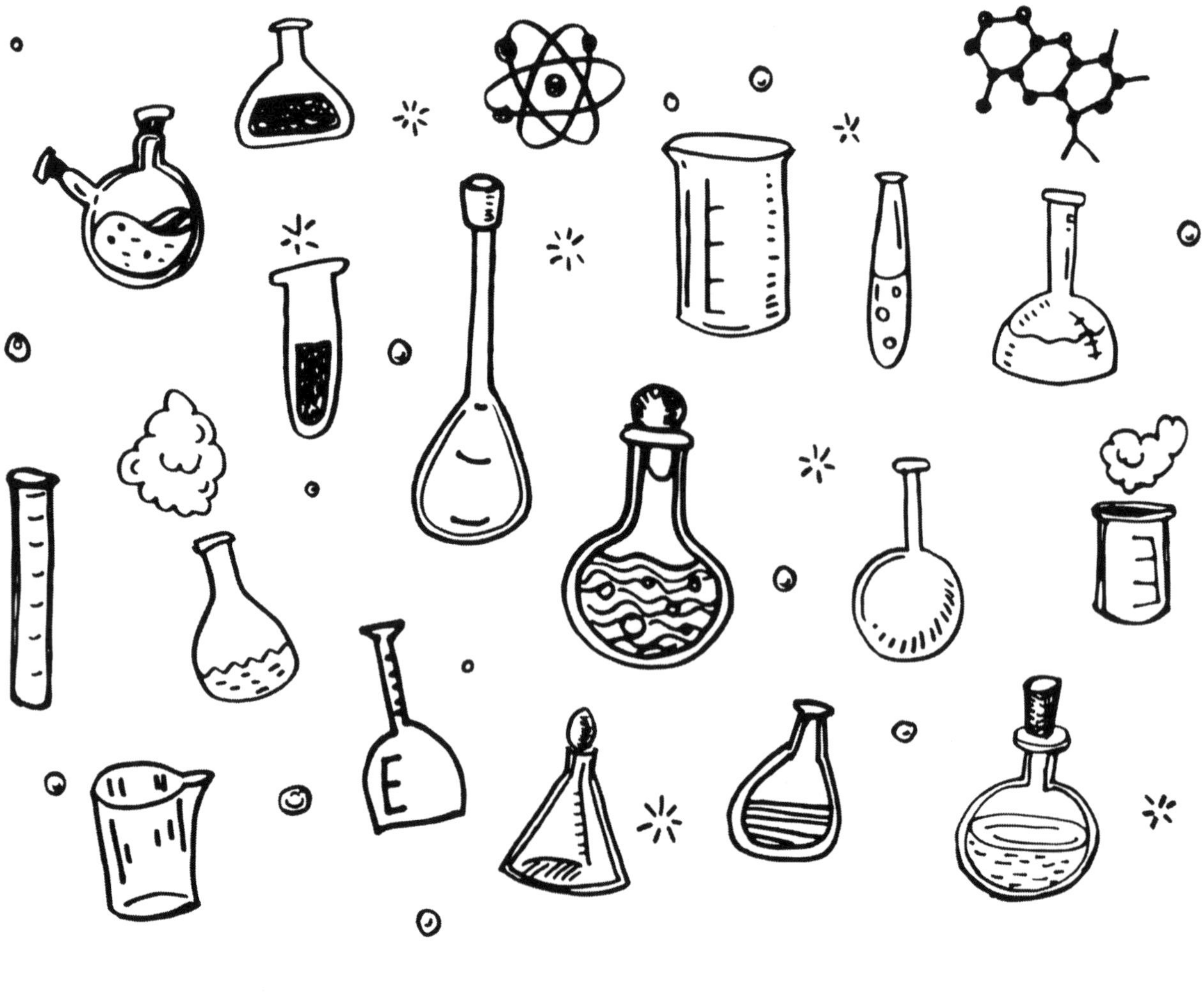

Projects, Observations & Experiments

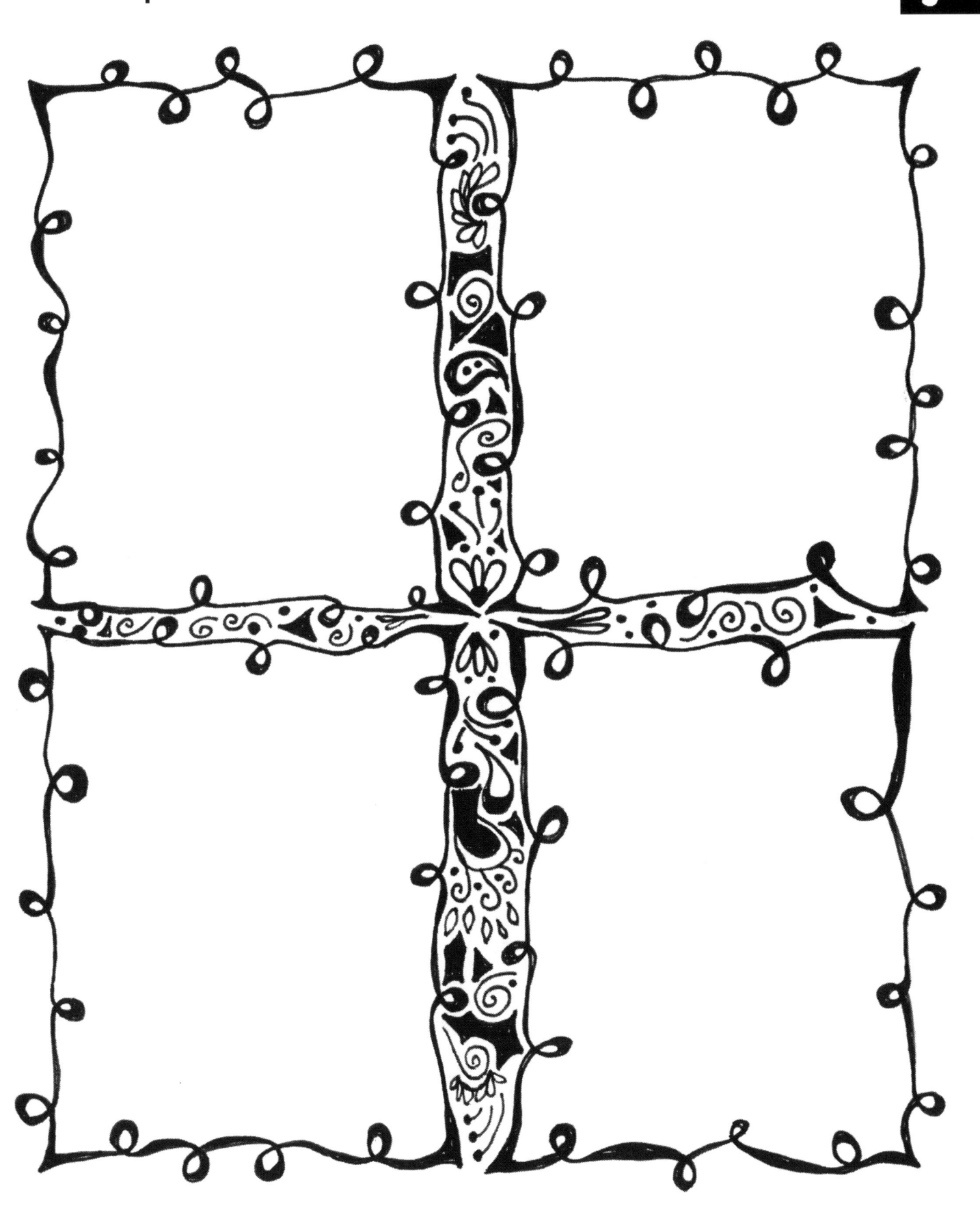

S

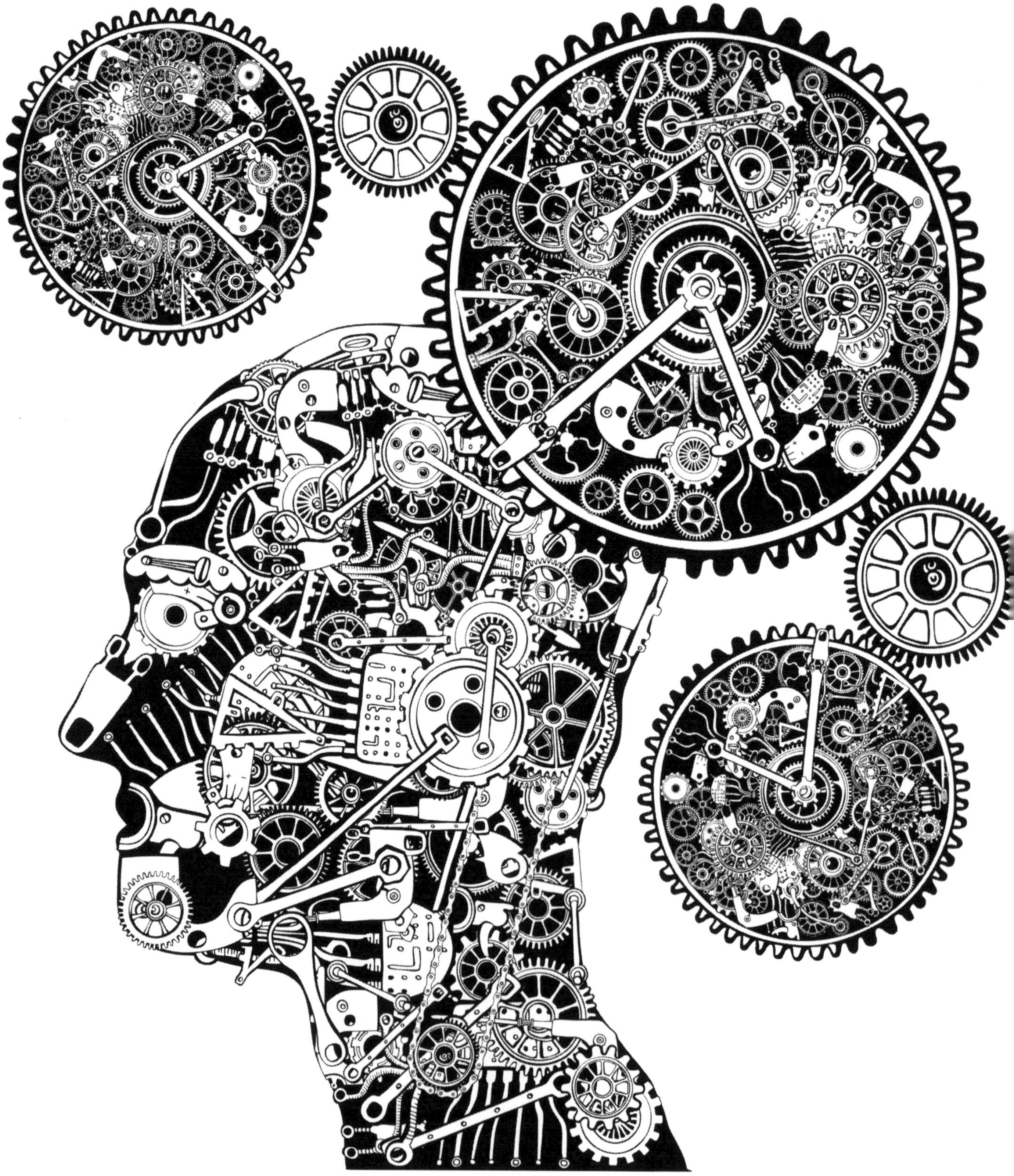

S

Projects, Observations & Experiments

Projects, Observations & Experiments

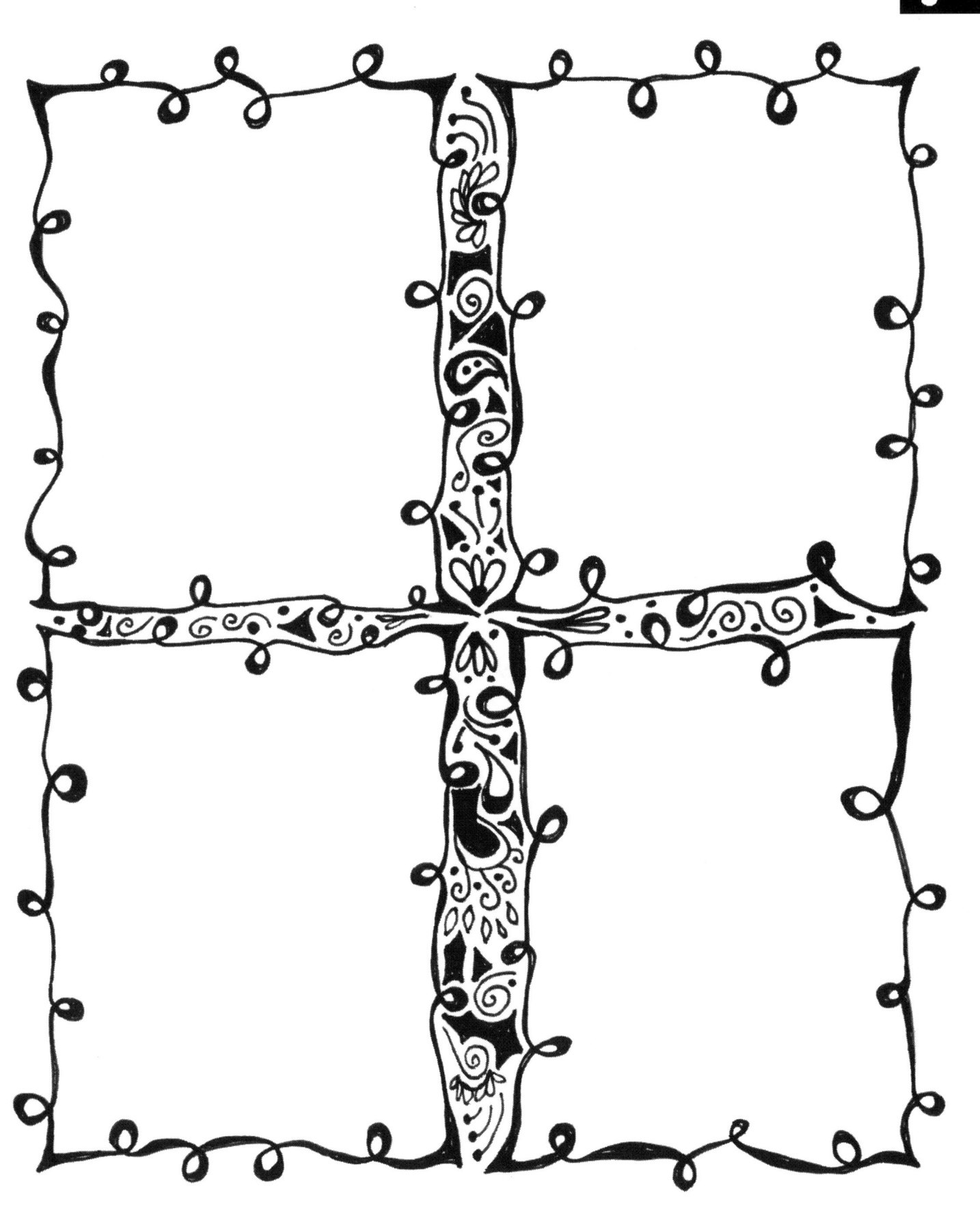

TOPIC:_____DATE:_____TITLE: _____

S

Projects, Observations & Experiments

Projects, Observations & Experiments

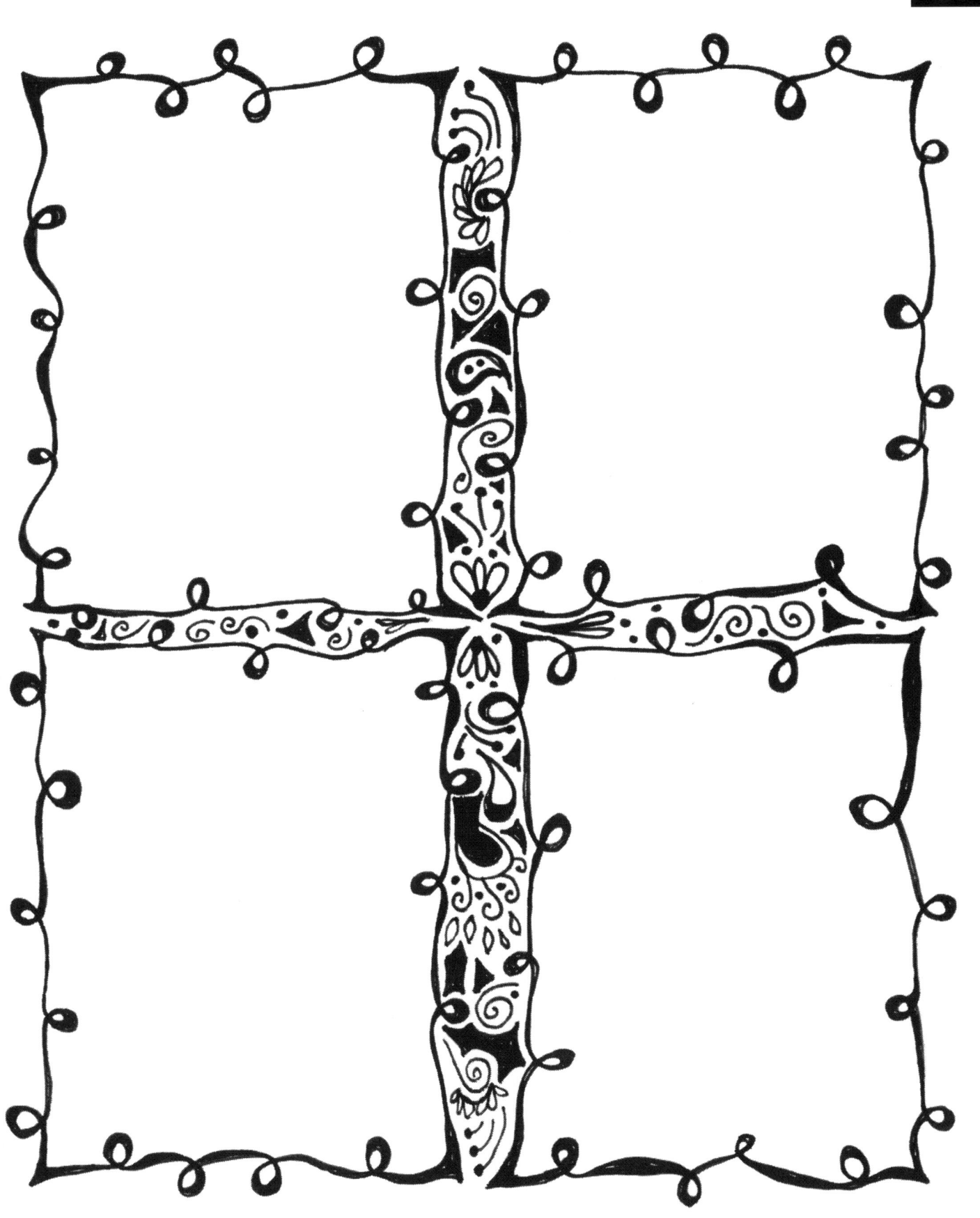

S

Projects, Observations & Experiments

Projects, Observations & Experiments

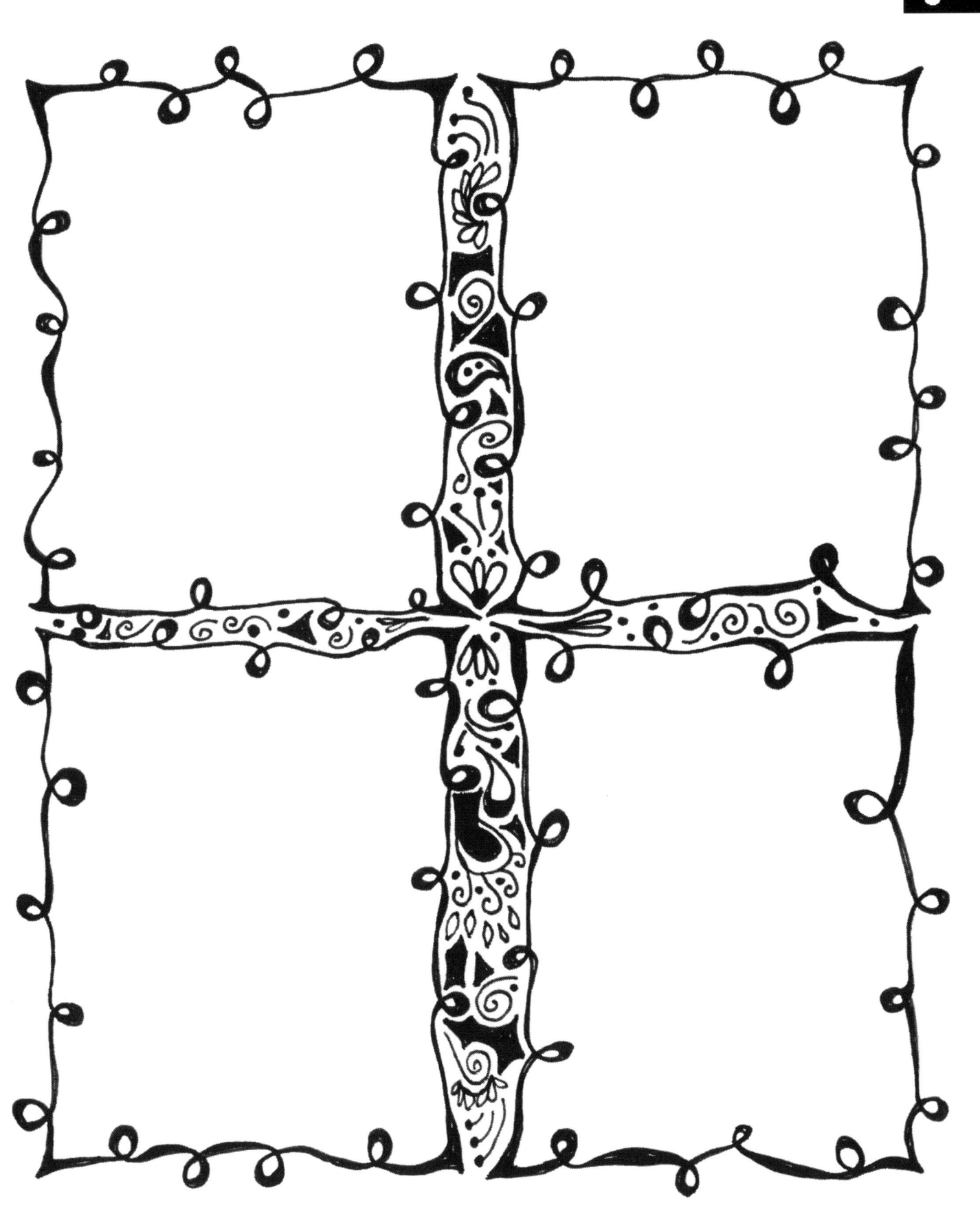

TOPIC:_____DATE:_____TITLE: _____

S

Projects, Observations & Experiments

Projects, Observations & Experiments

S

TOPIC:_____DATE:_____TITLE: _____

S

H₂O   E=mc²

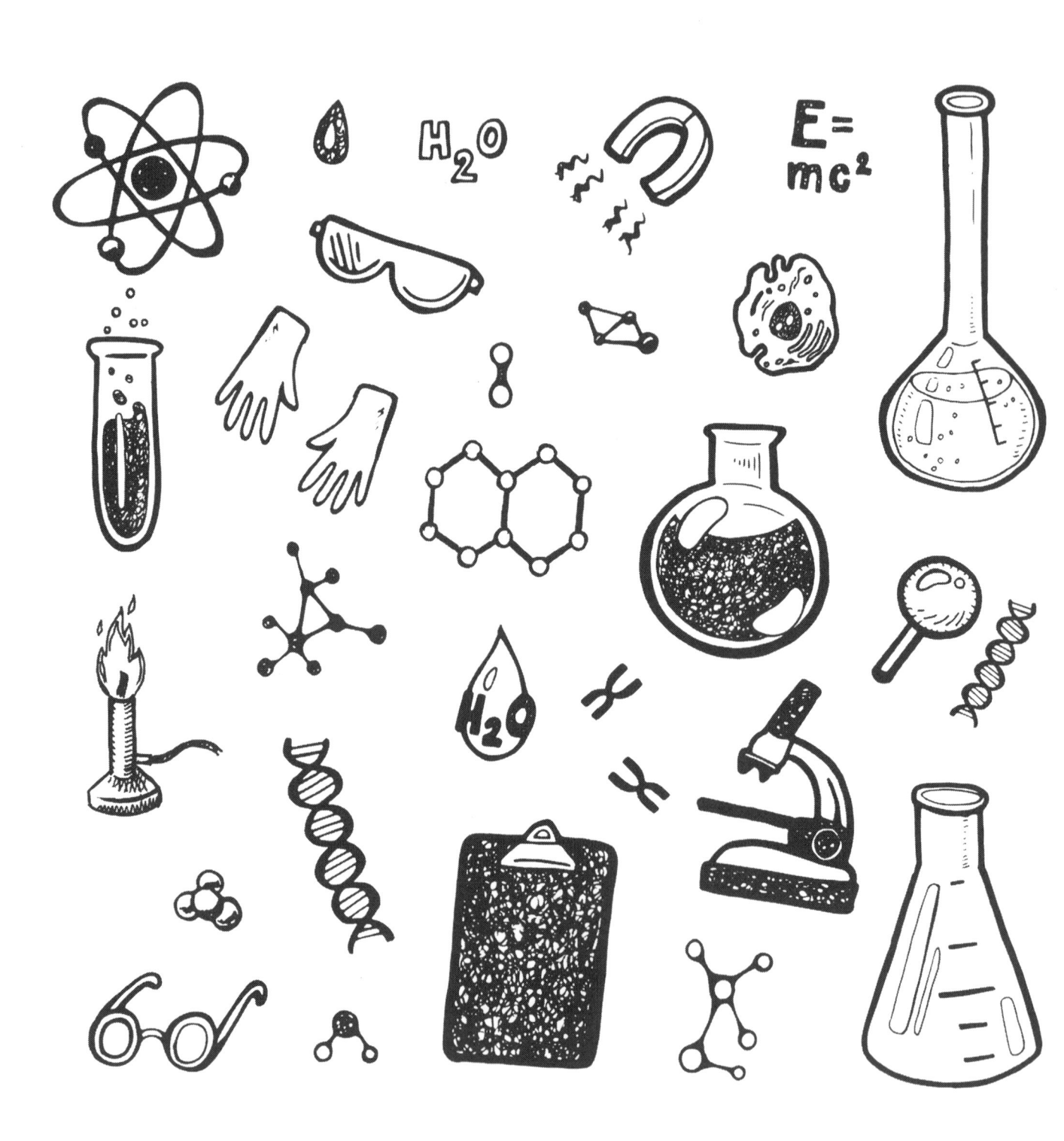

Projects, Observations & Experiments

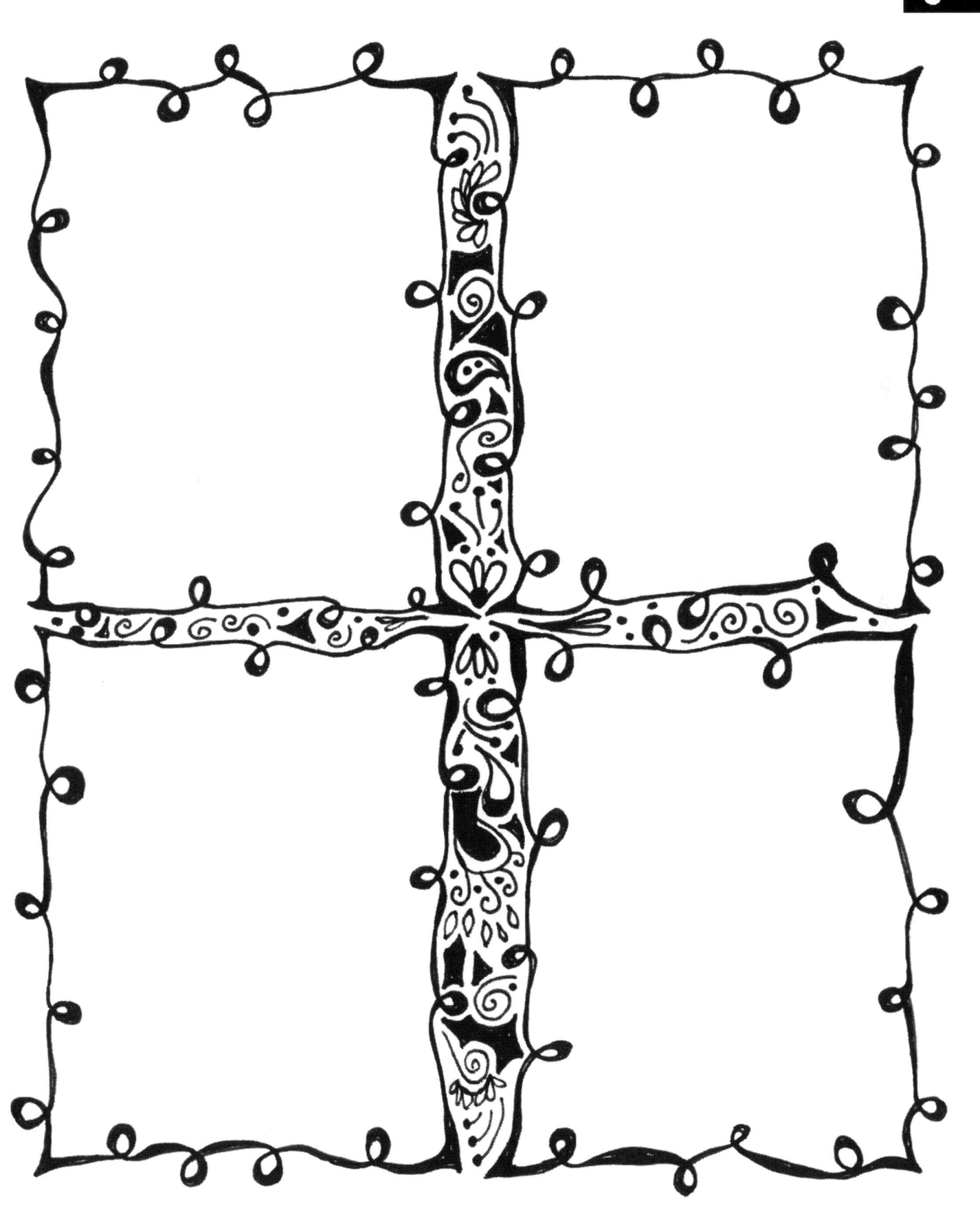

TOPIC:_____DATE:_____TITLE:_____

S

Projects, Observations & Experiments

Projects, Observations & Experiments

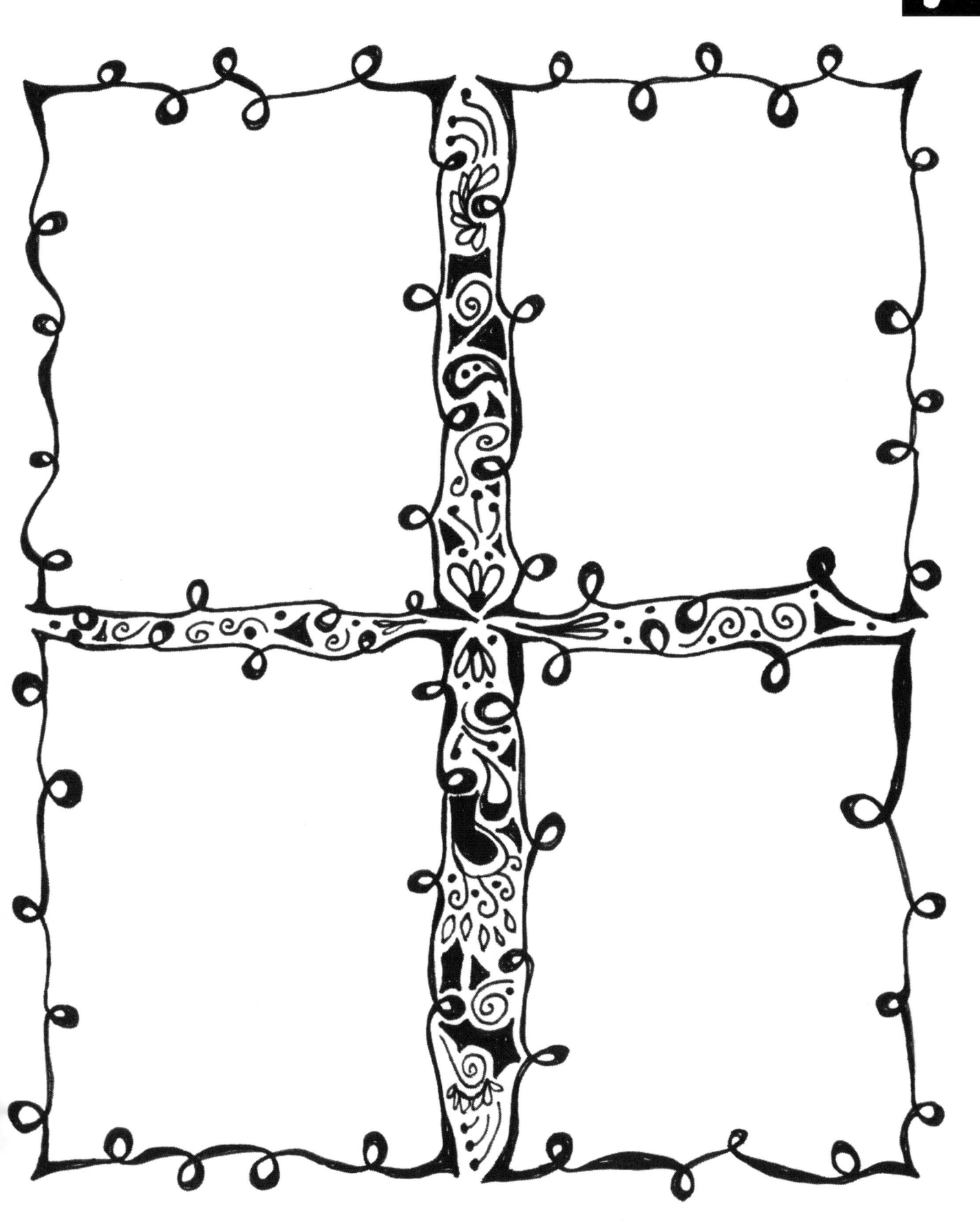

S

TOPIC:_____DATE:_____TITLE:_____

S

Projects, Observations & Experiments

Projects, Observations & Experiments

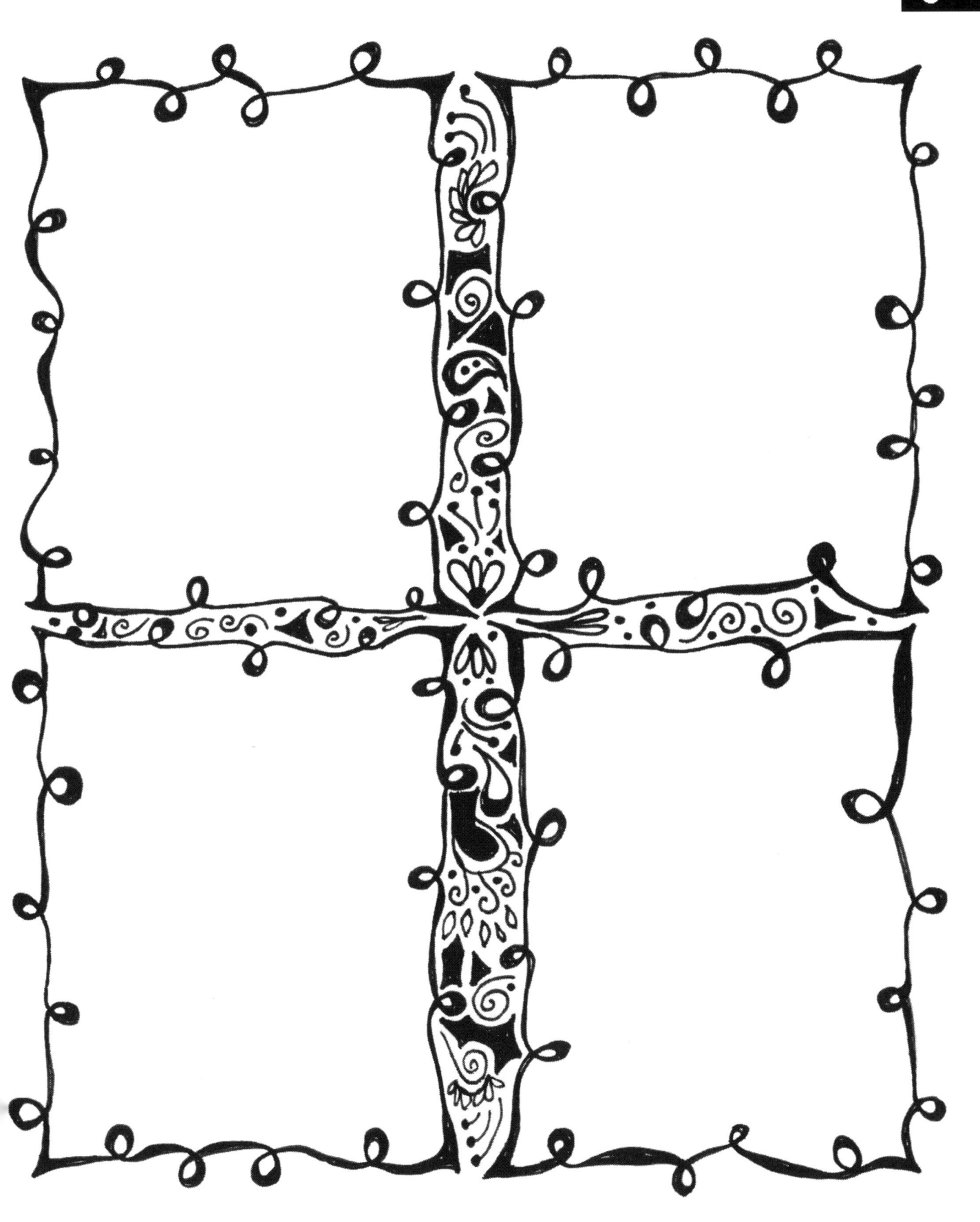

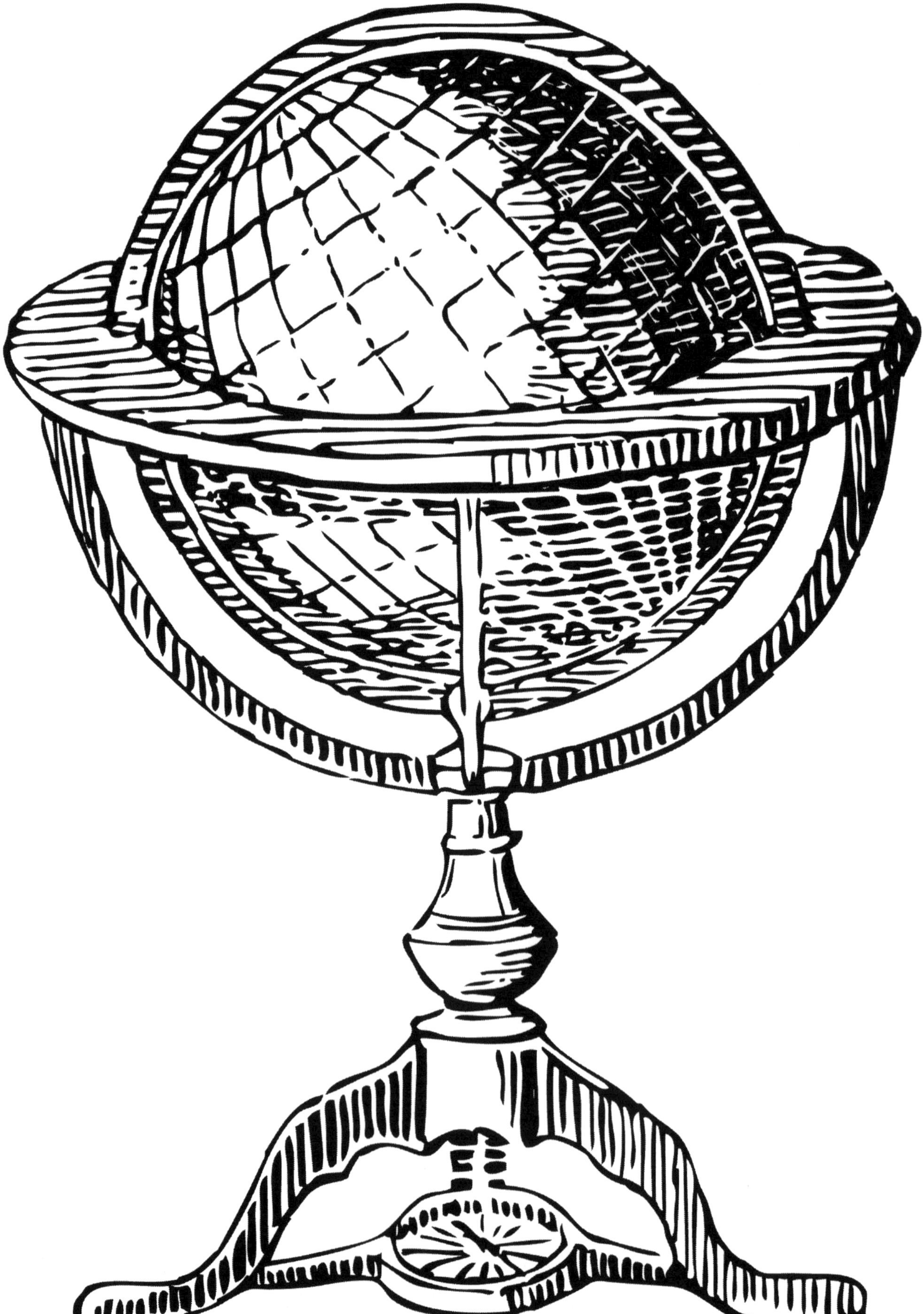

S

Projects, Observations & Experiments

Projects, Observations & Experiments

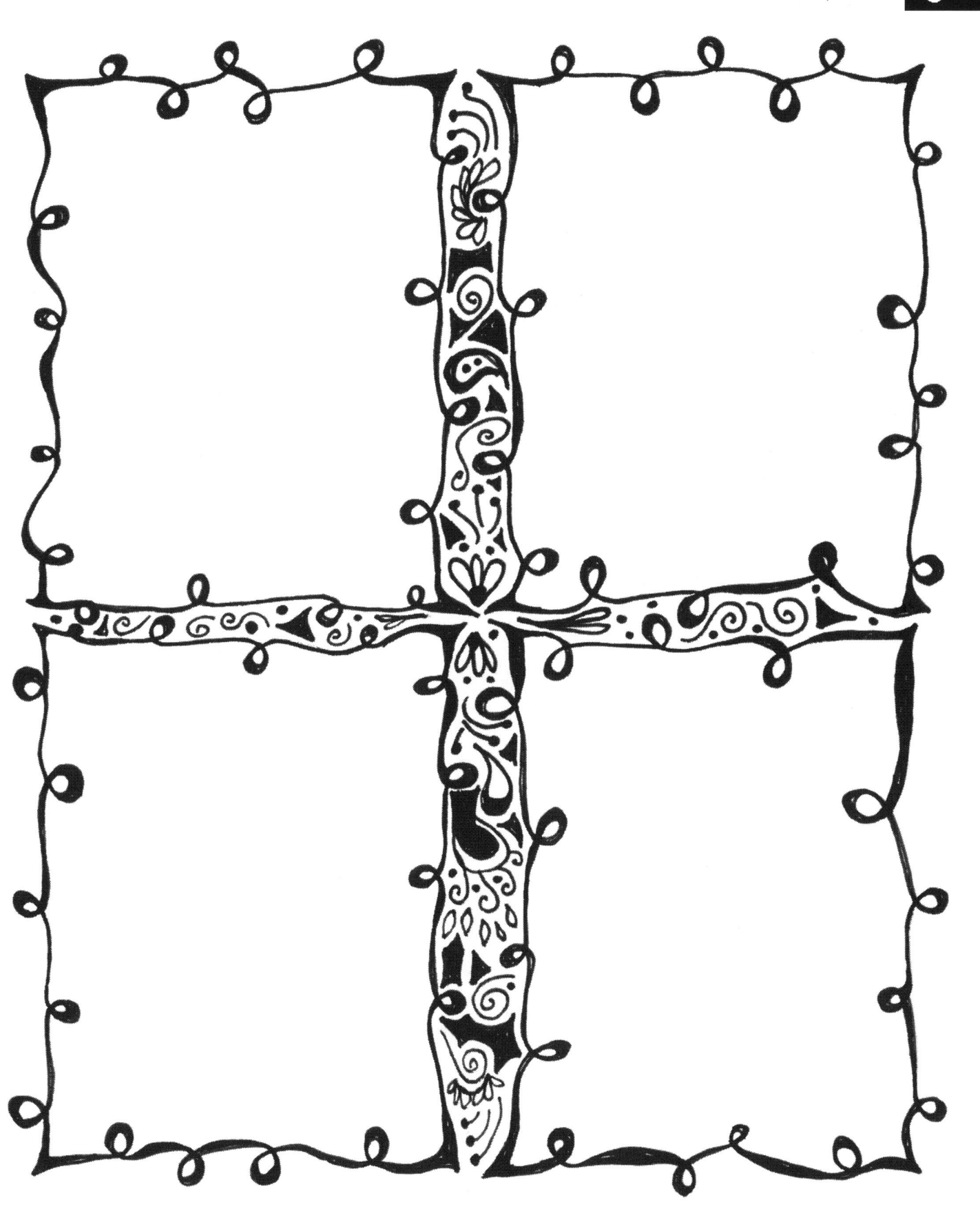

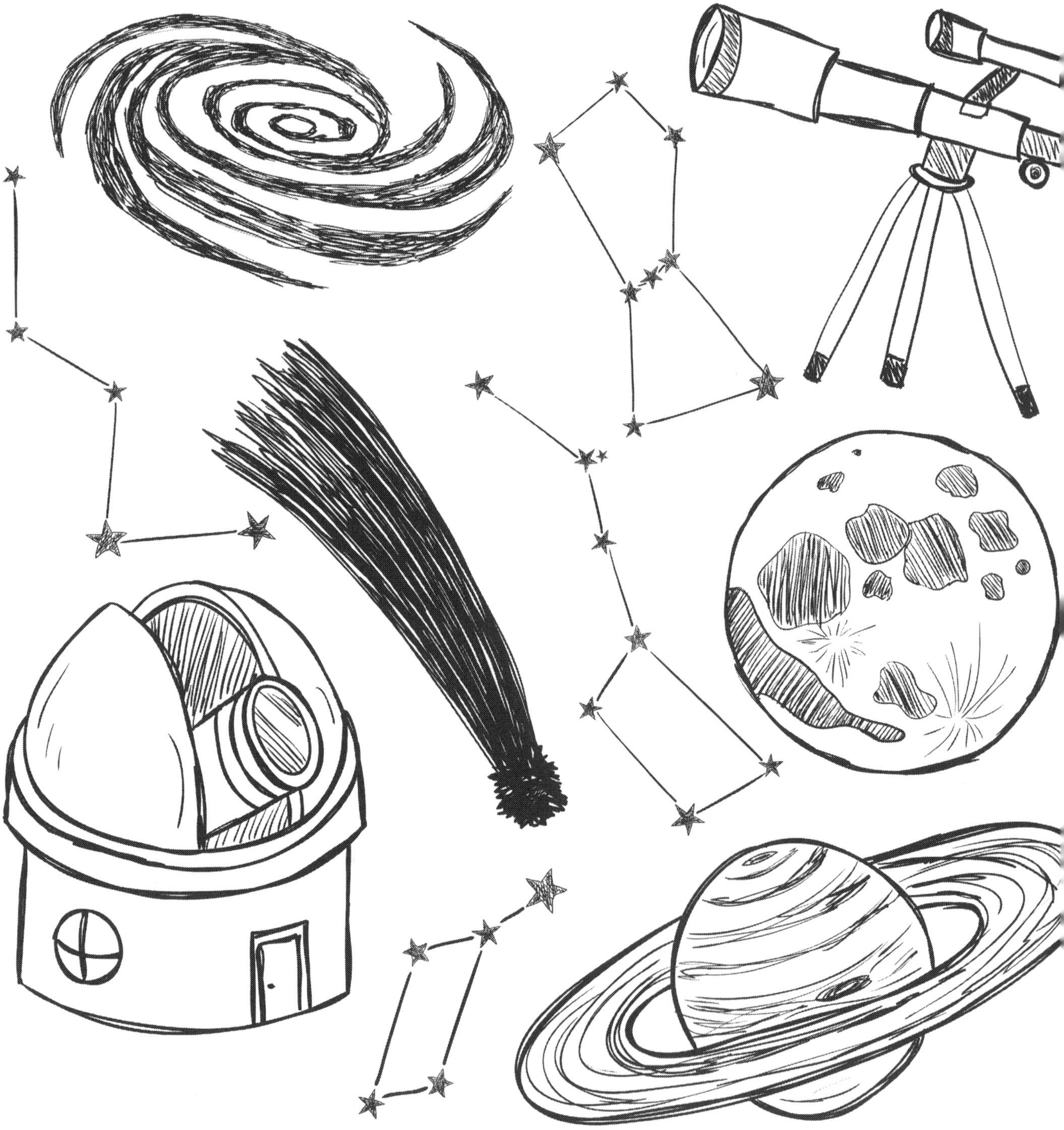

Projects, Observations & Experiments

Projects, Observations & Experiments

History

Watch
Clock
Clock
Clock
Timer
Clock
Watch
Clock
Clock
Timer
Clock
Watch
Clock

History

What do you want to learn about history?

1.

2.

3.

4.

5.

Action Steps:

1. Go to the library or bookstore.

2. Bring home a stack of at least FOUR interesting books about history. Choose some that have diagrams, instructions and illustrations.

3. Plan to watch historical movies, documentaries and take field trips to historic land marks.

Supplies Needed:

You will need pencils, black drawing pens, colored pencils, gel pens and markers.

What past events are you curious about?

Choose FOUR Books About History To Use As School Books!

1. Write down the titles on each cover below.
2. You may also choose Videos, Tutorials and Documenteries to help you learn about these topics.

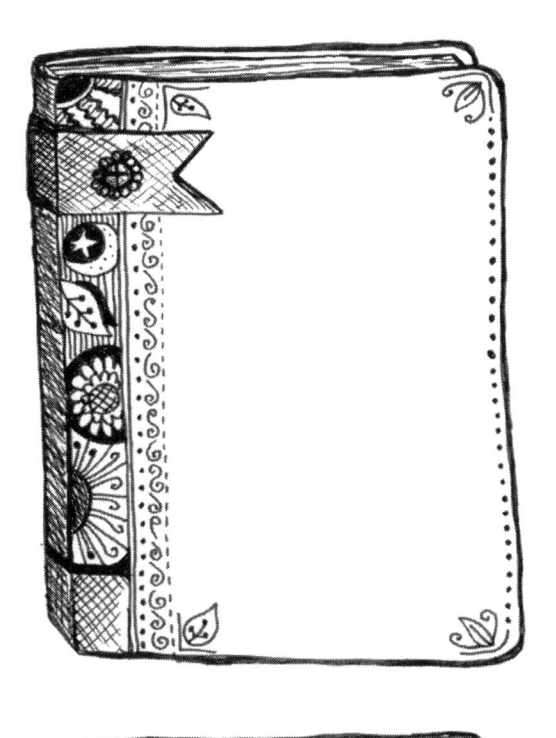

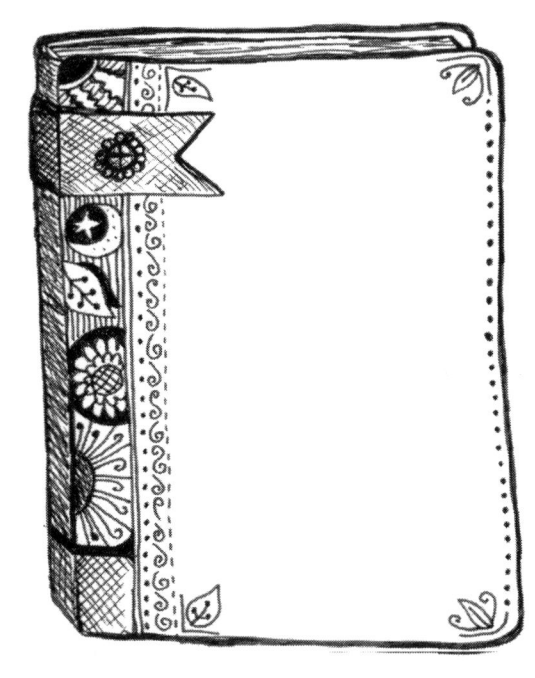

H

A Study of the Historic Events

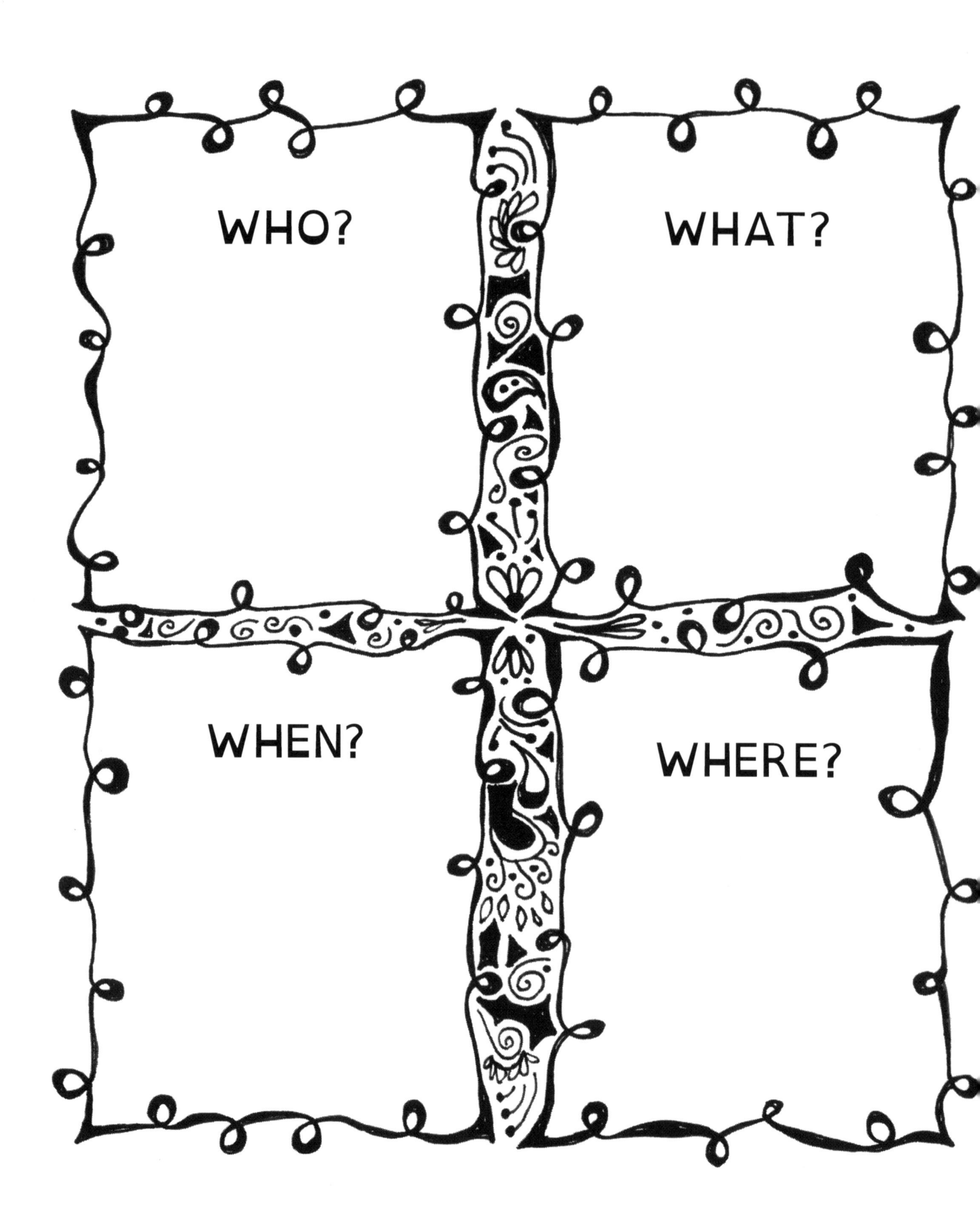

WHO?	**WHAT?**
WHEN?	**WHERE?**

Drawings, Photos & Images:

H

Tell the Story in Your Own Words:

A Study of the Historic Events

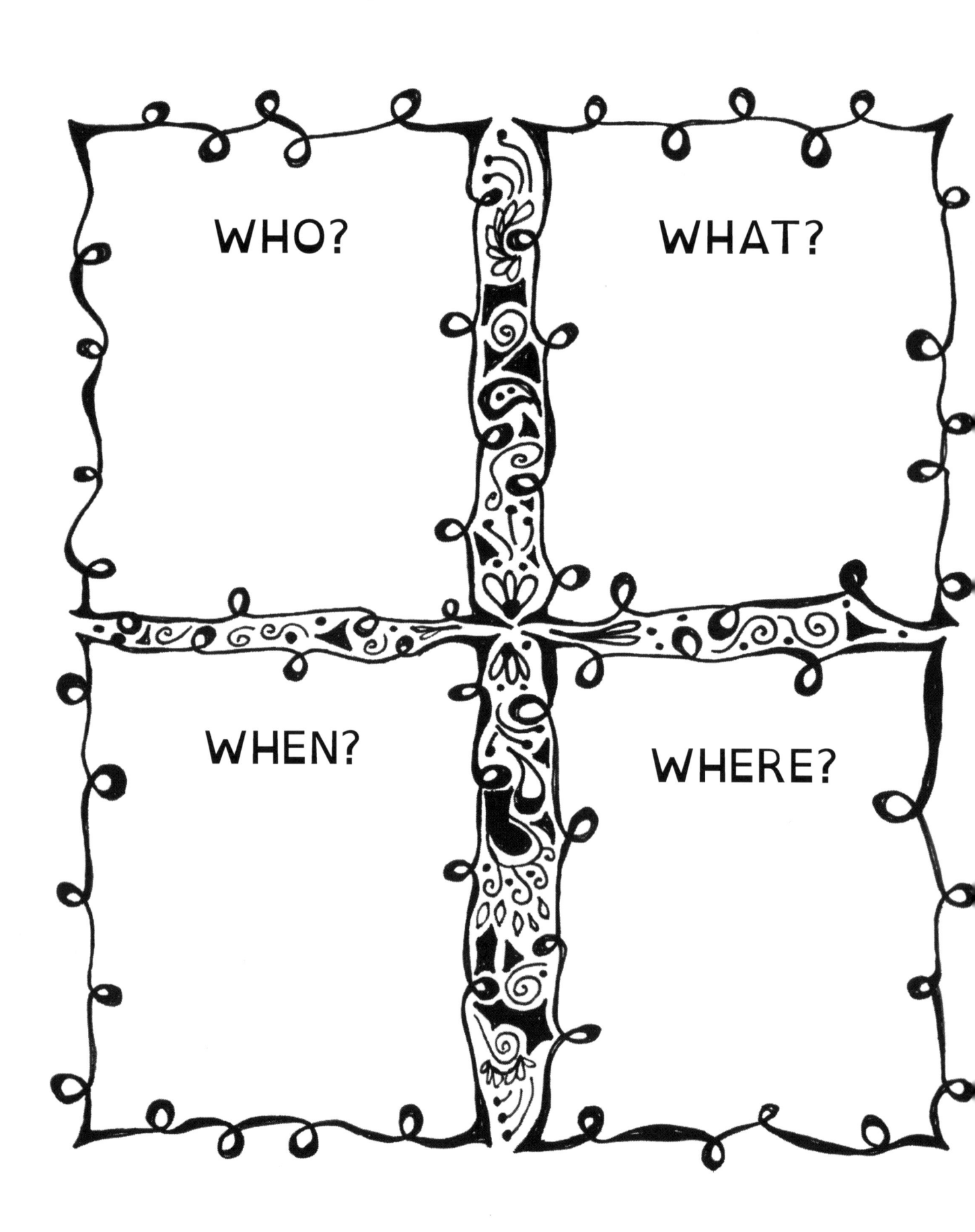

WHO?

WHAT?

WHEN?

WHERE?

Drawings, Photos & Images:

H

Tell the Story in Your Own Words:

A Study of the Historic Events

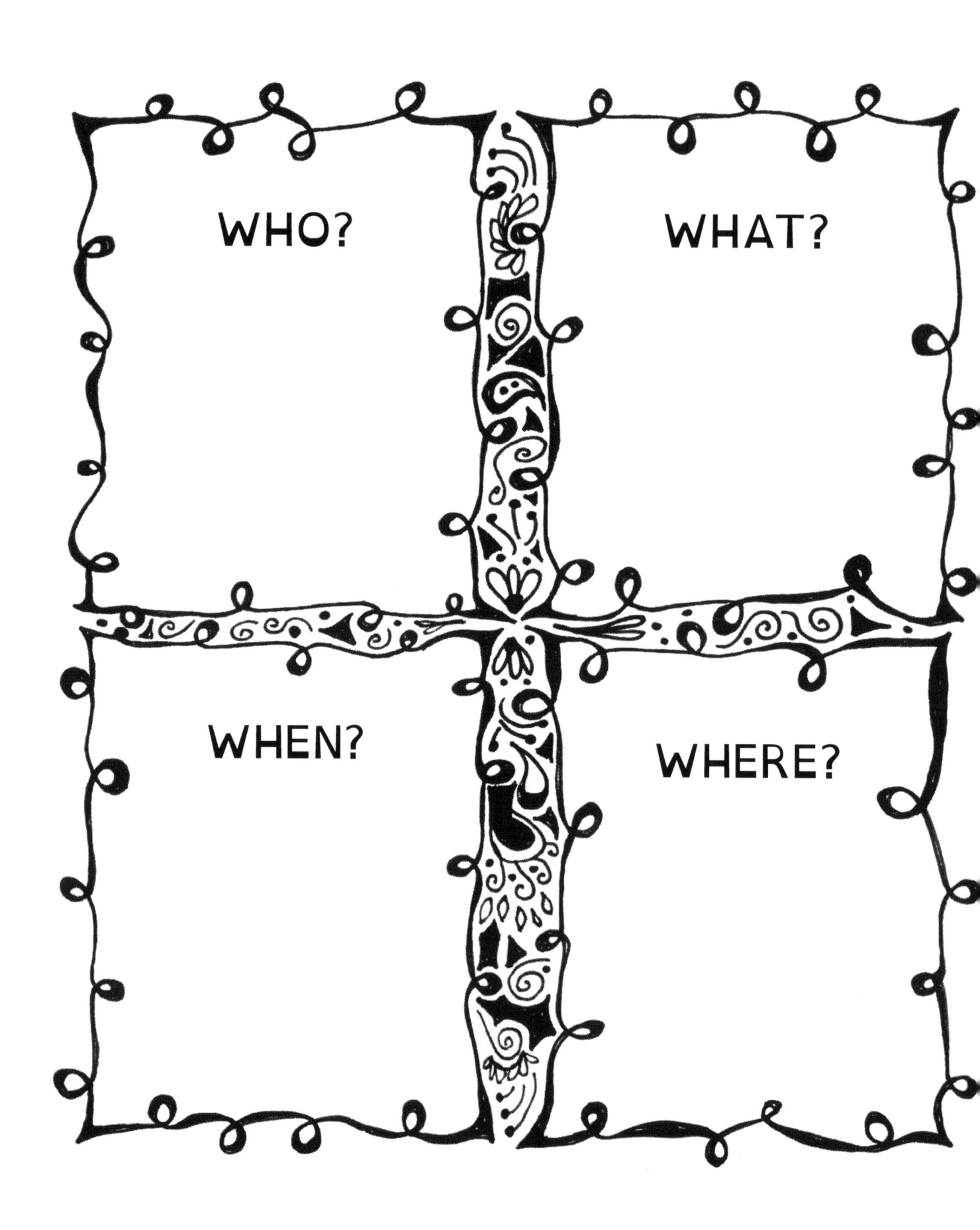

WHO?

WHAT?

WHEN?

WHERE?

Drawings, Photos & Images:

H

Tell the Story in Your Own Words:

A Study of the Historic Events

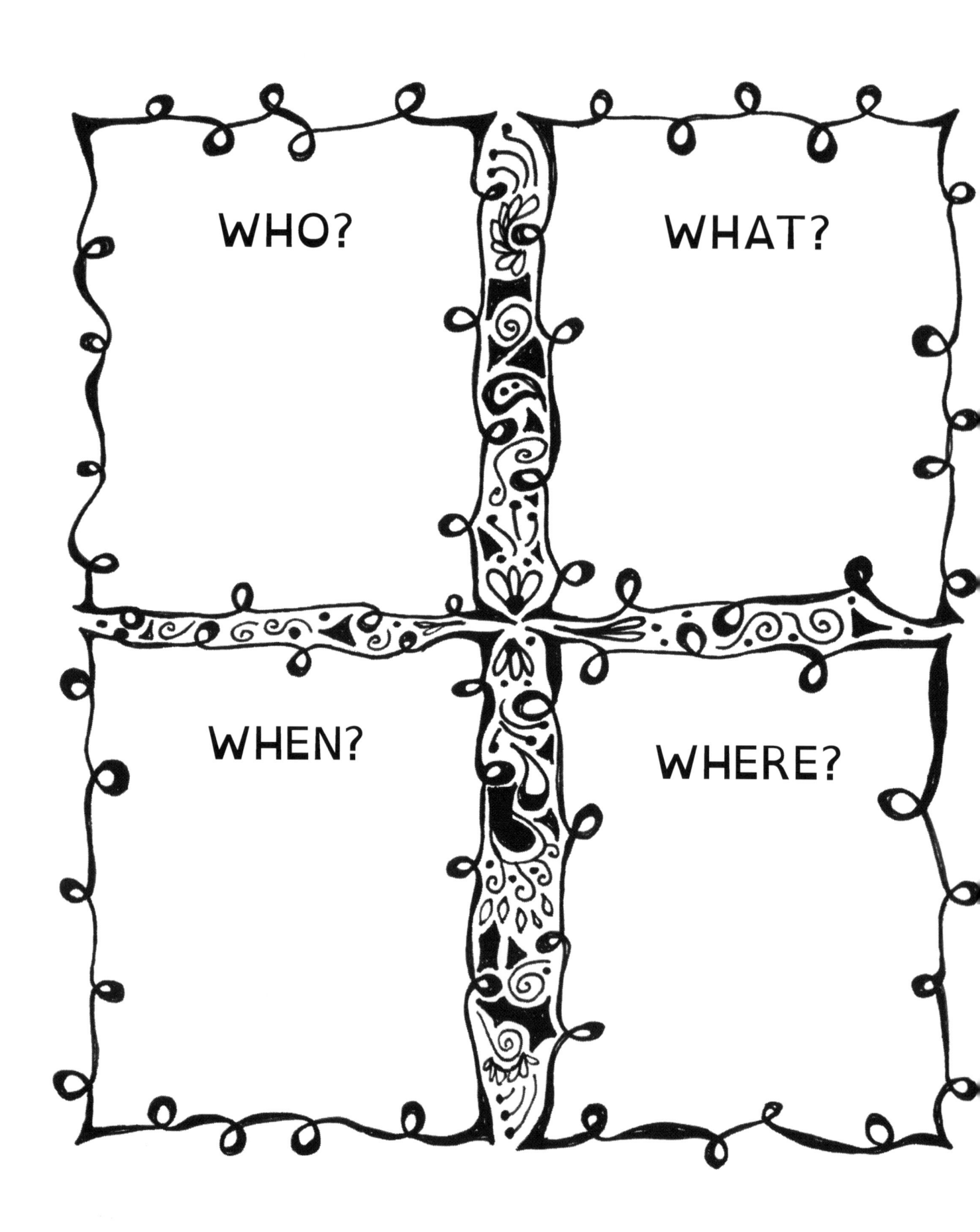

WHO?	**WHAT?**
WHEN?	**WHERE?**

Drawings, Photos & Images:

H

Tell the Story in Your Own Words:

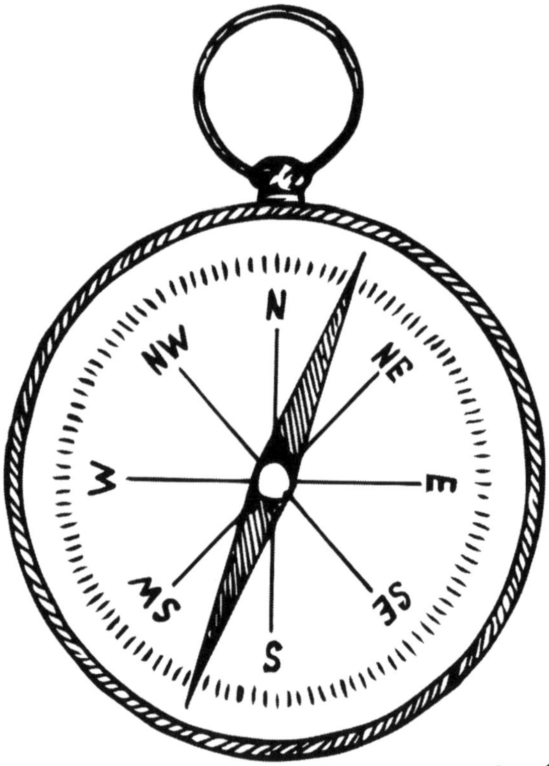
N
NW
NE
W
E
SW
SE
S

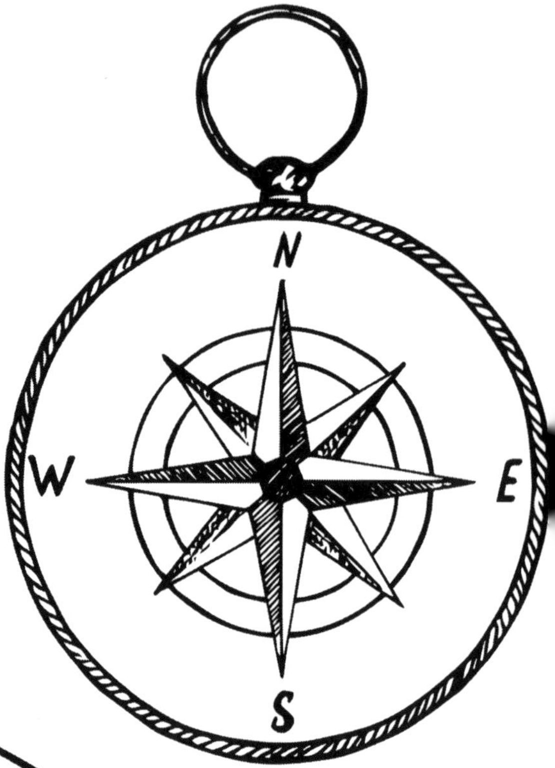
N
W
E
S

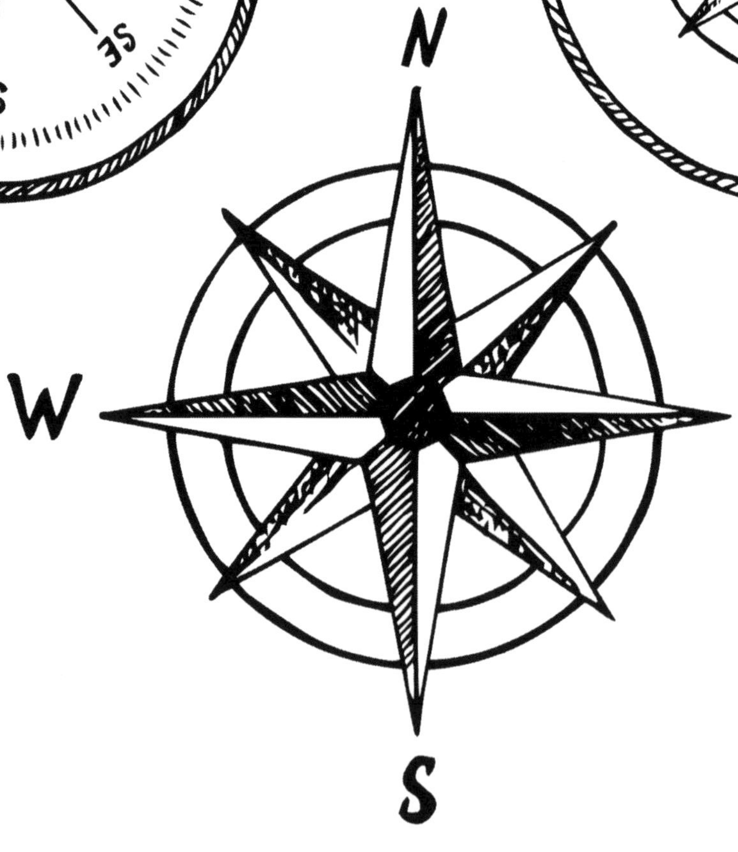
N
W
E
S

H

A Study of the Historic Events

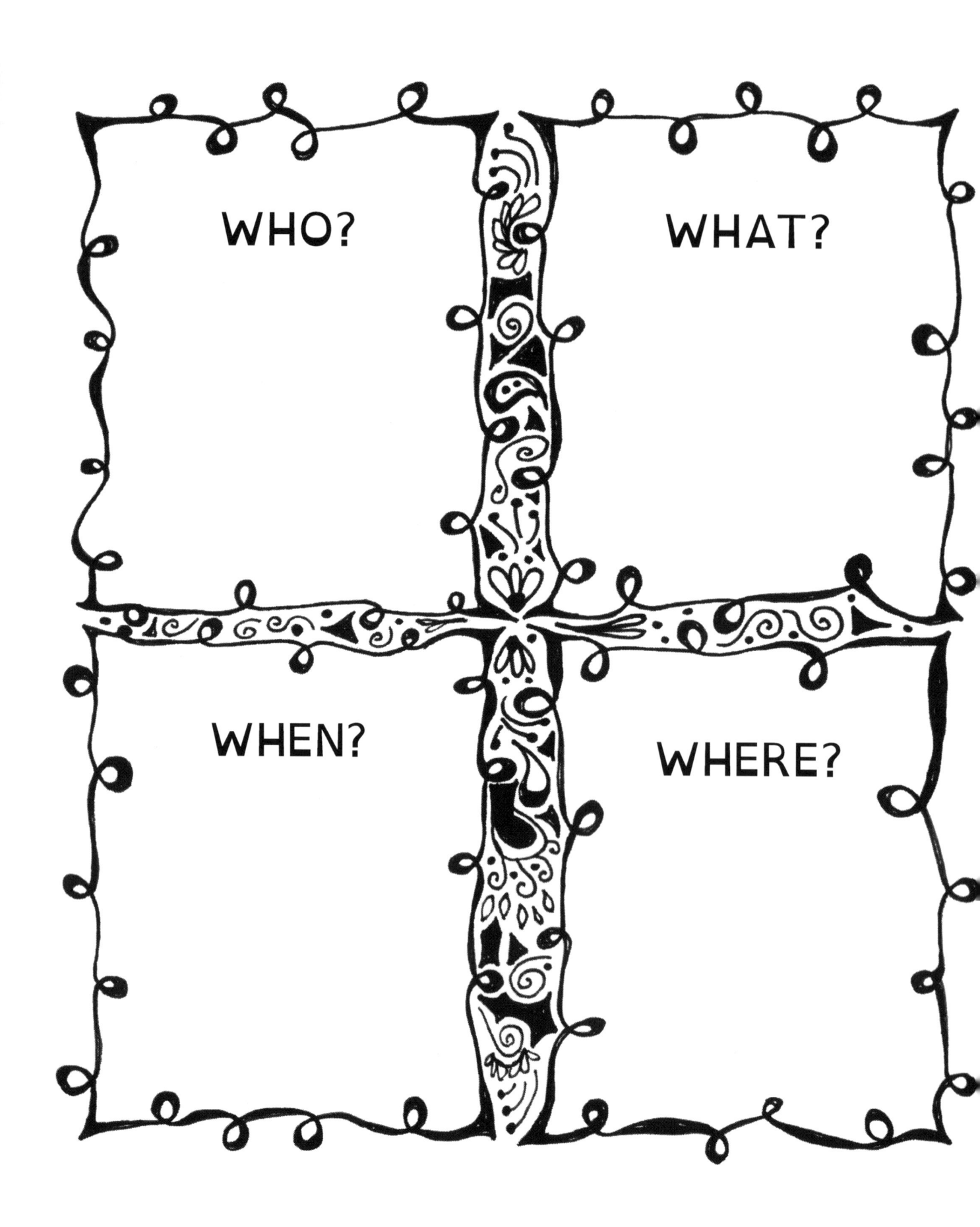

WHO?	**WHAT?**
WHEN?	**WHERE?**

Drawings, Photos & Images:

H

Tell the Story in Your Own Words:

A Study of the Historic Events

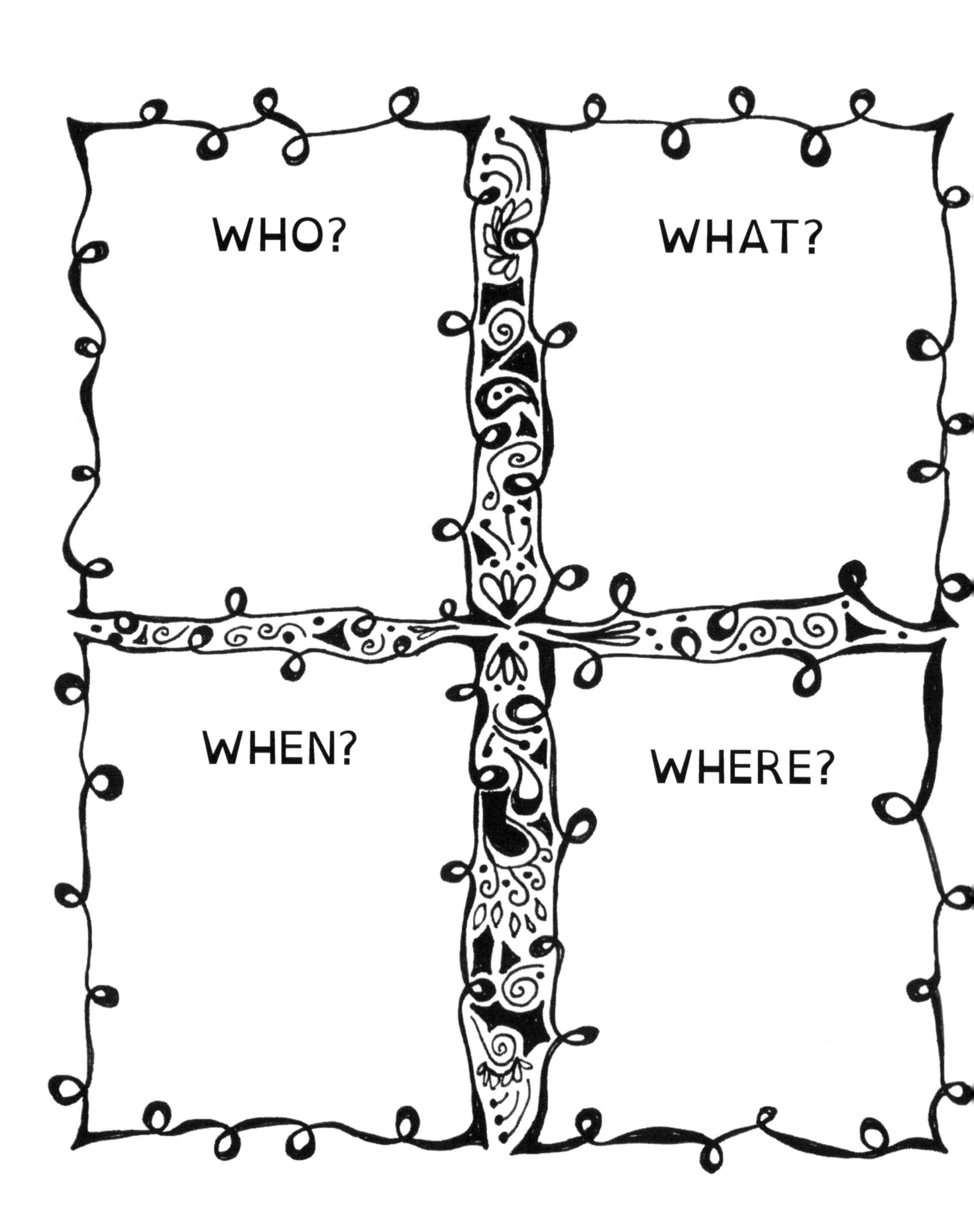

WHO?	**WHAT?**
WHEN?	**WHERE?**

Drawings, Photos & Images:

H

Tell the Story in Your Own Words:

A Study of the Historic Events

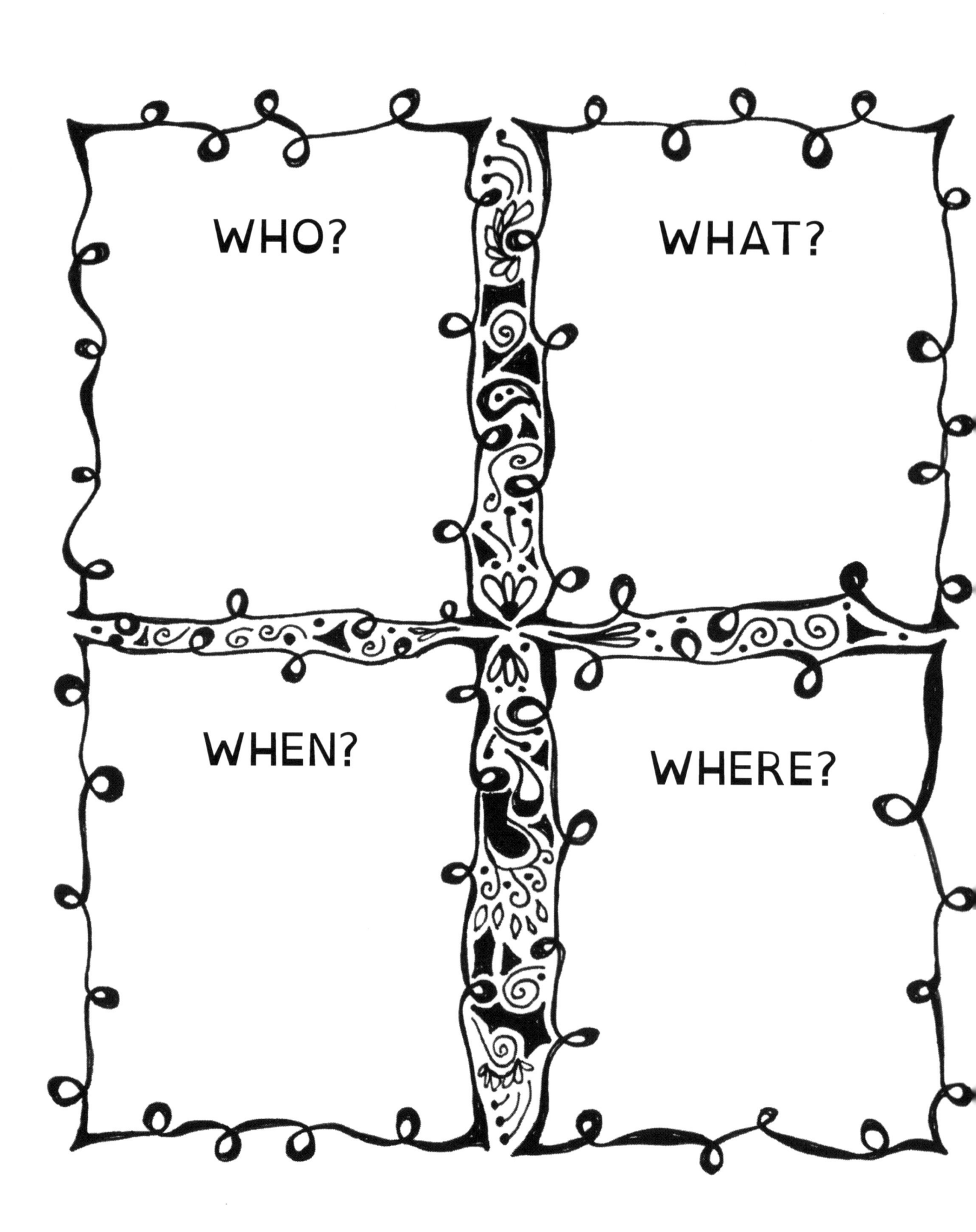

WHO?	**WHAT?**
WHEN?	**WHERE?**

Drawings, Photos & Images:

H

Tell the Story in Your Own Words:

A Study of the Historic Events

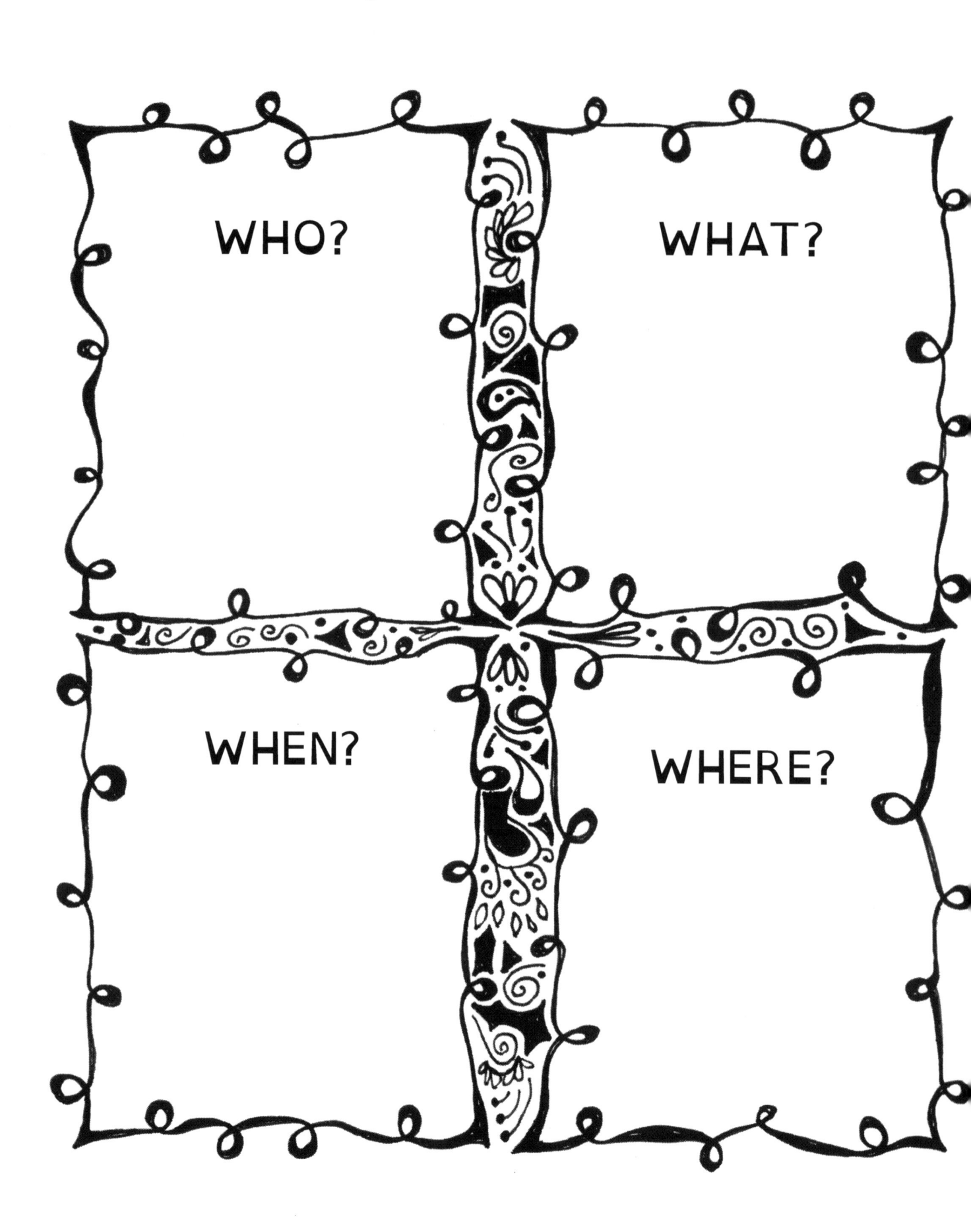

WHO?	**WHAT?**
WHEN?	**WHERE?**

Drawings, Photos & Images:

H

Tell the Story in Your Own Words:

A Study of the Historic Events

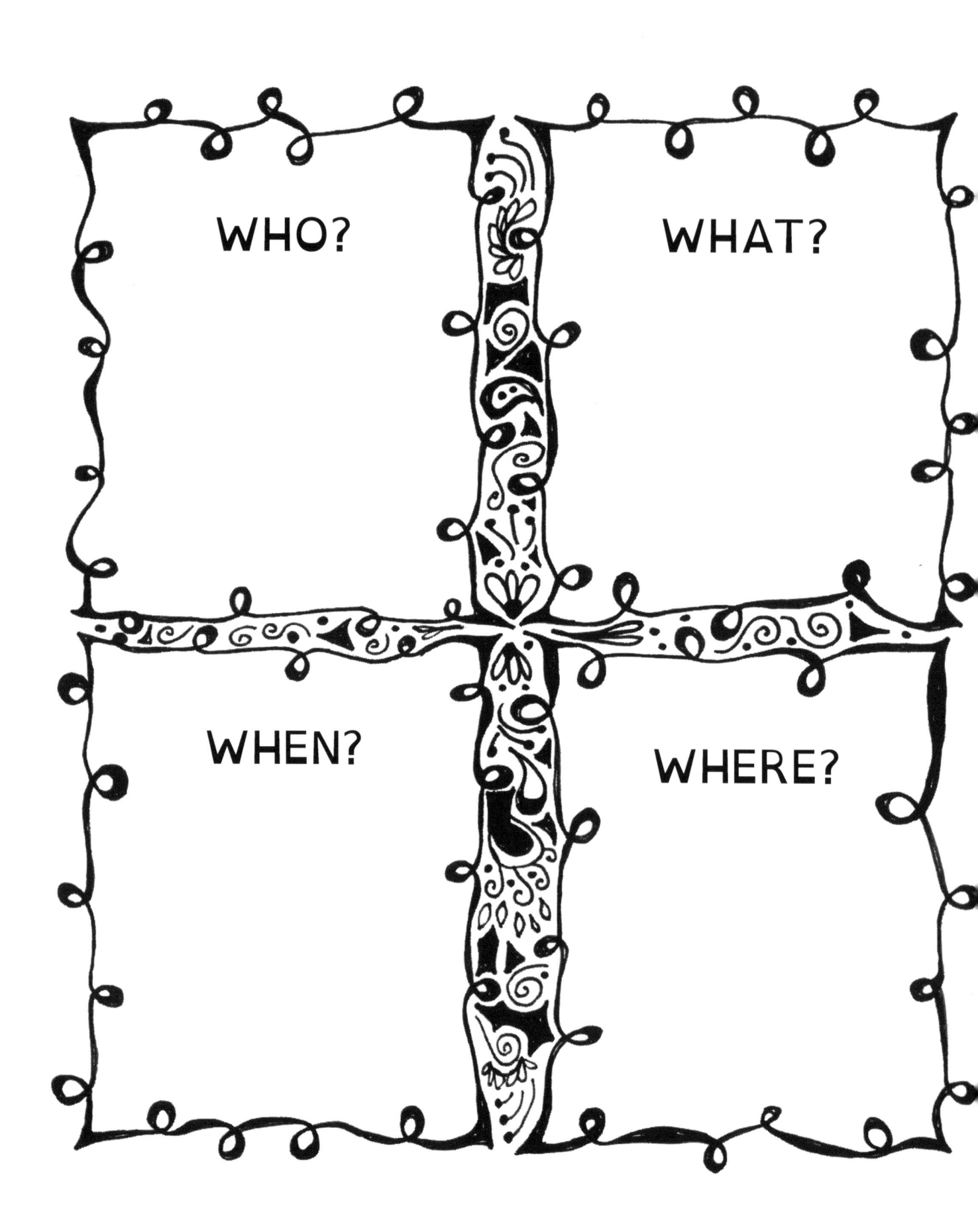

WHO?	**WHAT?**
WHEN?	**WHERE?**

Drawings, Photos & Images:

H

Tell the Story in Your Own Words:

A Study of the Historic Events

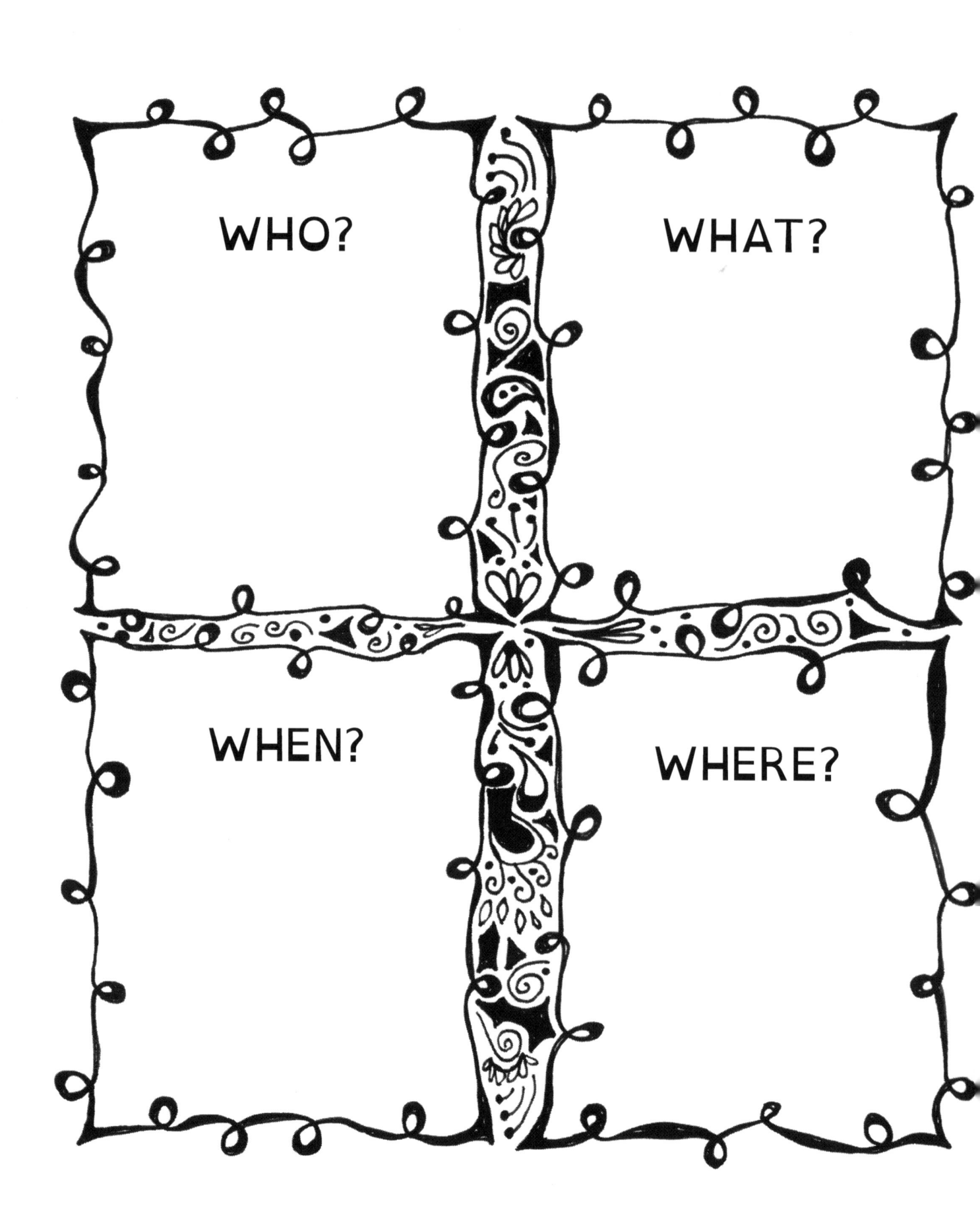

WHO?

WHAT?

WHEN?

WHERE?

Drawings, Photos & Images:

H

Tell the Story in Your Own Words:

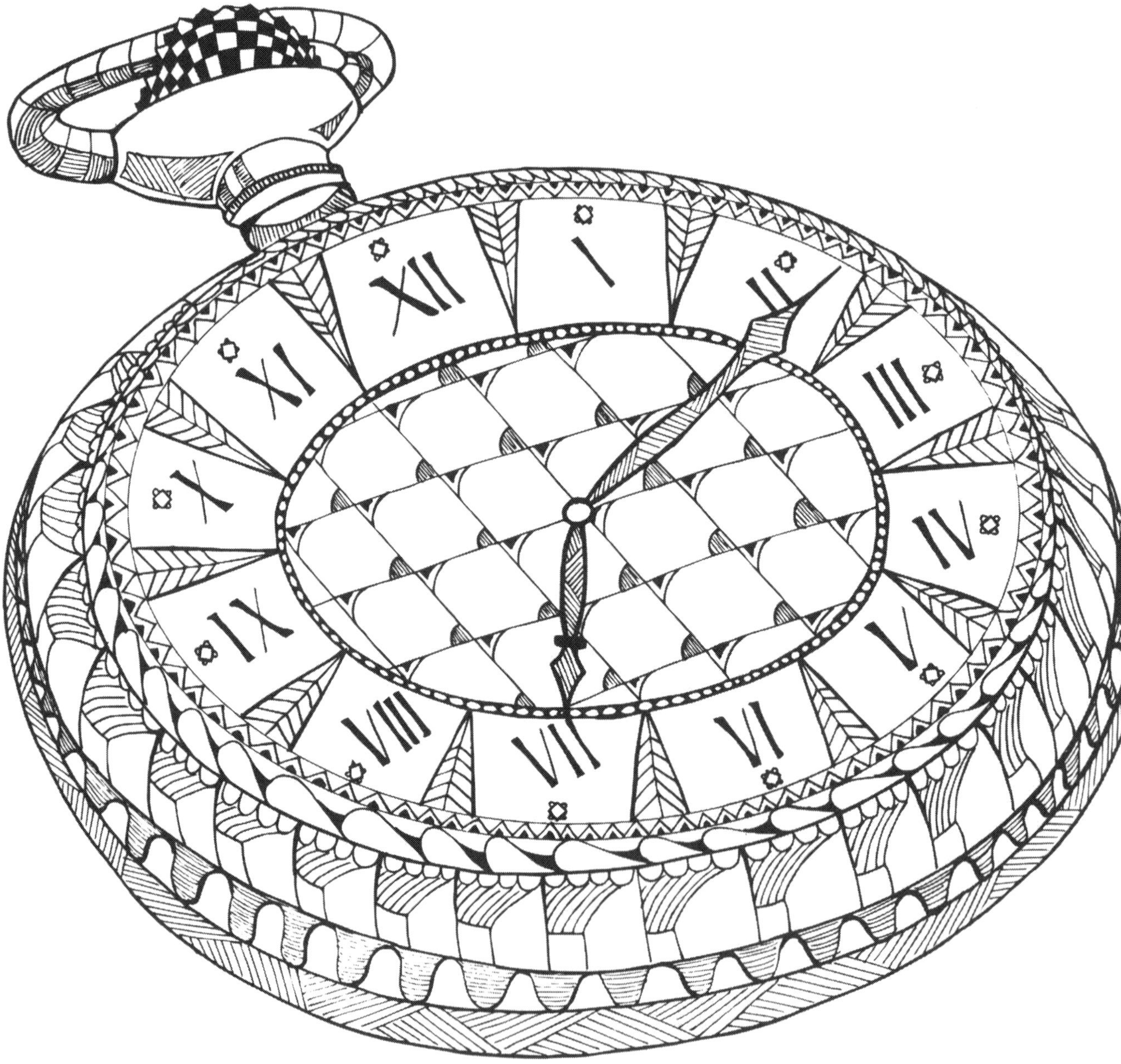

H

A Study of the Historic Events

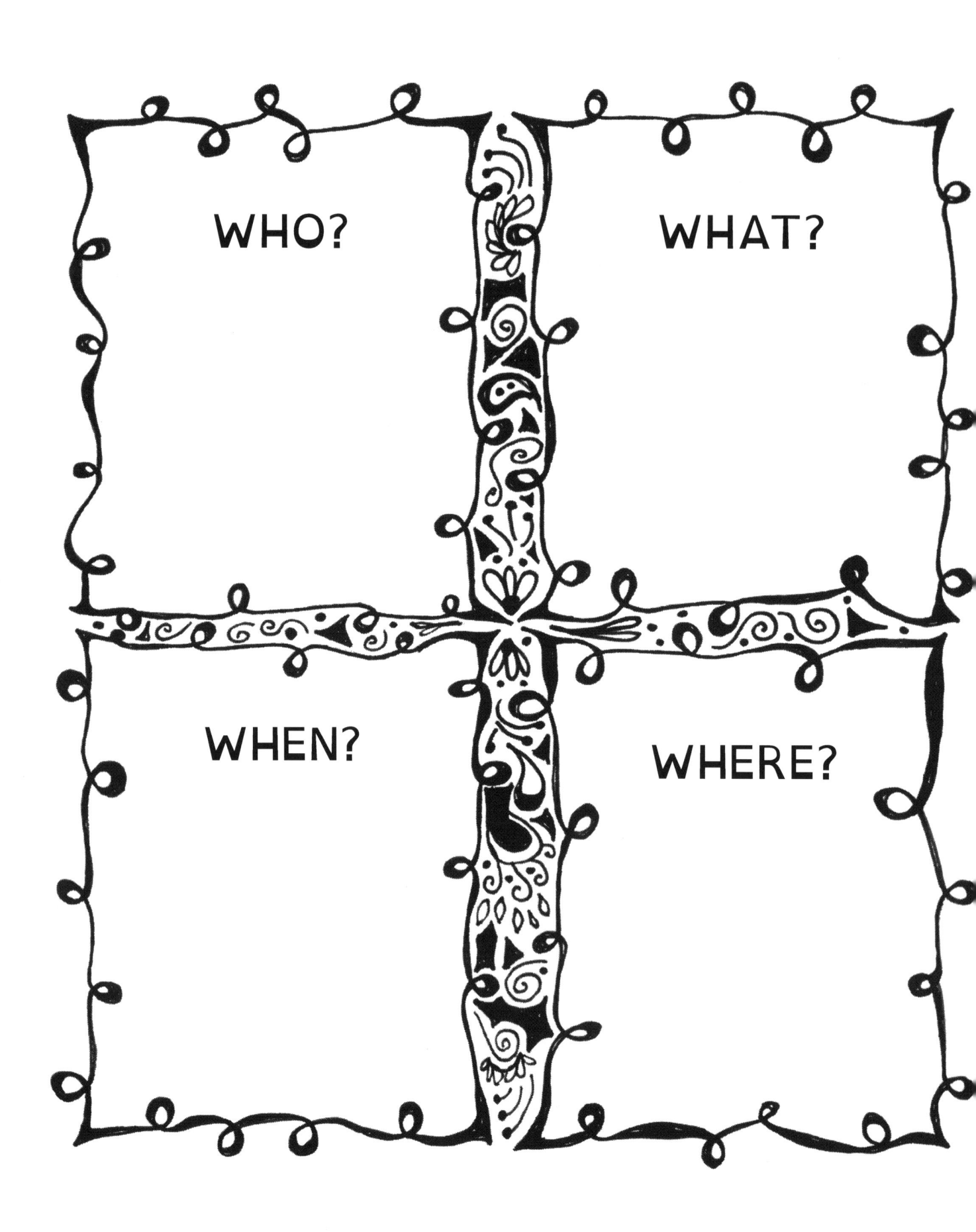

WHO?	**WHAT?**
WHEN?	**WHERE?**

Drawings, Photos & Images:

H

Tell the Story in Your Own Words:

A Study of the Historic Events

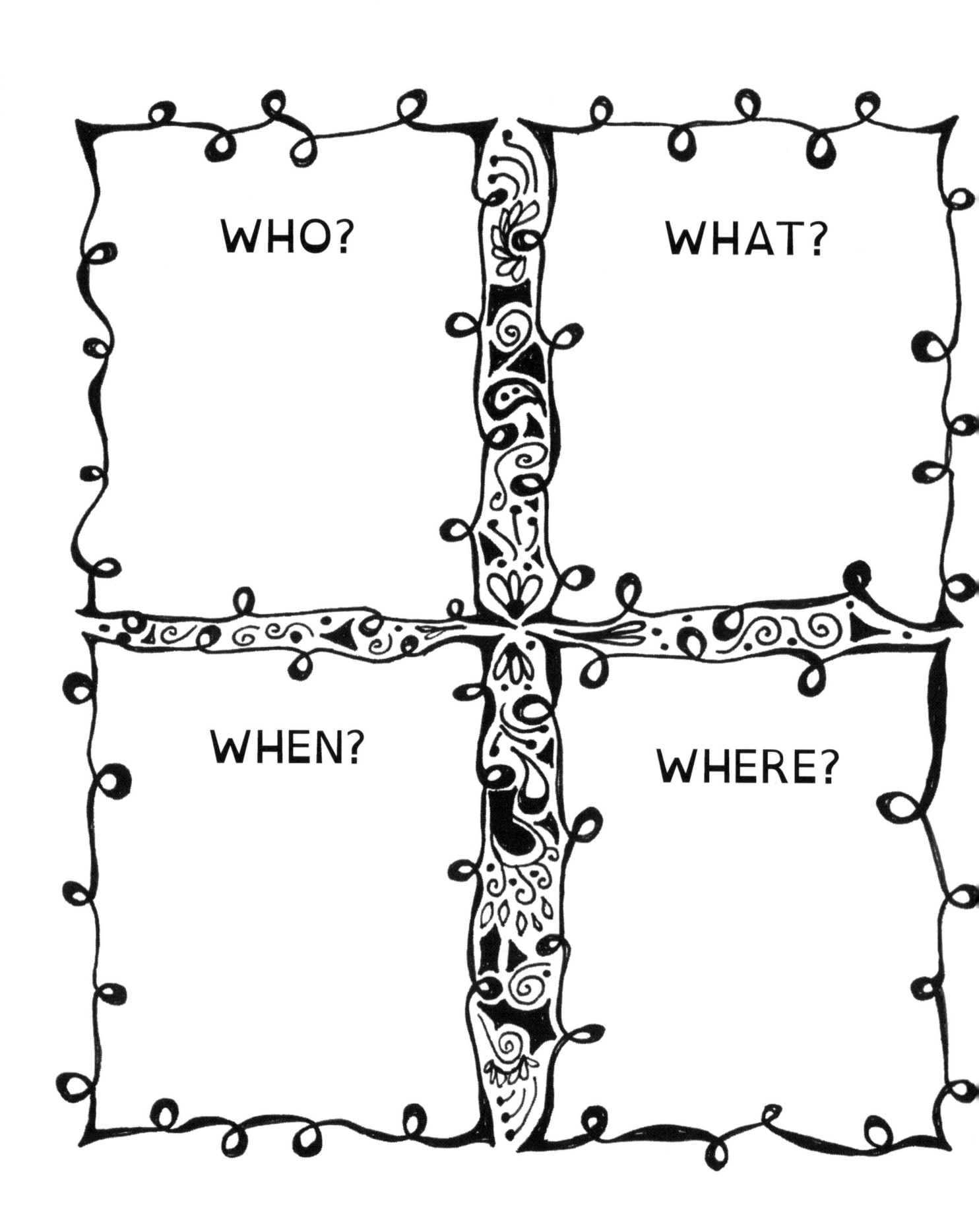

WHO?

WHAT?

WHEN?

WHERE?

Drawings, Photos & Images:

H

Tell the Story in Your Own Words:

A Study of the Historic Events

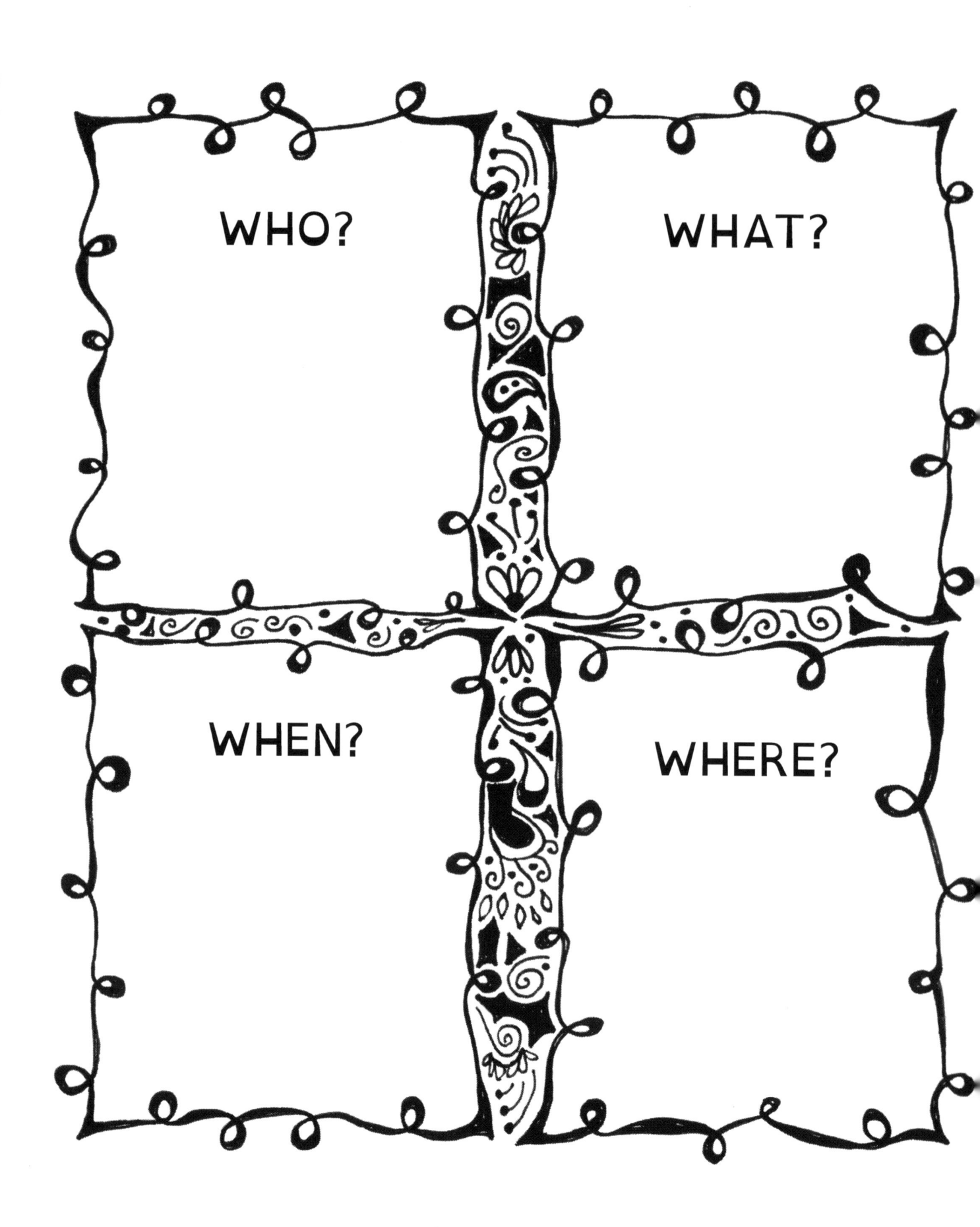

WHO?	**WHAT?**
WHEN?	**WHERE?**

Drawings, Photos & Images:

H

Tell the Story in Your Own Words:

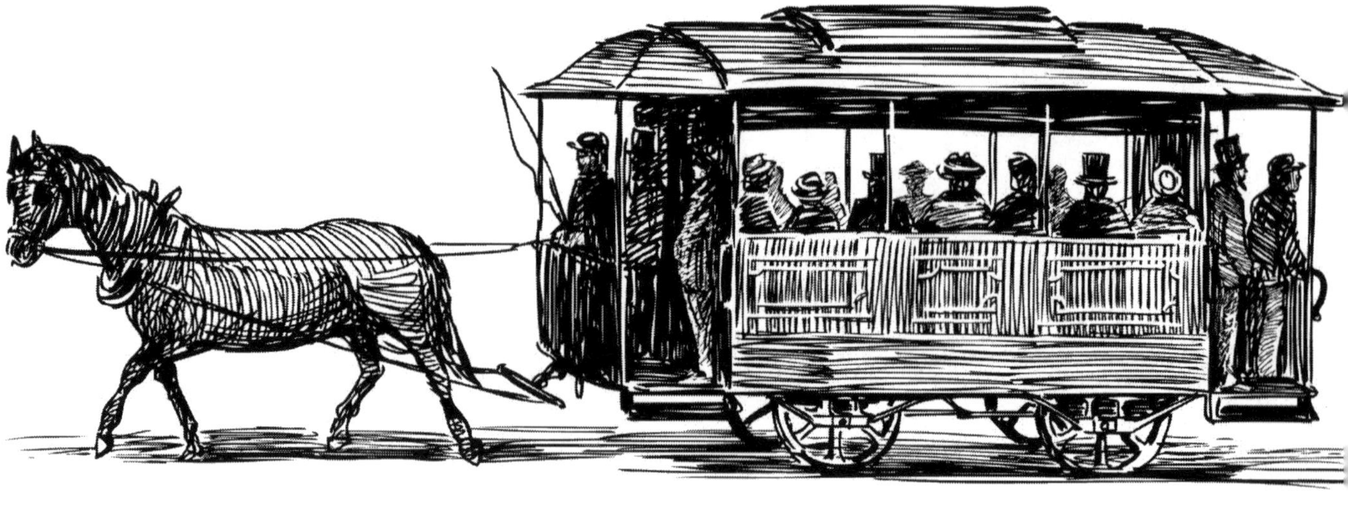
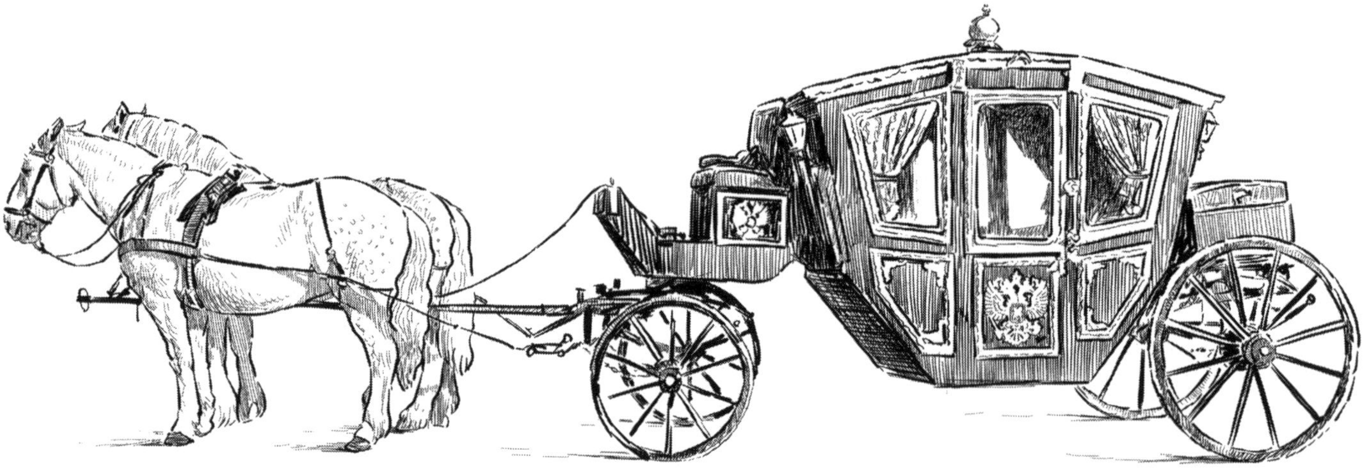
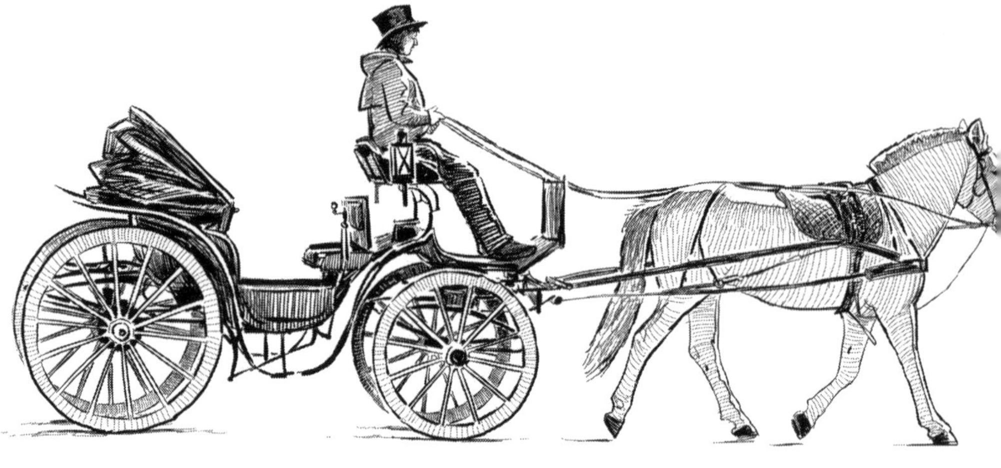

H

A Study of the Historic Events

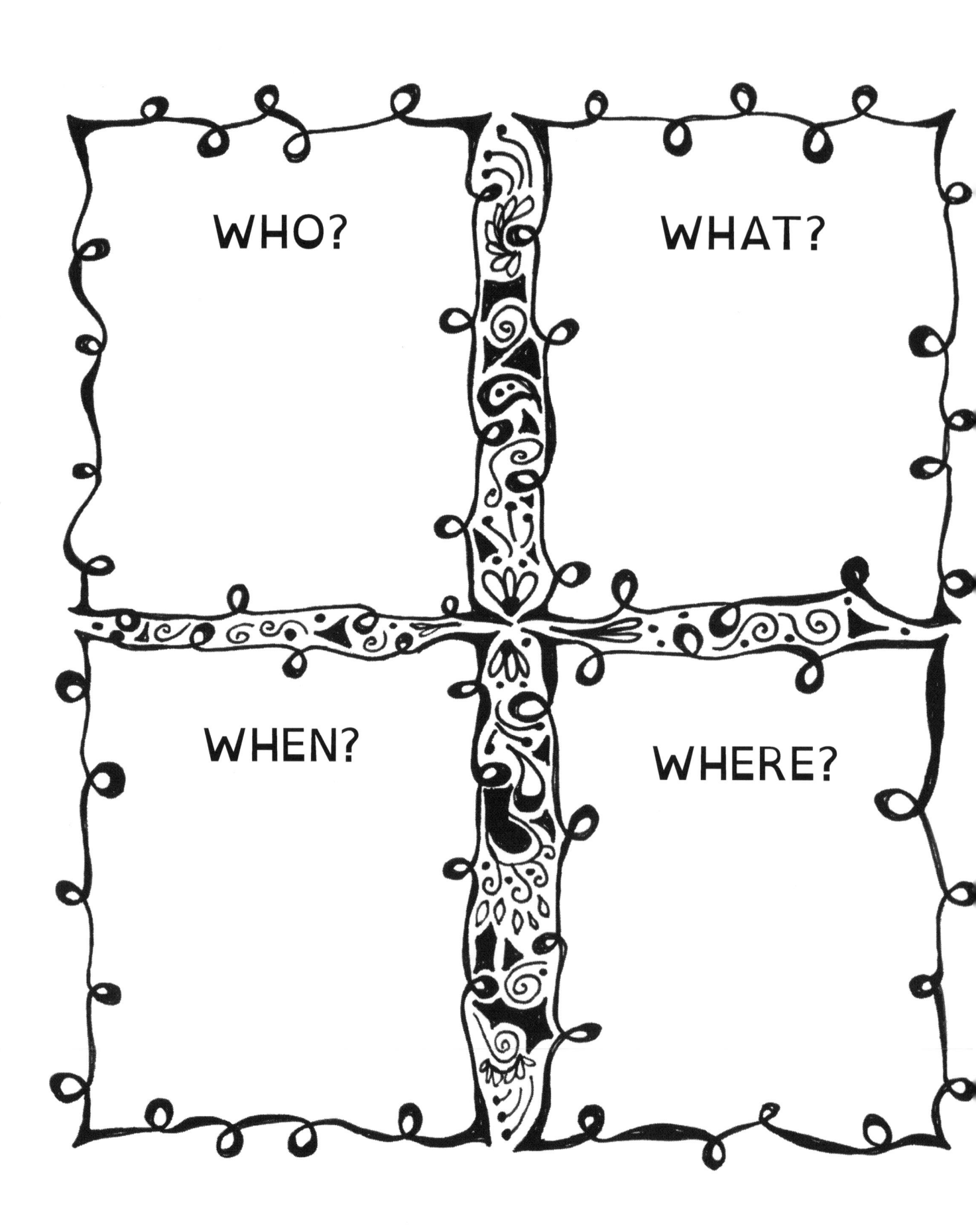

WHO?	**WHAT?**
WHEN?	**WHERE?**

Drawings, Photos & Images:

H

Tell the Story in Your Own Words:

A Study of the Historic Events

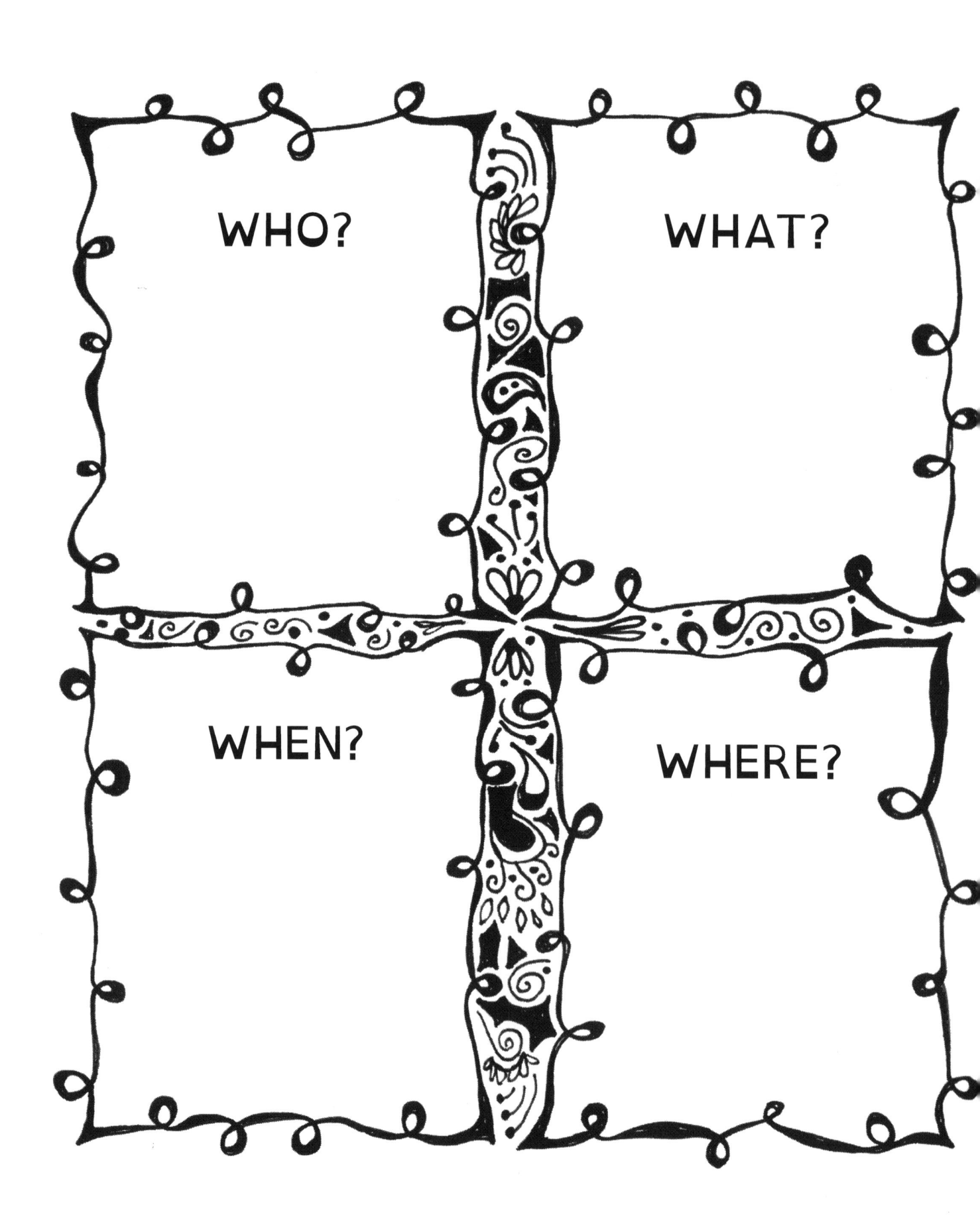

WHO?	**WHAT?**
WHEN?	**WHERE?**

Drawings, Photos & Images:

H

Tell the Story in Your Own Words:

Geography & Travel

What do you want to learn about geography and travel?

1.

2.

3.

4.

5.

Action Steps:

1. Go to the library or bookstore.

2. Bring home a stack of at least SIX interesting books about geography and travel.

Choose some that have diagrams, instructions and illustrations.

3. Plan to watch travel documentaries online!

Supplies Needed:

You will need pencils, black drawing pens, colored pencils, gel pens and markers.

What are your Travel Dreams?

Choose FOUR Books About Geography & Travel To Use As School Books!

1. Write down the titles on each cover below.
2. You may also choose Videos, Tutorials and Documenteries to help you learn about these topics.

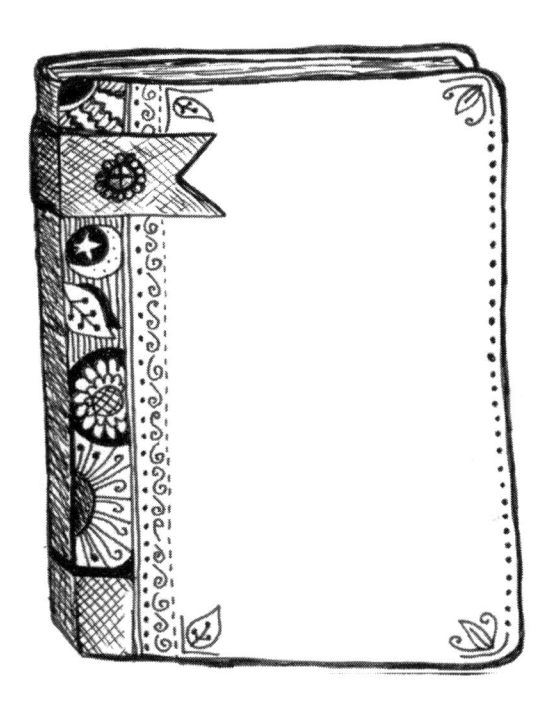

GT

TITLE:_____

Date_____

GT

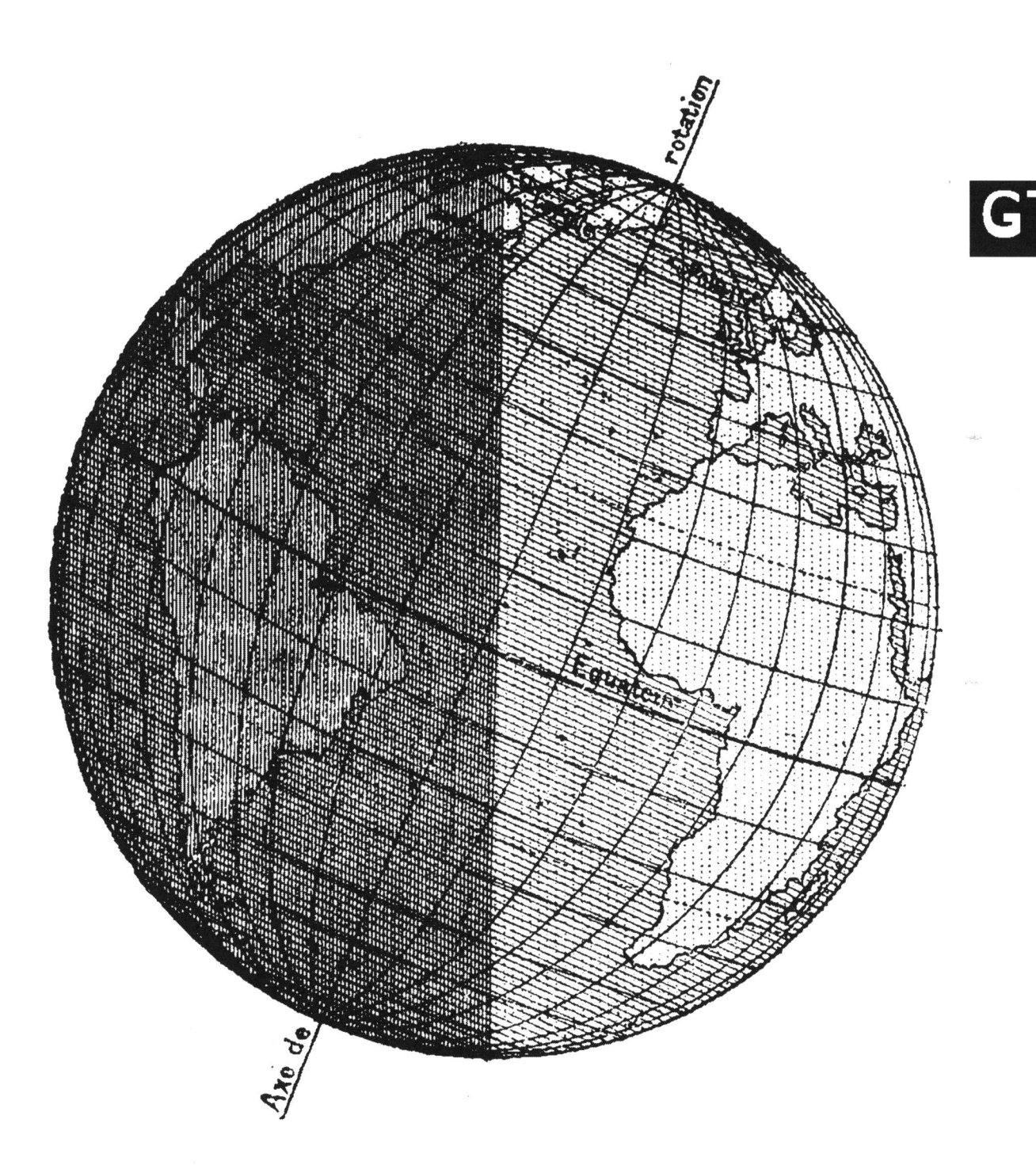

TITLE:_____

Date_____

GT

TITLE:_____

Date_____

GT

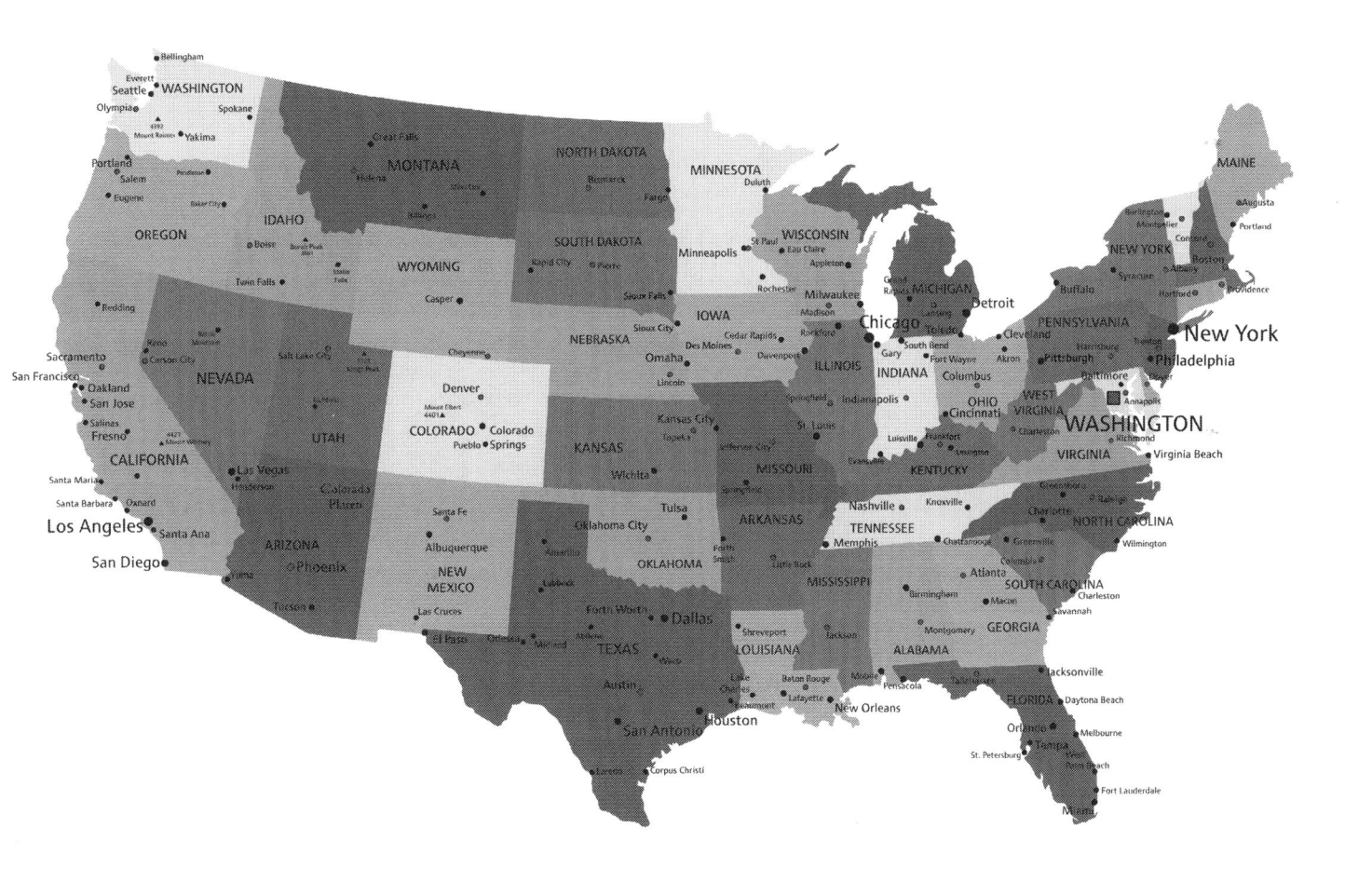

TITLE:_____

Date_____

GT

TITLE:_____

Date_____

GT

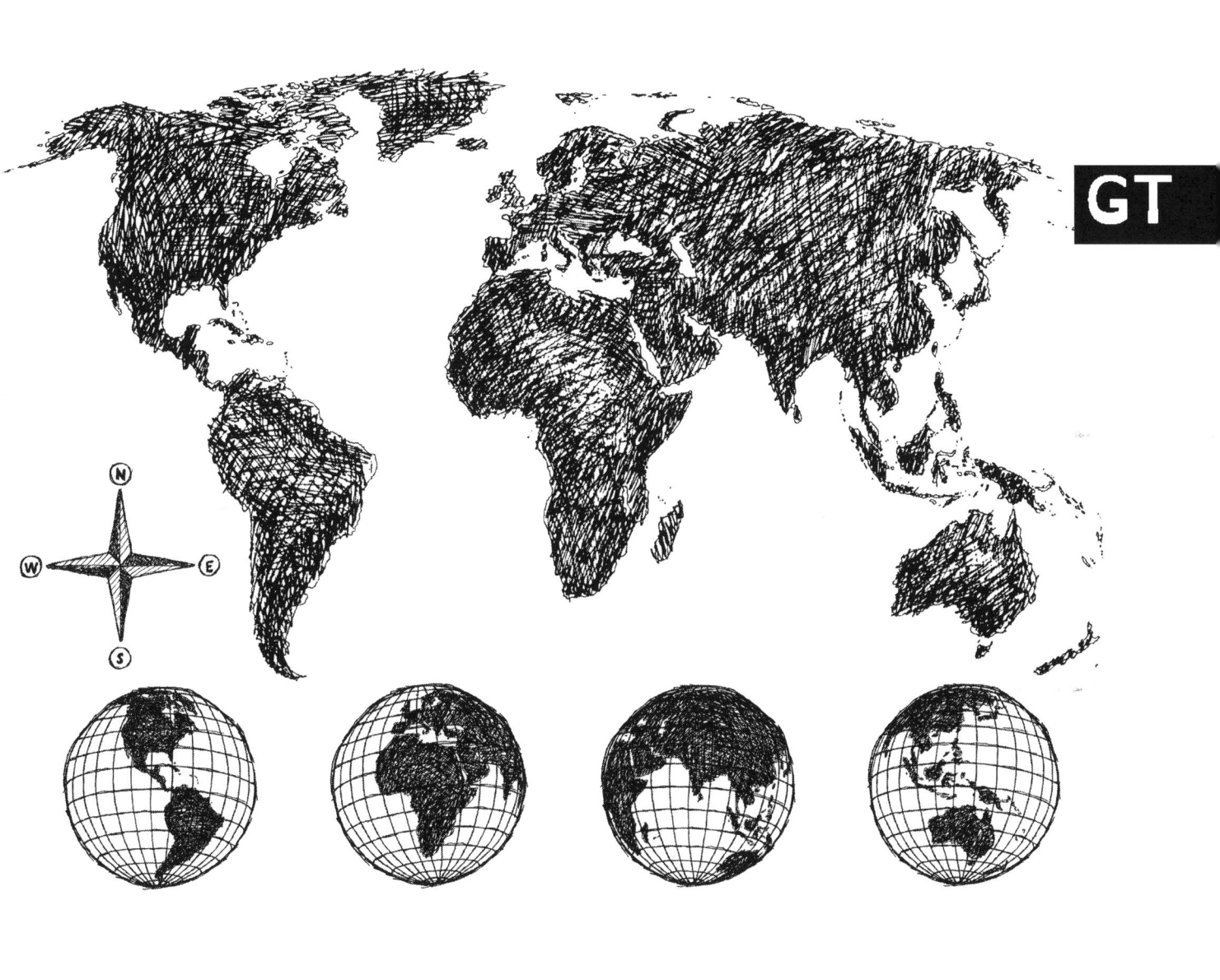

TITLE:_____

Date_____

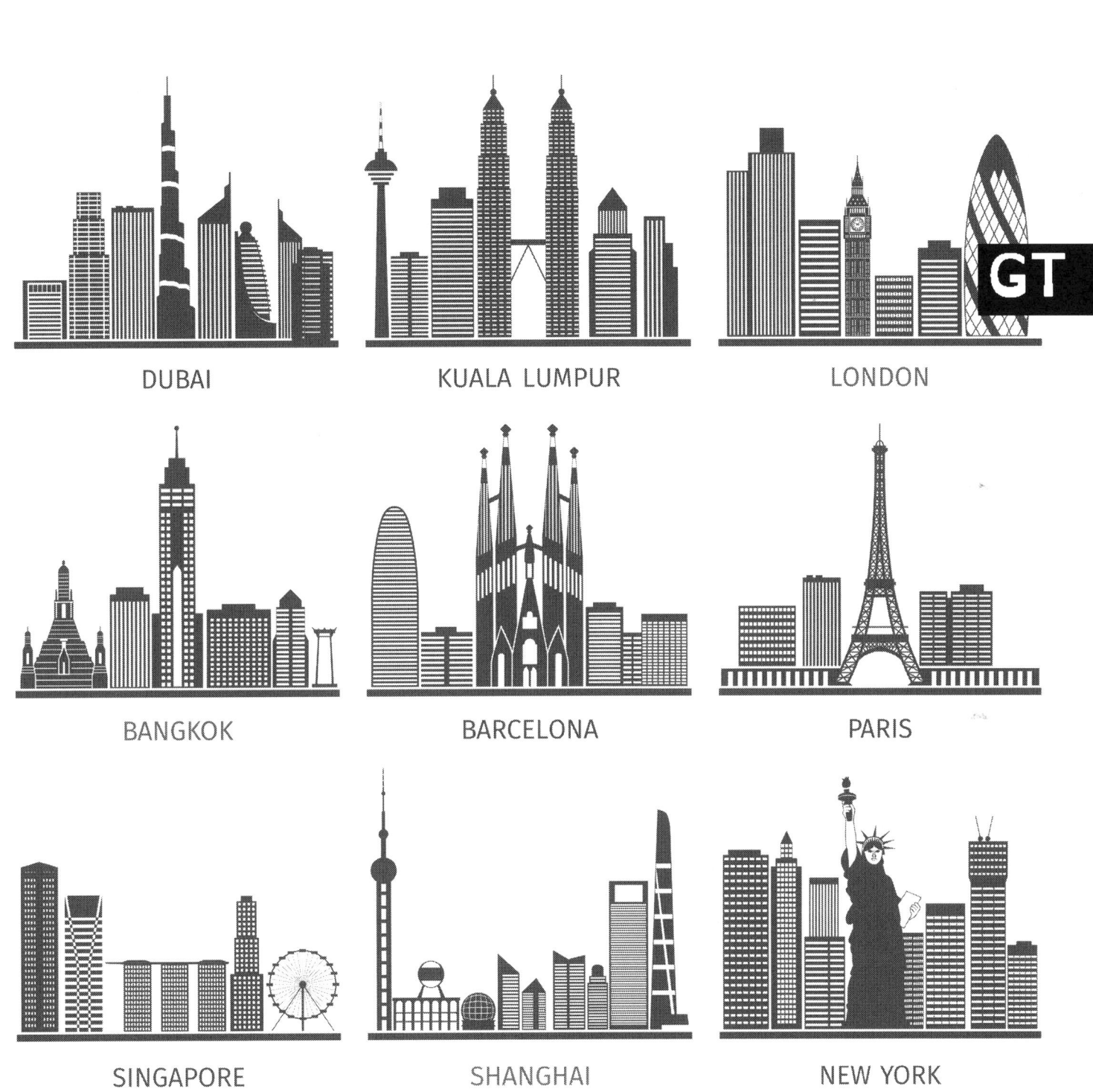

DUBAI	KUALA LUMPUR	LONDON
BANGKOK	BARCELONA	PARIS
SINGAPORE	SHANGHAI	NEW YORK

TITLE:_____

Date_____

Dubai Prague Shanghai Rome

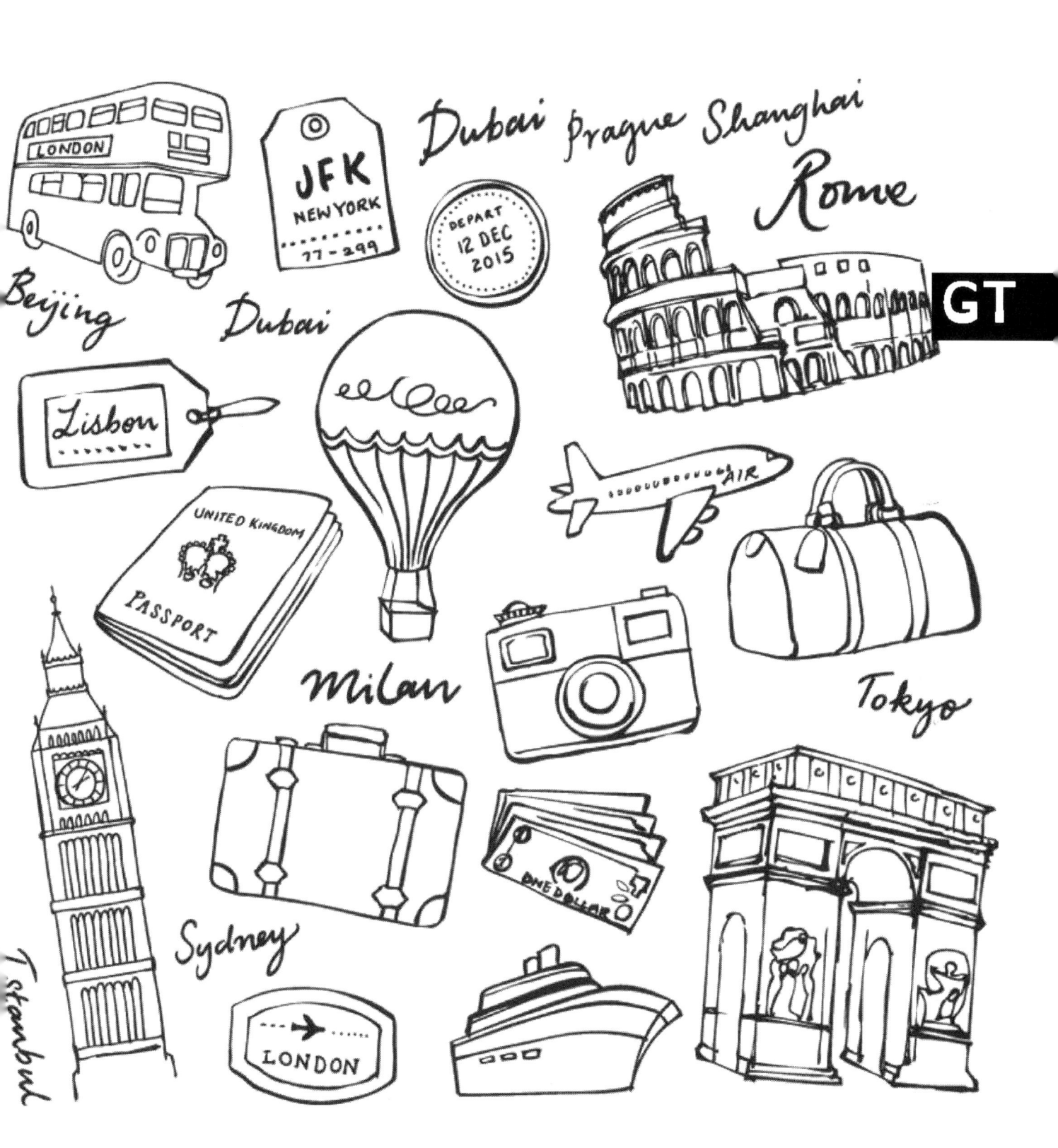

Beijing Dubai

GT

Lisbon

Milan

Tokyo

Sydney

Istanbul LONDON

TITLE:_____

Date_____

GT

North America

Atlantic Ocean

South America

Pacific Ocean

Africa

Antarctic

Eurasia

Pacific Ocean

Indian Ocean

Australia

GT

TITLE:_____

Date_____

GT

TITLE:_____

Date_____

GT

TITLE:_____

Date_____

GT

TITLE:_____

Date_____

GT

TITLE:_____

Date_____

GT

TITLE:_____

Date_____

GT

Mathematics

What do you want to learn about mathematics?

1.

2.

3.

4.

5.

Action Steps:

1. Go to the library or bookstore.

2. Bring home TWO interesting books about math.

Choose some that have diagrams, instructions and illustrations.

3. Choose a Computer Based Math Program.

Supplies Needed:

You will need pencils, black drawing pens, colored pencils, gel pens and markers.

List of Tutorials:

Choose TWO Books About Mathematics
To Use As School Books!

1. Write down the titles on each cover below.
2. You may also choose Videos, Tutorials and Documenteries to help you learn about these topics.

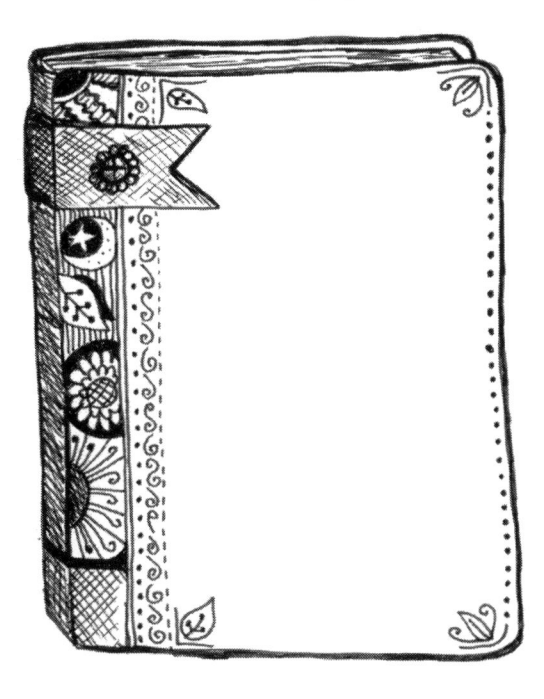

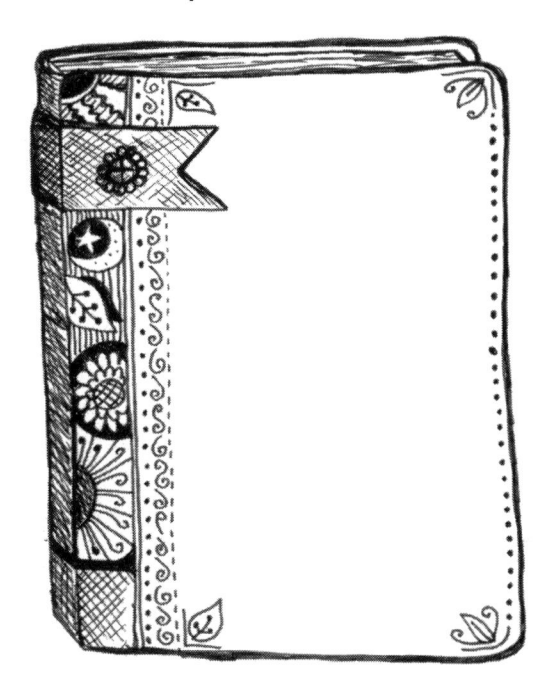

Computer Based Mathematics

What Learning Programs will you use?

1.

2.

3.

4.

LIKE

Timeline

SOCIAL MEDIA
INTERNET
EMAIL

0% 15% 50% 75% 100%

POPULATION
RELATIONSHIPS

RATING

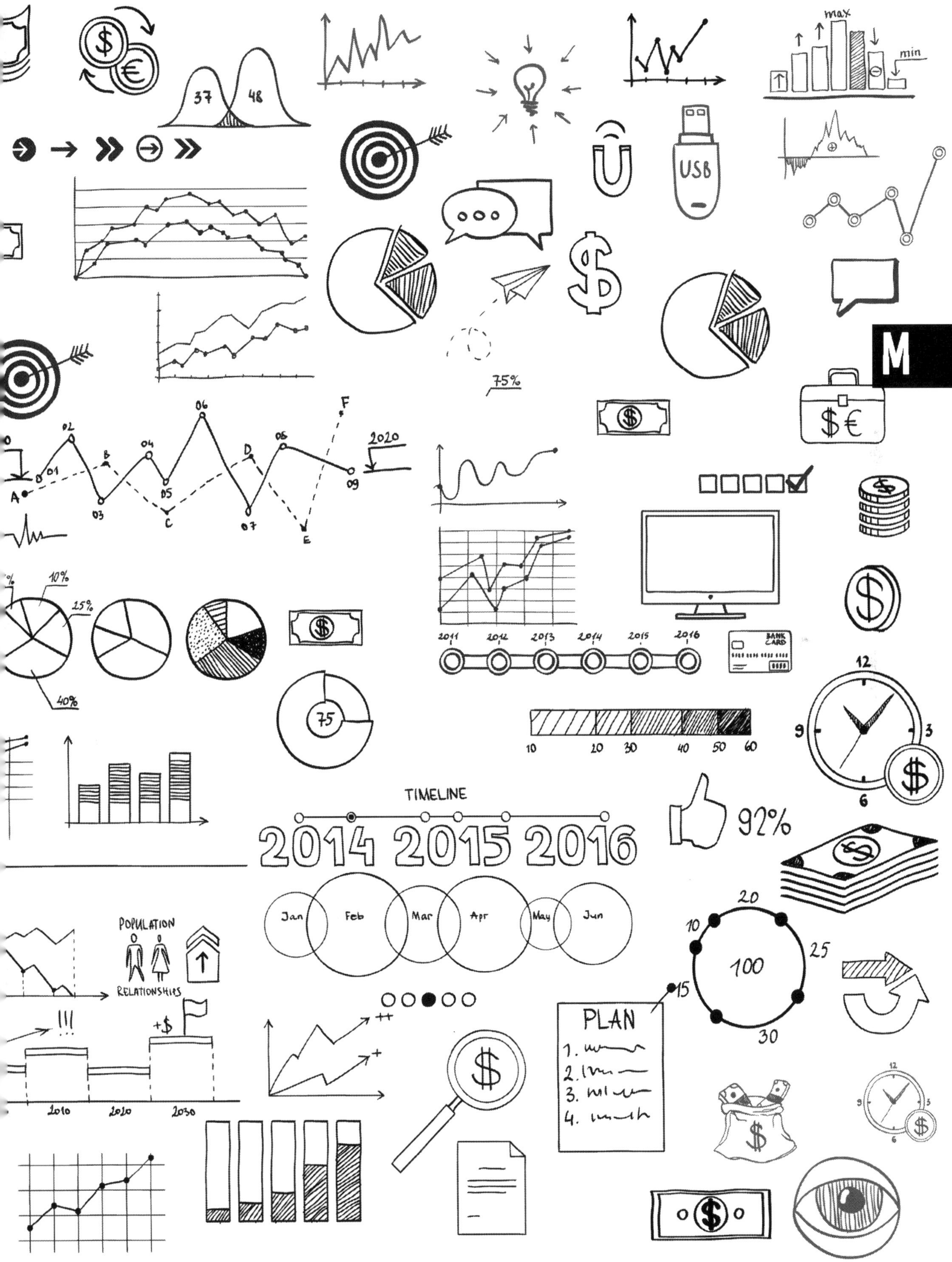

37
48
max
min
USB
75%
2020
TIMELINE
2014 2015 2016
Jan
Feb
Mar
Apr
May
Jun
92%
10%
25%
40%
75
2011
2012
2013
2014
2015
2016
BANK CARD
10 20 30 40 50 60
12
3
6
9
POPULATION
RELATIONSHIPS
!!!
+$
2010
2020
2030
PLAN
100
20
25
30
15
10

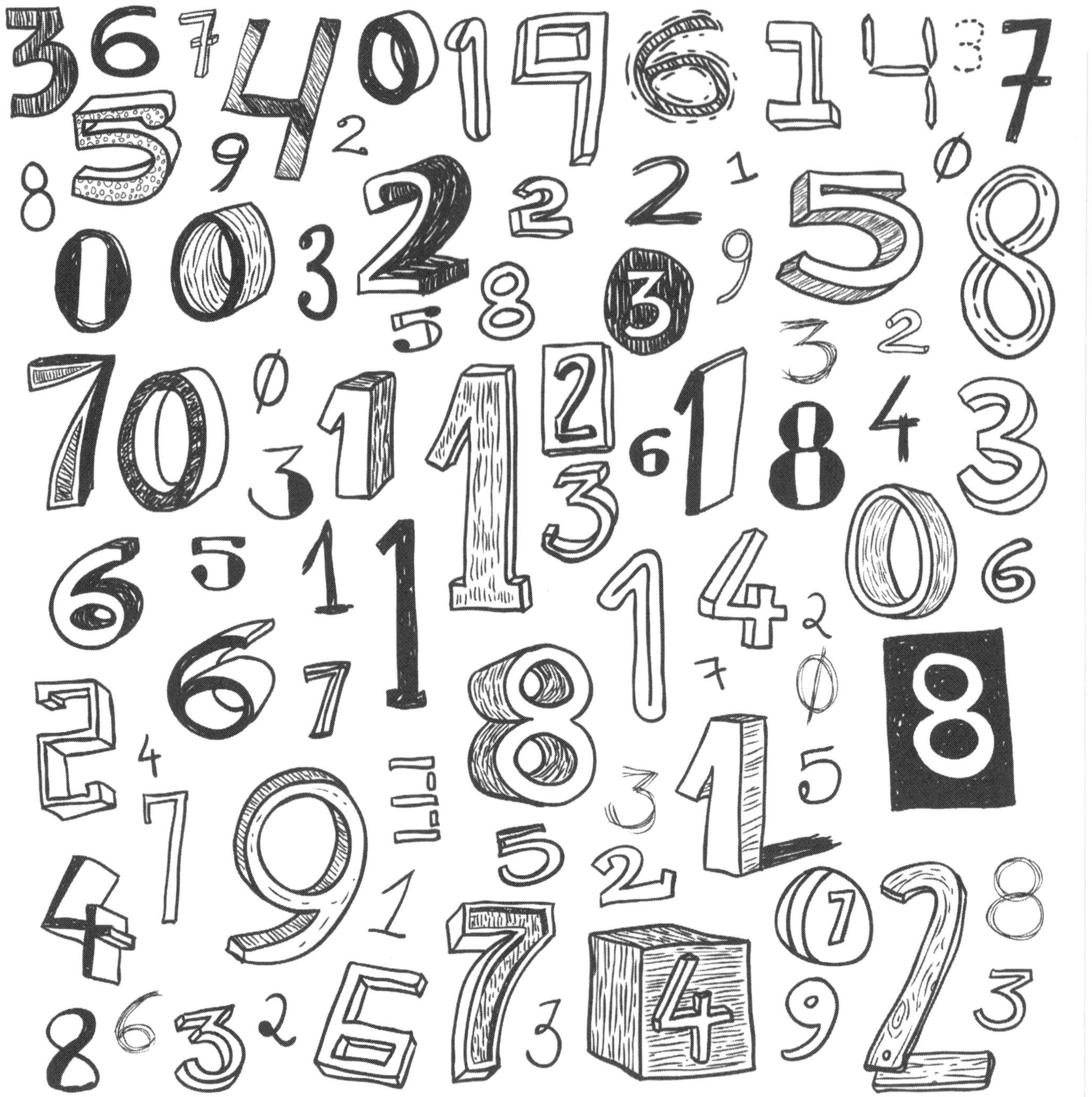

M

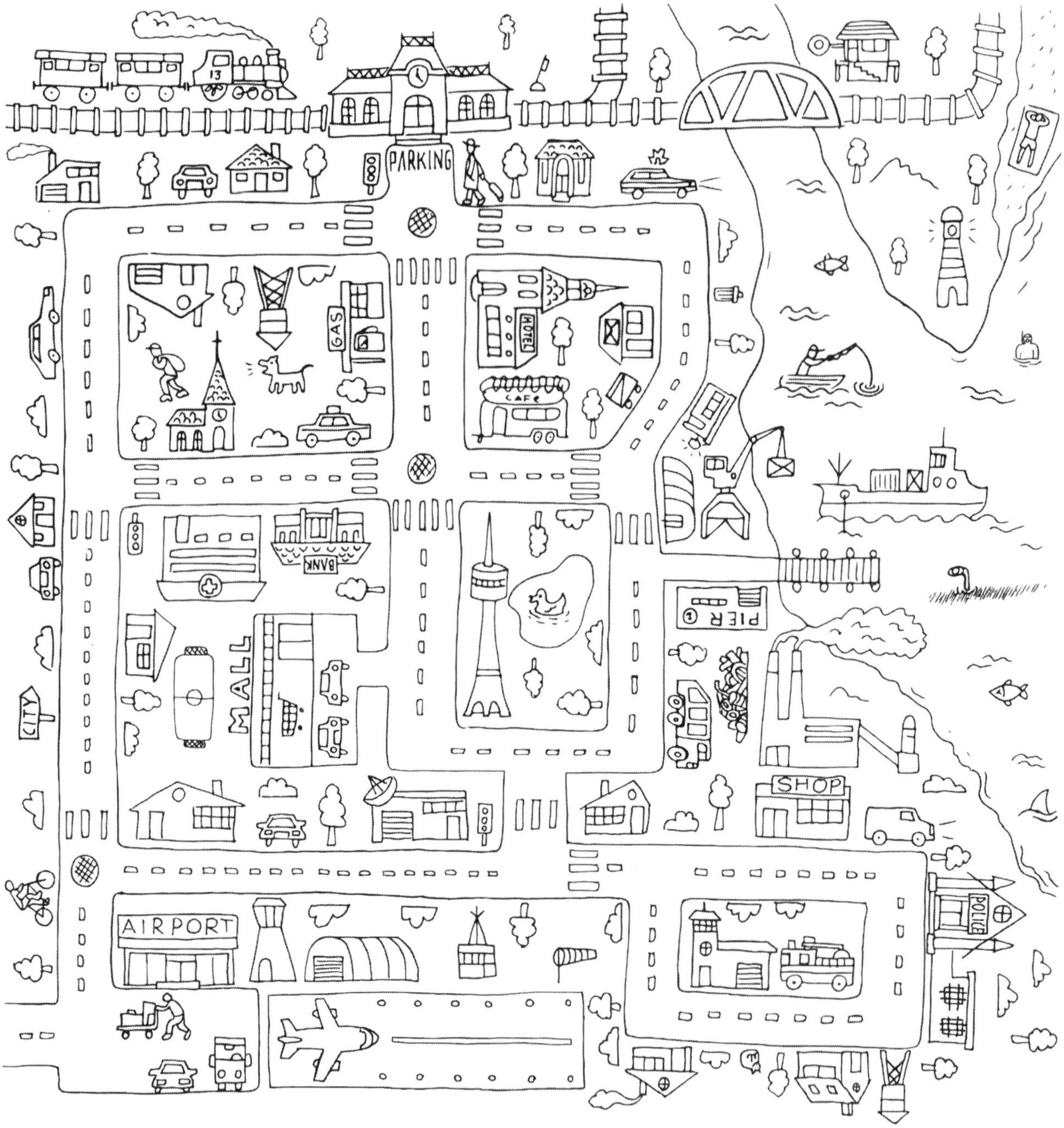

M

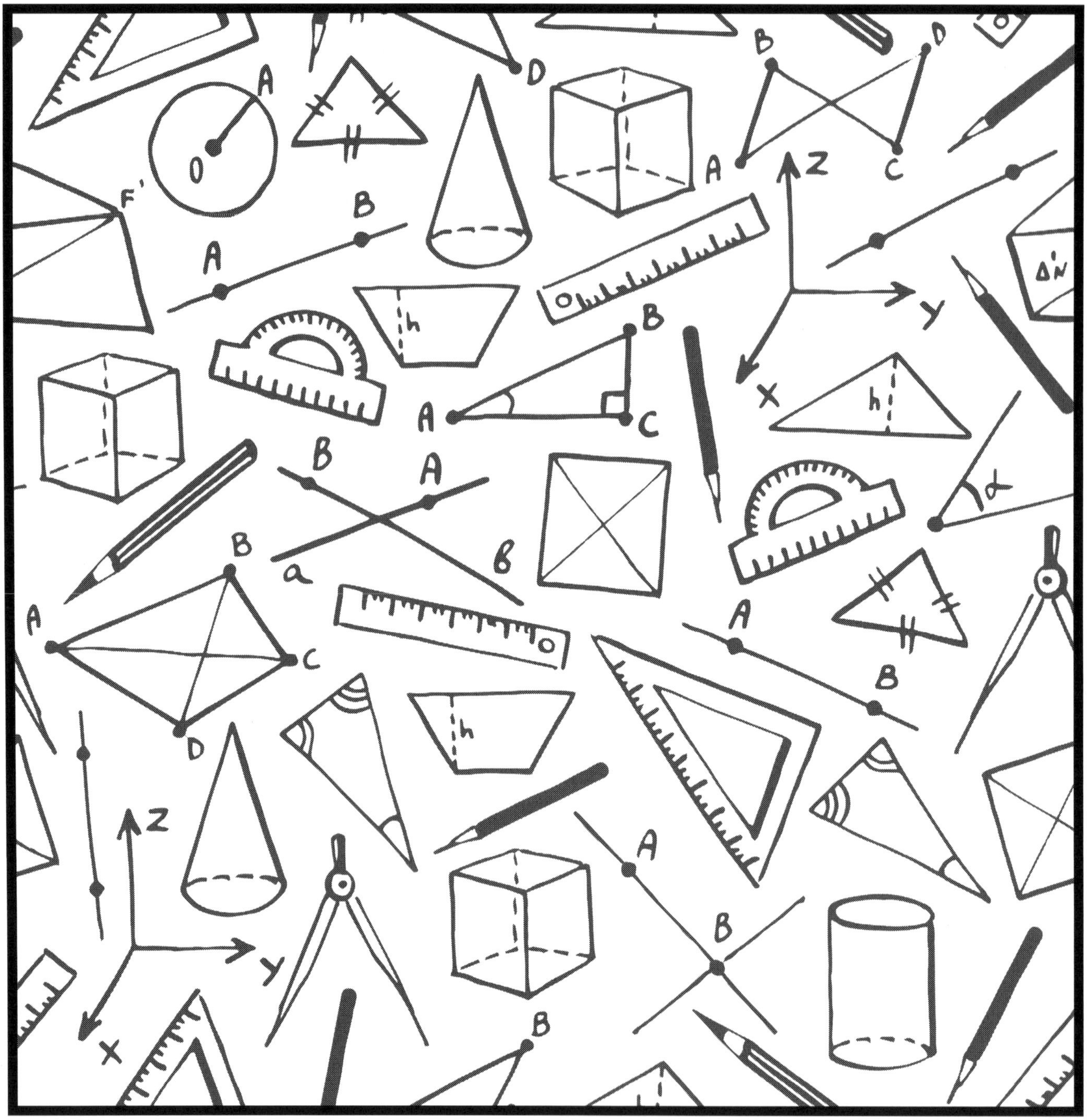

M

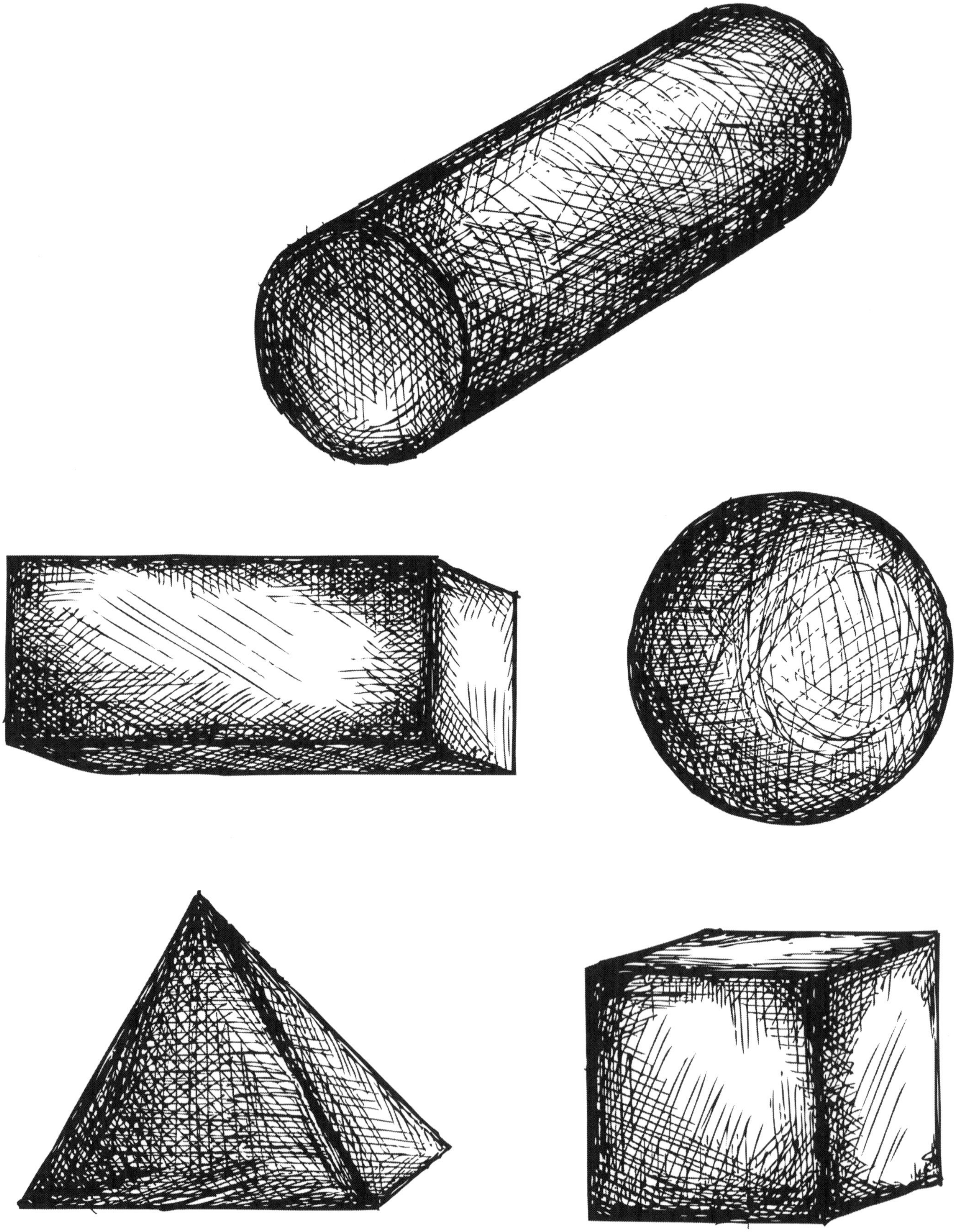

M

149

CREDIT

M

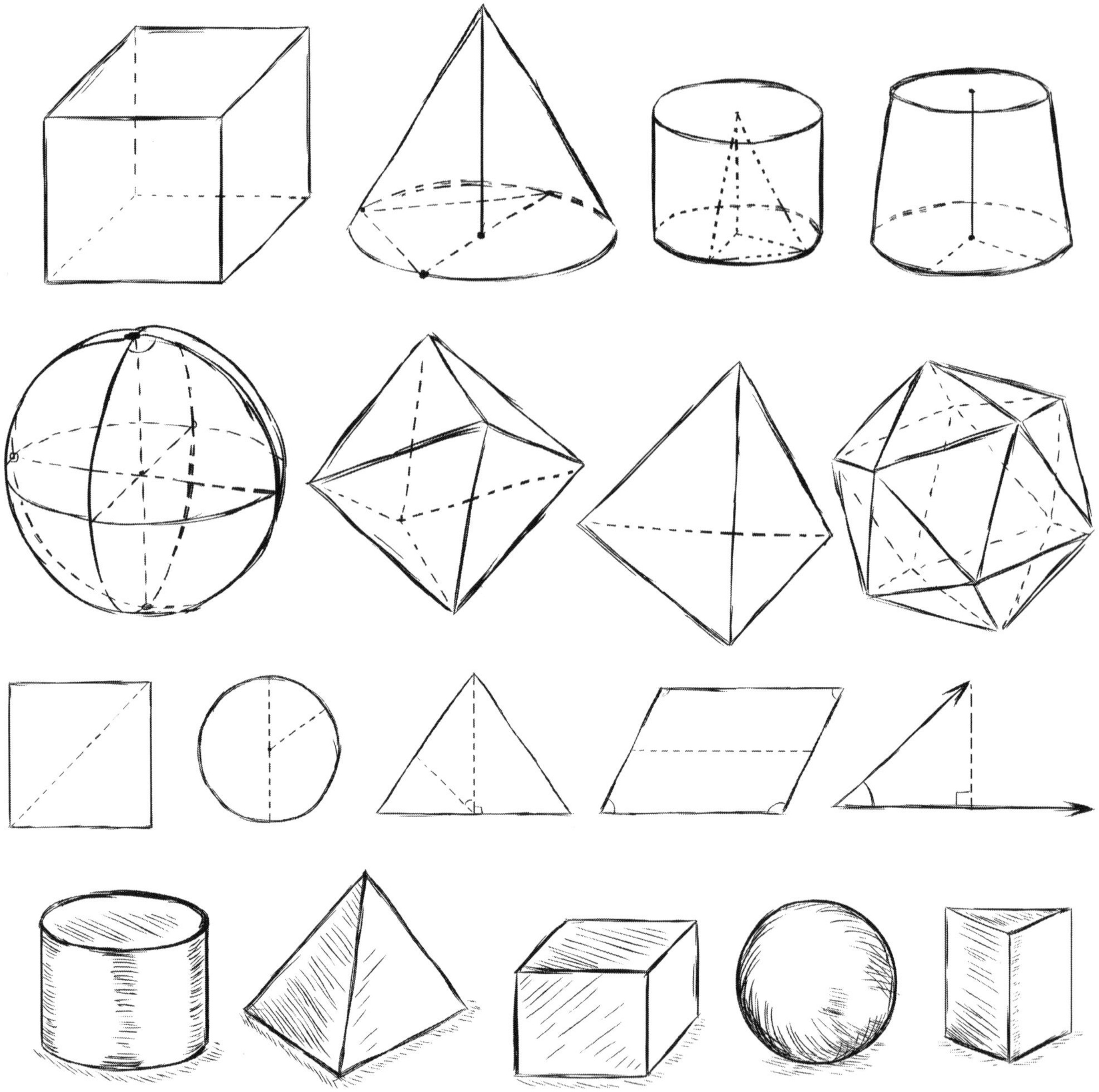

M

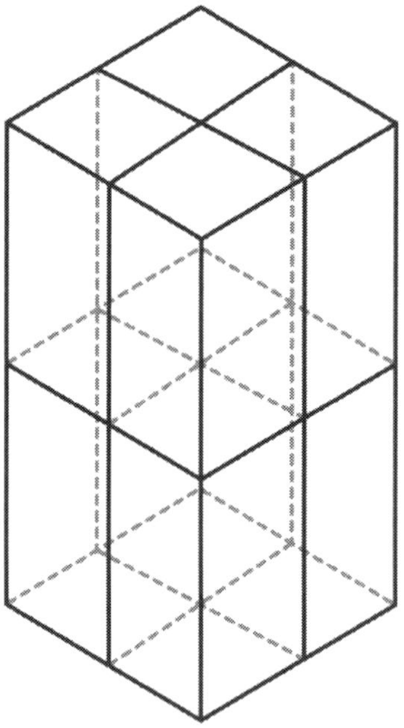
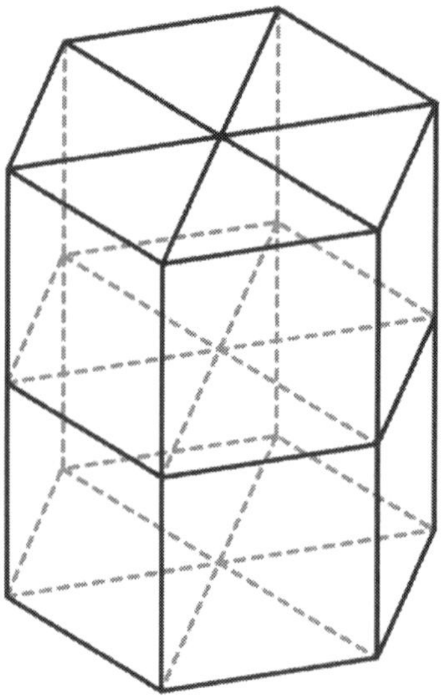
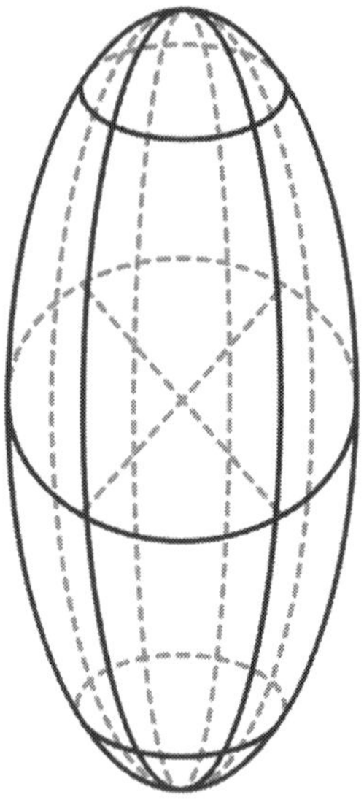
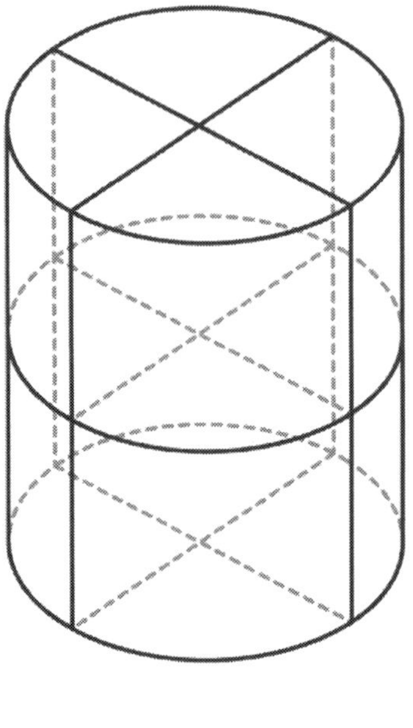
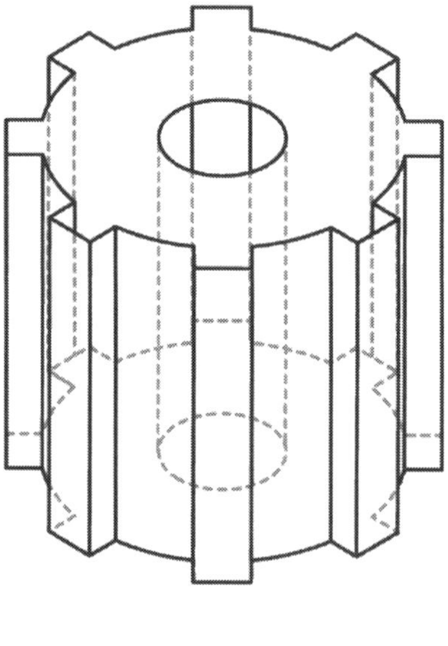
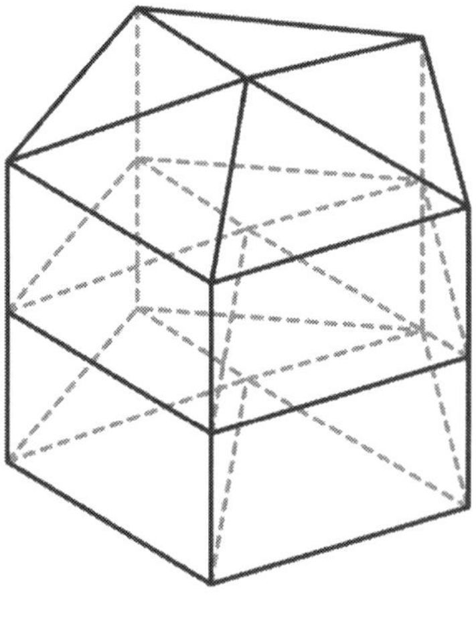

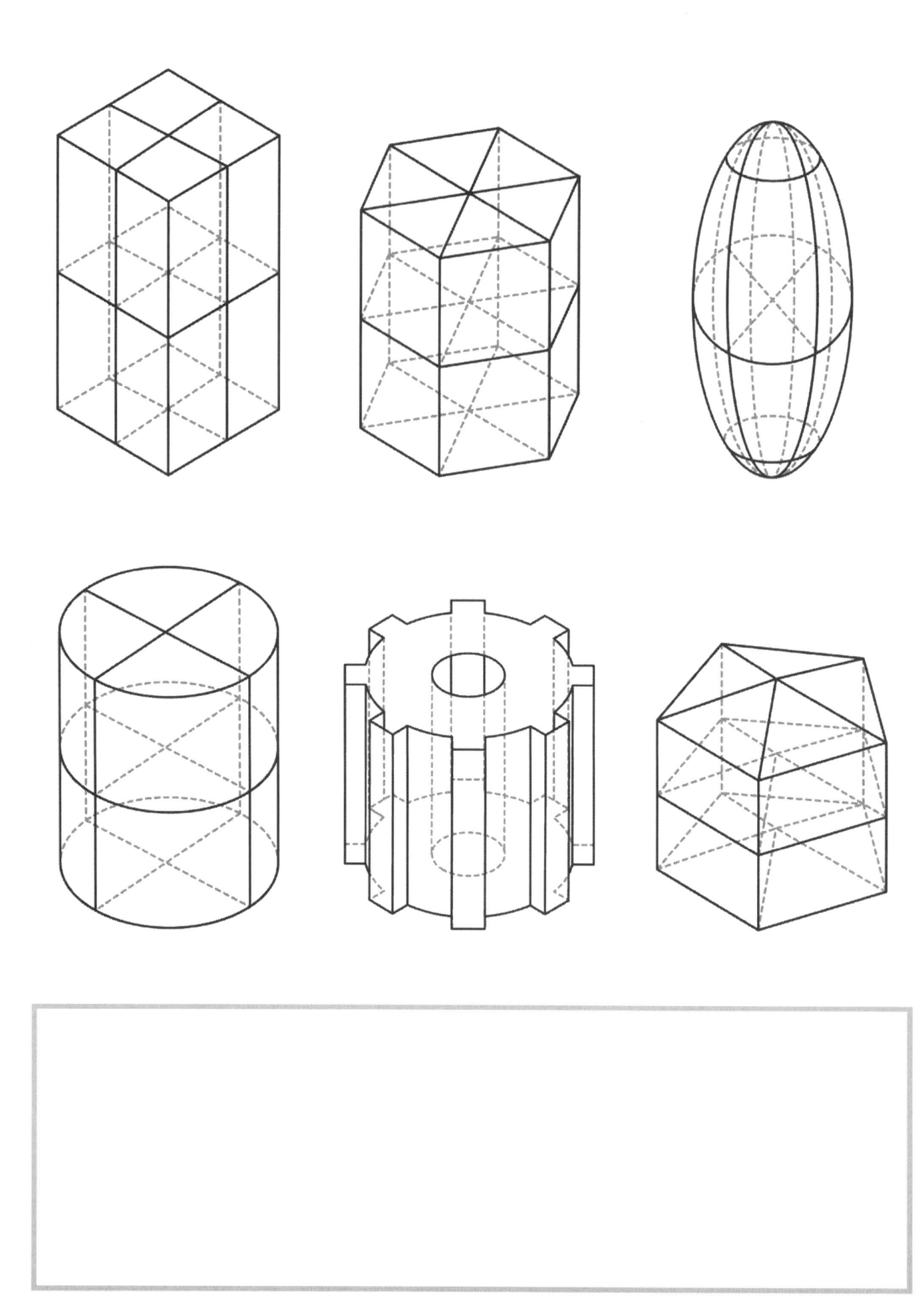

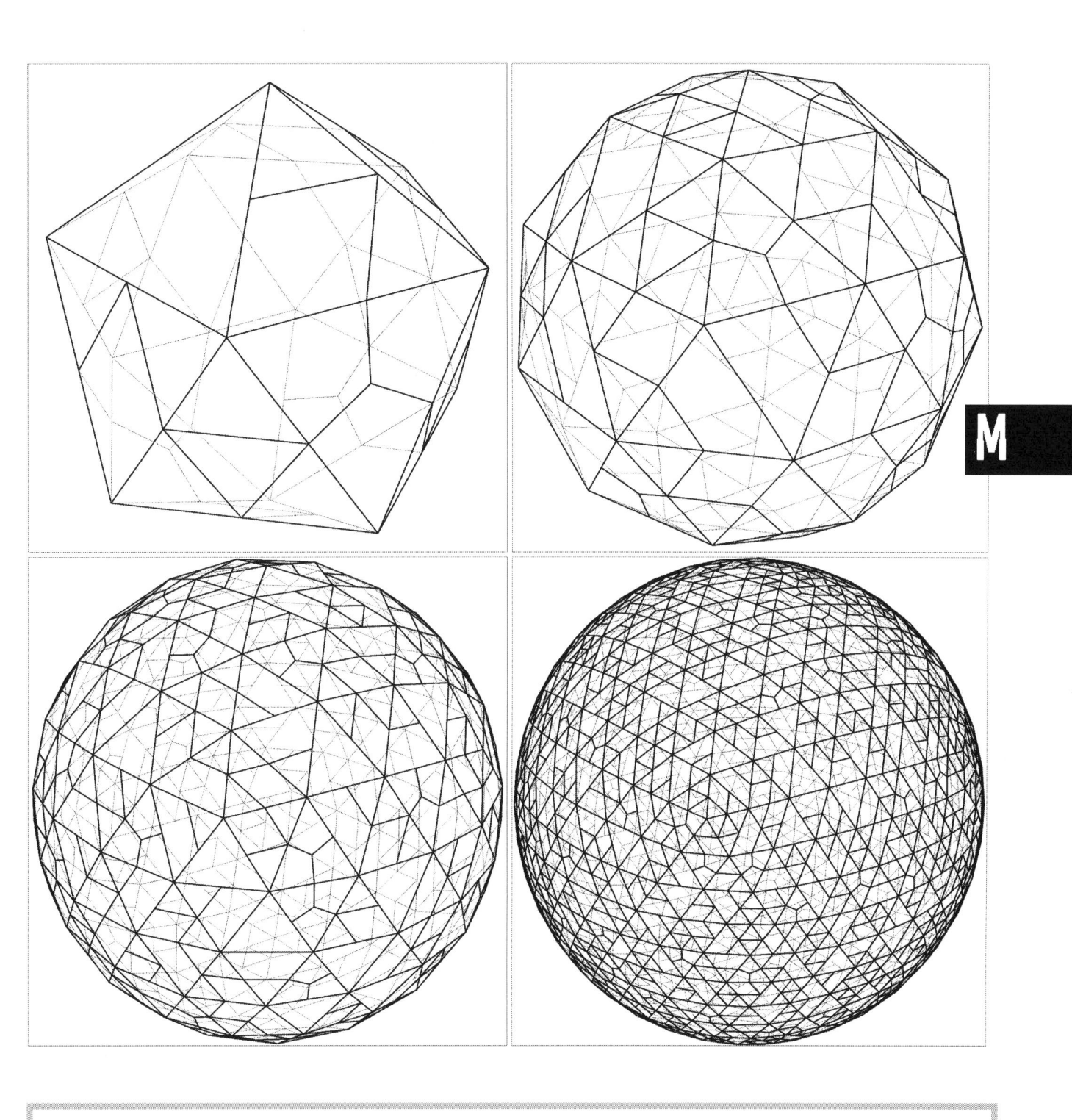

M

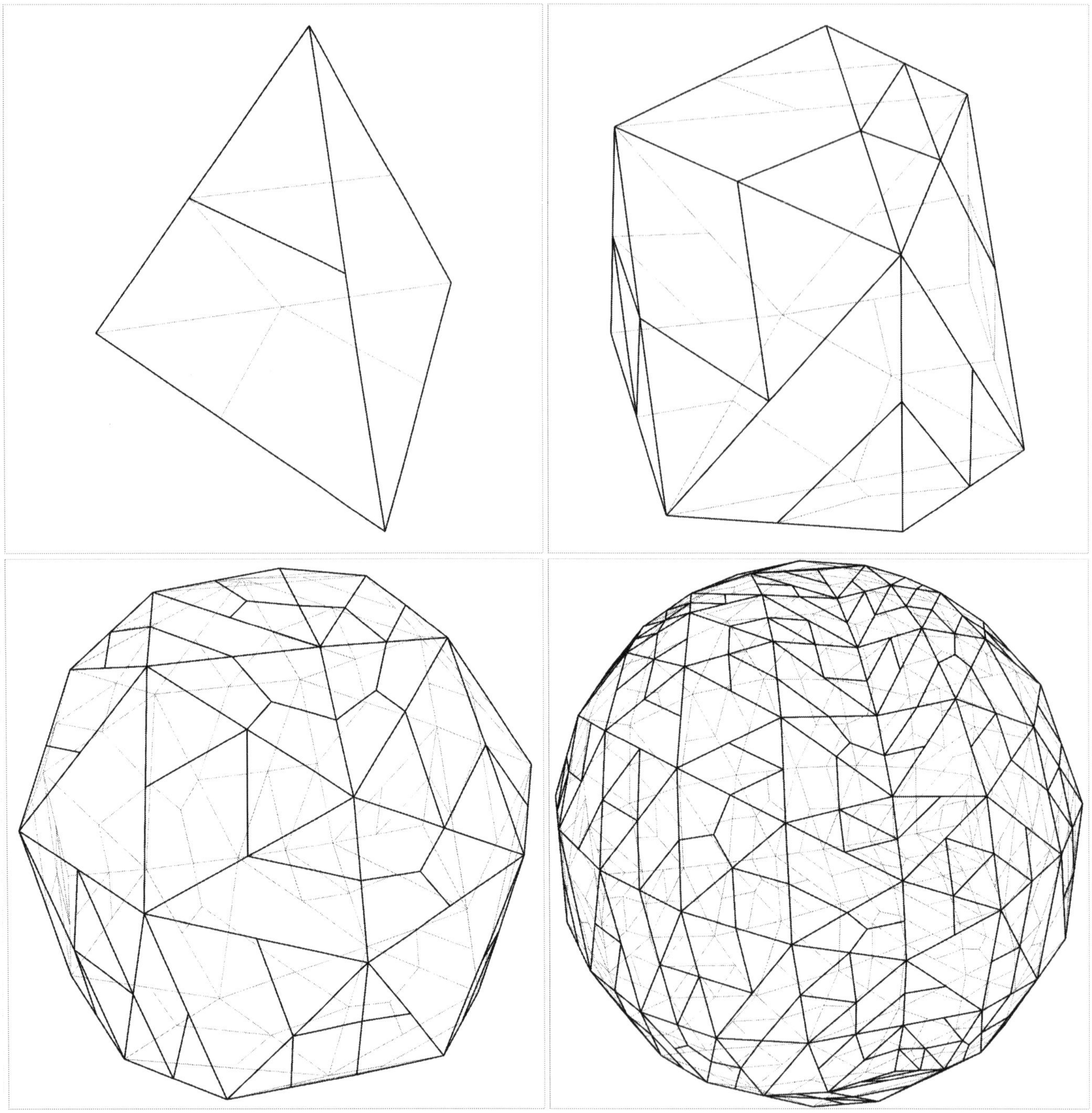

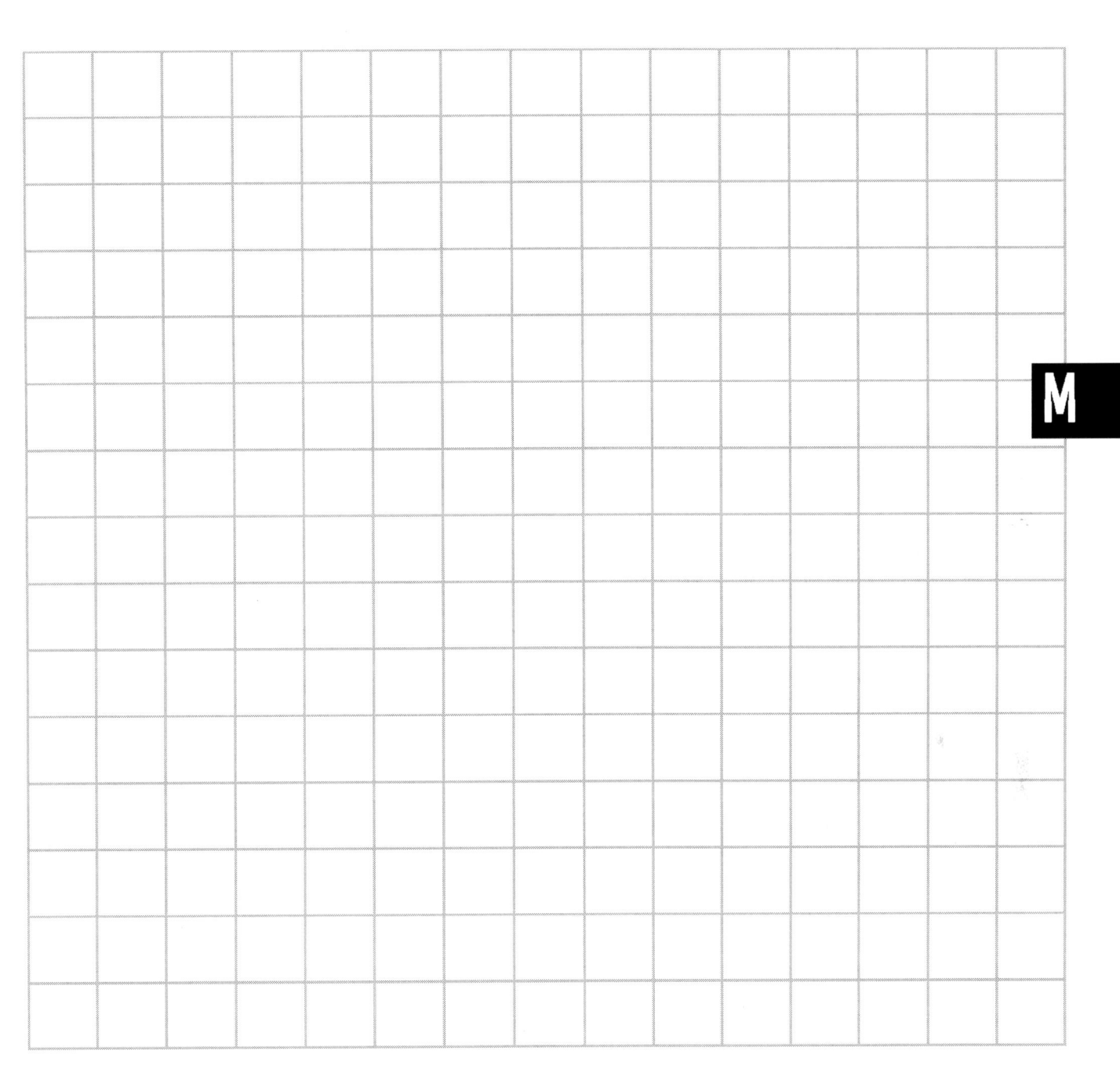

M

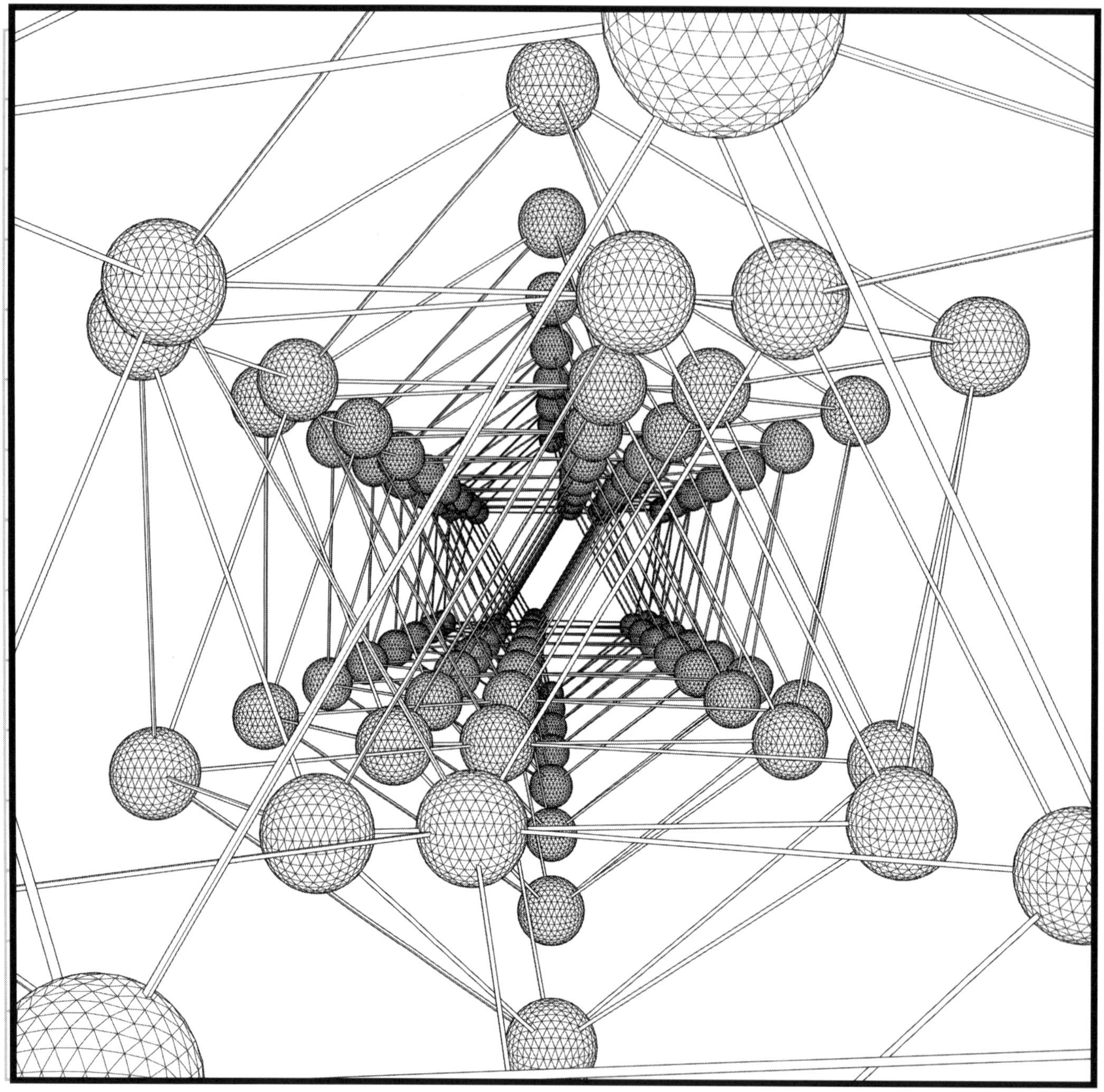

M

TEAM
SECURE
1. Design
2. Built
3. Profit
IDEA
A. D. G.
B. E. H.
C. F. I.
GRAPH
STARTUP
¥ $ £ €
3 7 5 6 8 2
CONTRACT
40 60 20
PROFIT
DEAL
Investment
%

M

$a^2 - b^2 = (a+b)(a-b)$

GEOMETRY

$a^0 = 1$

$(ab)^n = a^n b^n$

$a^m \times a^n = a^{m+n}$

$S = vt$

11	16	15
18	14	10
13	12	17

π

$A = l \times w$

CIRCLE

$C = 2\pi r$
$A = 2\pi r^2$

Math

$a^{-n} = \dfrac{1}{a^n}$

TRIANGLE

SQUARE

$c^2 = a^2 + b^2$

$A = \dfrac{1}{2} bh$

$(a^m)^n = a^{mn}$

numbers

$\left(\dfrac{a}{b}\right)^n = \dfrac{a^n}{b^n}$

$\dfrac{a^m}{a^n} = a^{m-n}$

$(a+b)^2 = a^2 + 2ab + b^2$
$(a-b)^2 = a^2 - 2ab + b^2$

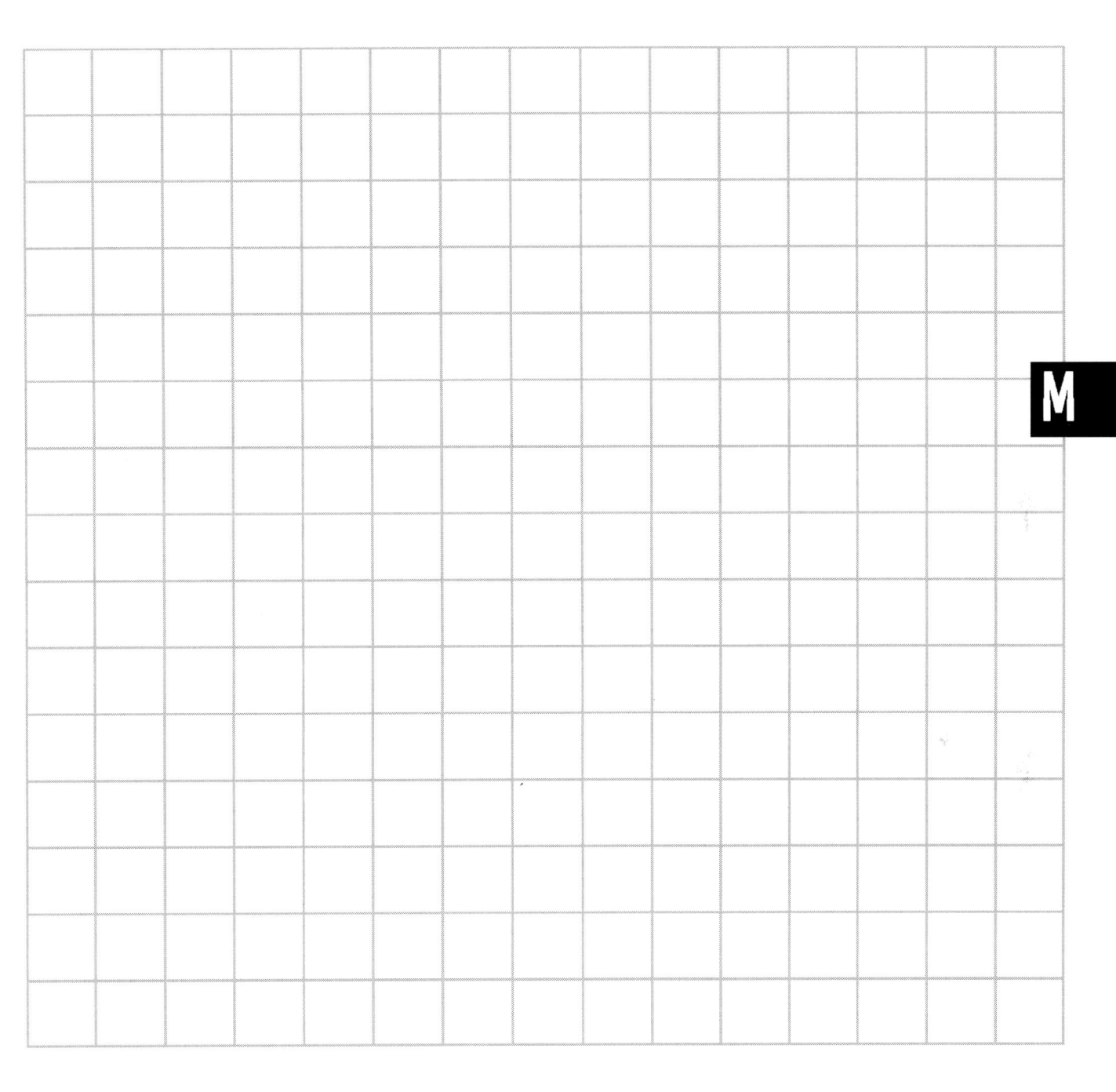

M

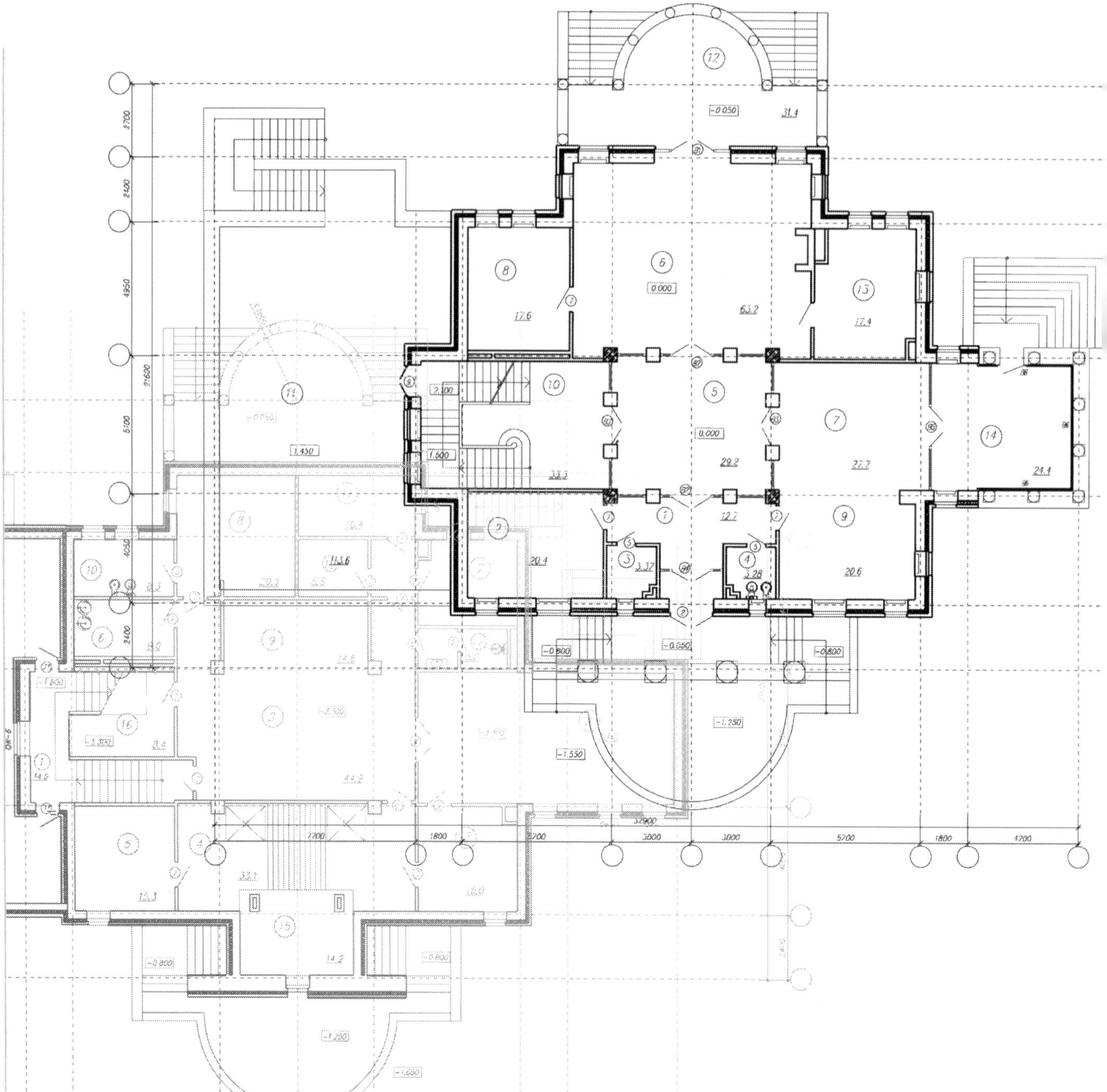

M

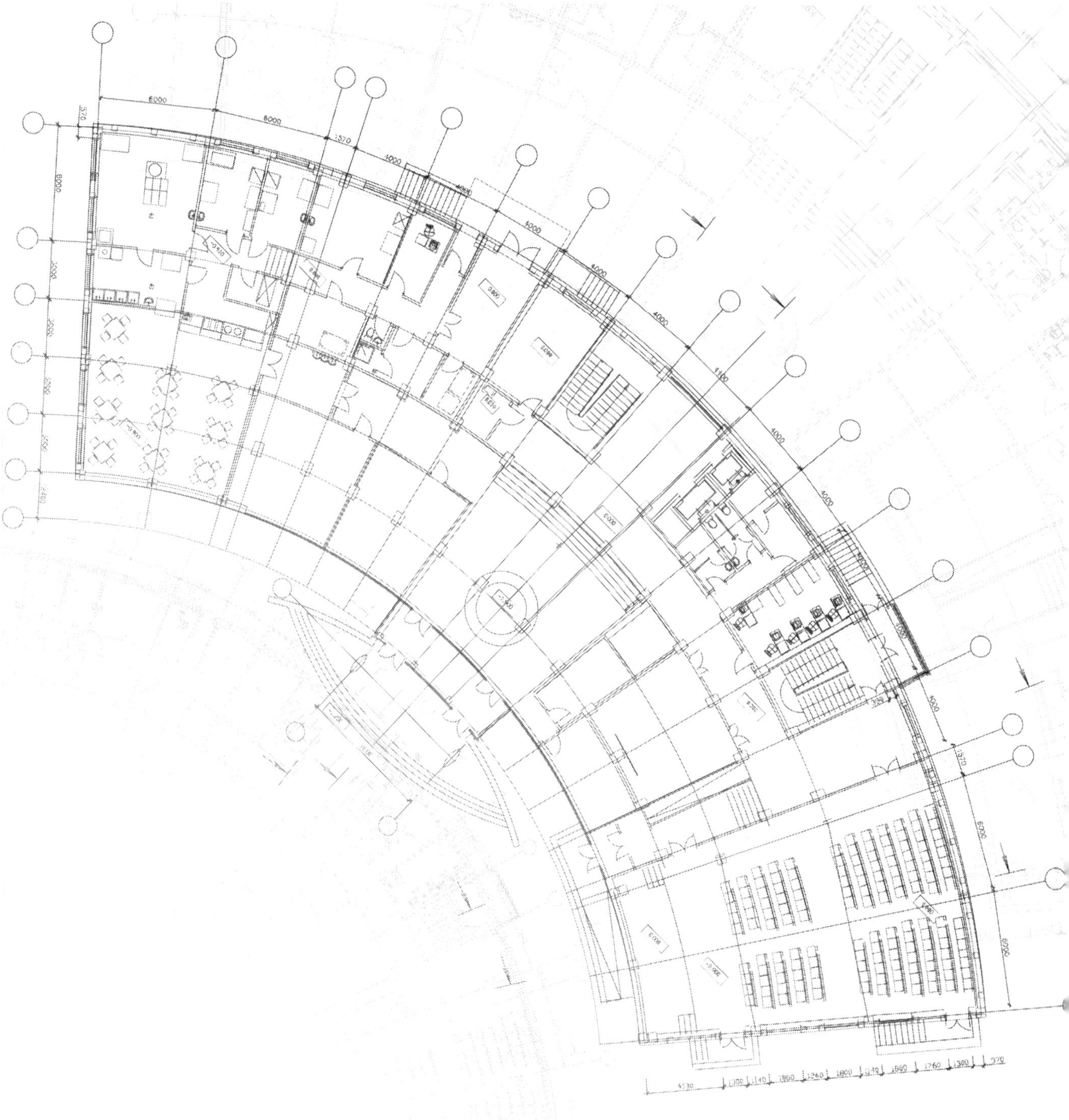

M

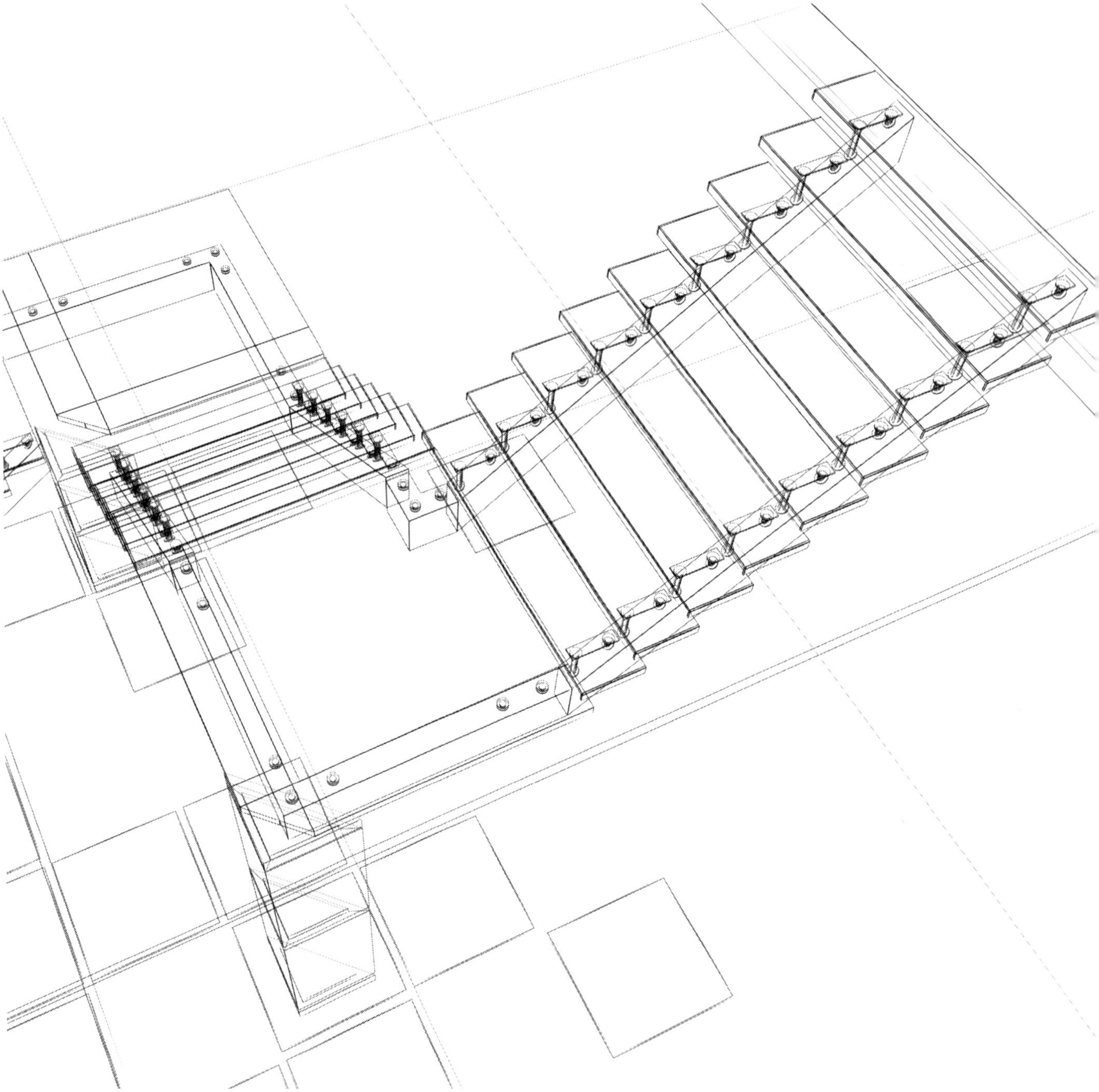

M

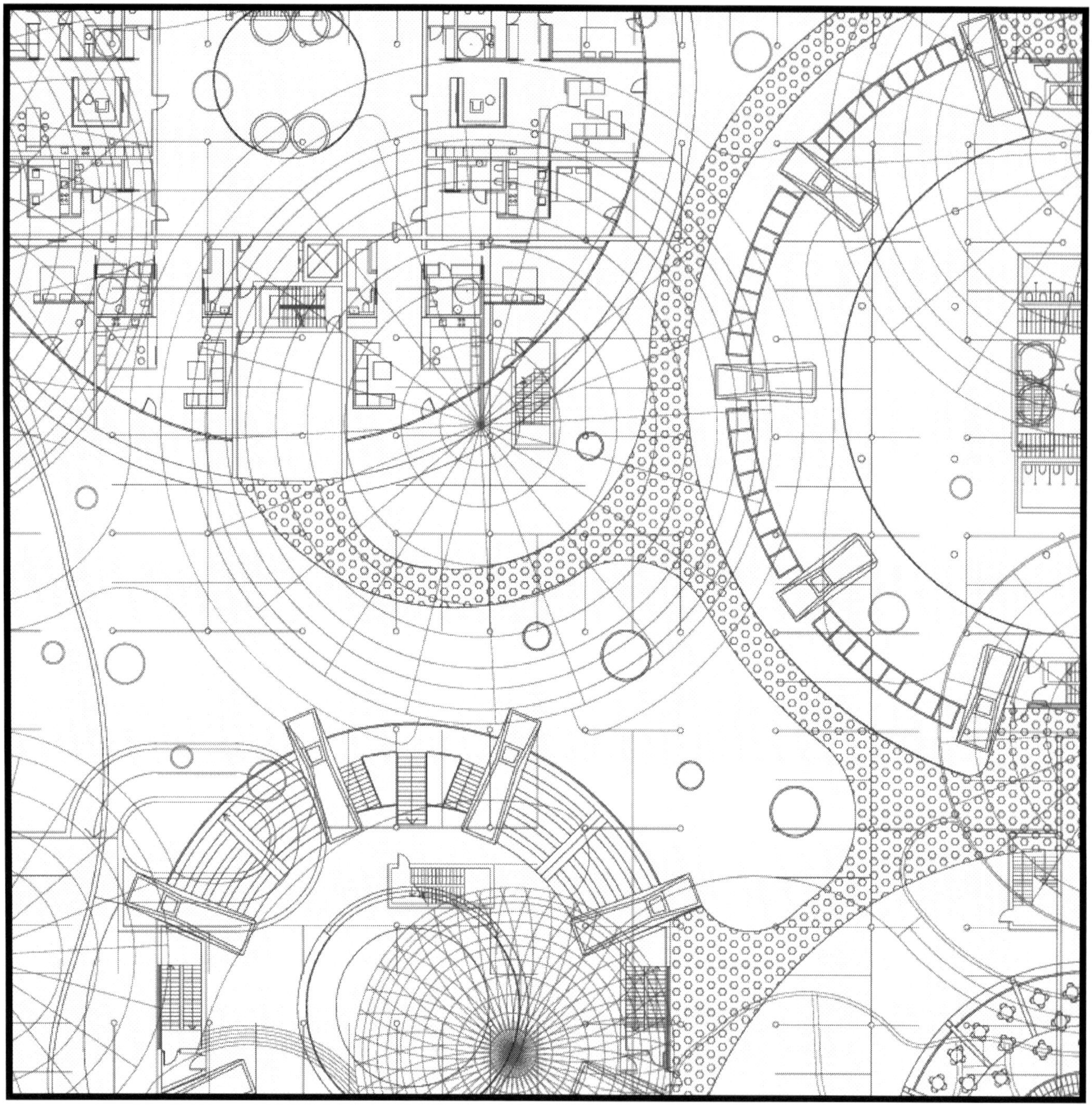

M

M

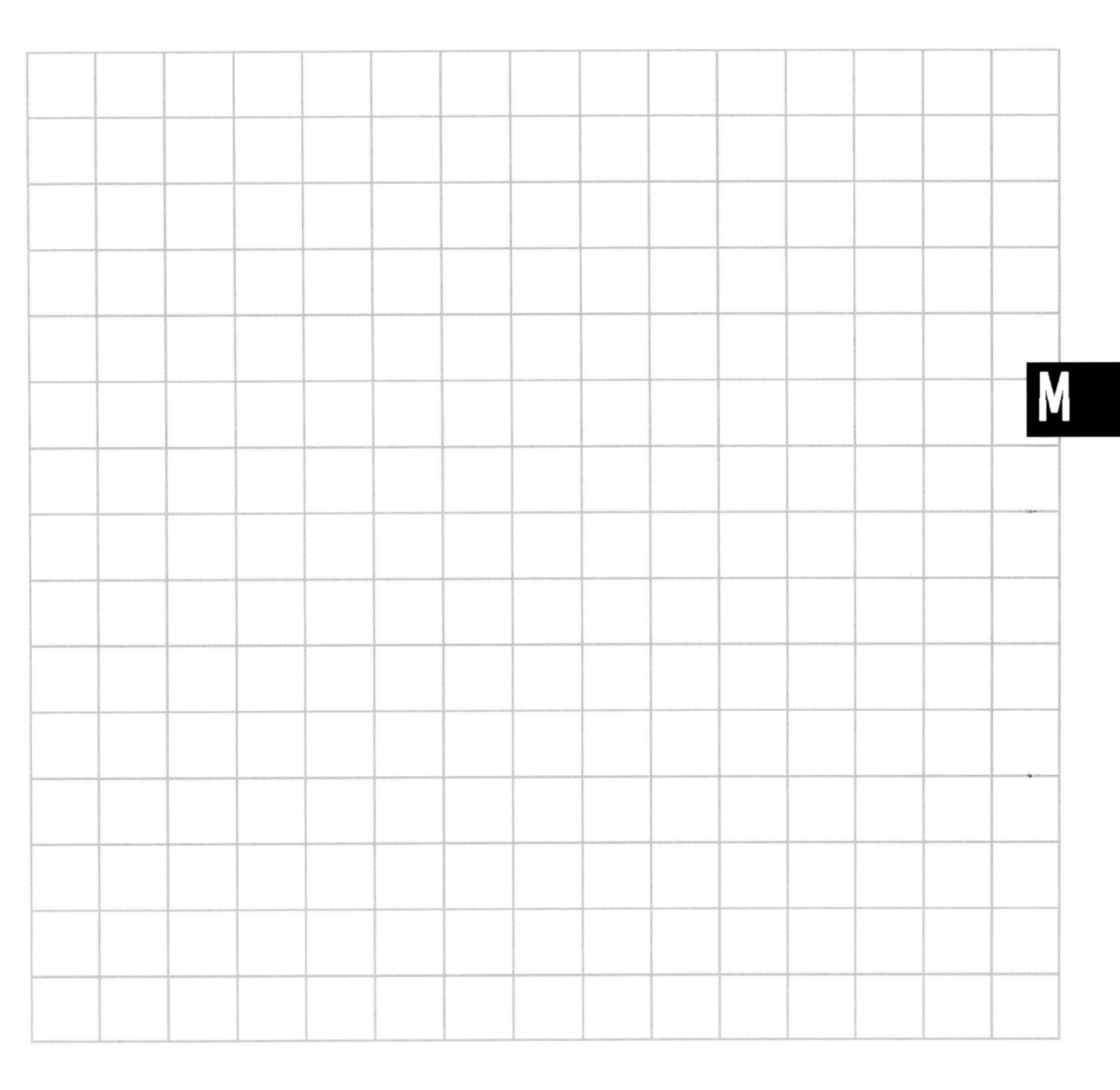

M

175

M

Business & Technology

What do you want to learn about business and technology?

1.

2.

3.

4.

5.

Action Steps:

1. Go to the library or bookstore.
2. Bring home a stack of at least FOUR interesting books about these topics. Choose some that have diagrams, instructions and illustrations.
3. Plan to watch online tutorials on this topic.

Supplies Needed:

You will need pencils, black drawing pens, colored pencils, gel pens and markers.

What are your Future Career Goals?

Choose FOUR Books About Buisness & Technology To Use As School Books!

1. Write down the titles on each cover below.
2. You may also choose Videos, Tutorials and Documenteries to help you learn about these topics.

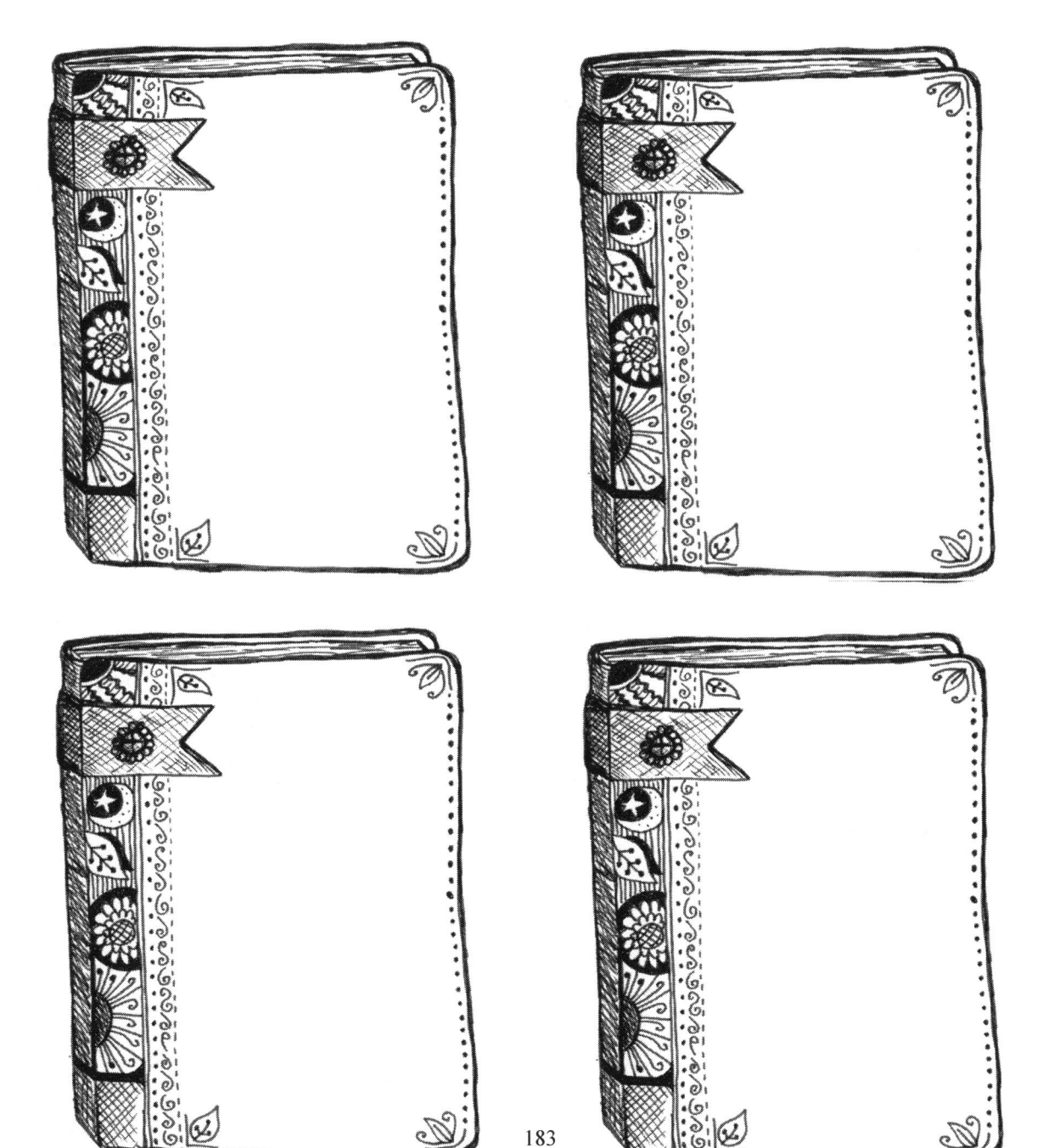

BT

TITLE:_____

Date_____

Quotes, Tips and Ideas

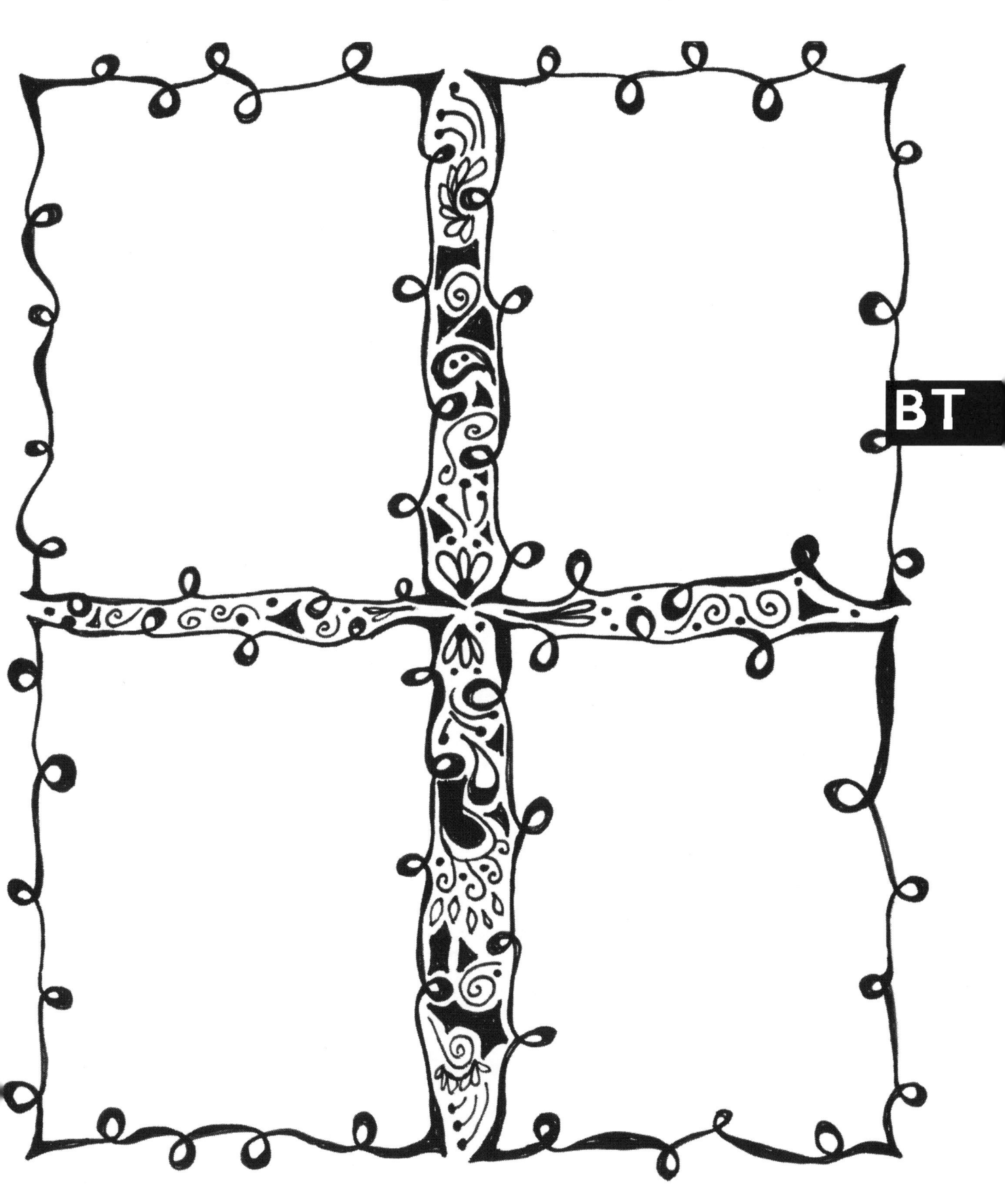

TITLE:_____

Date_____

Quotes, Tips and Ideas

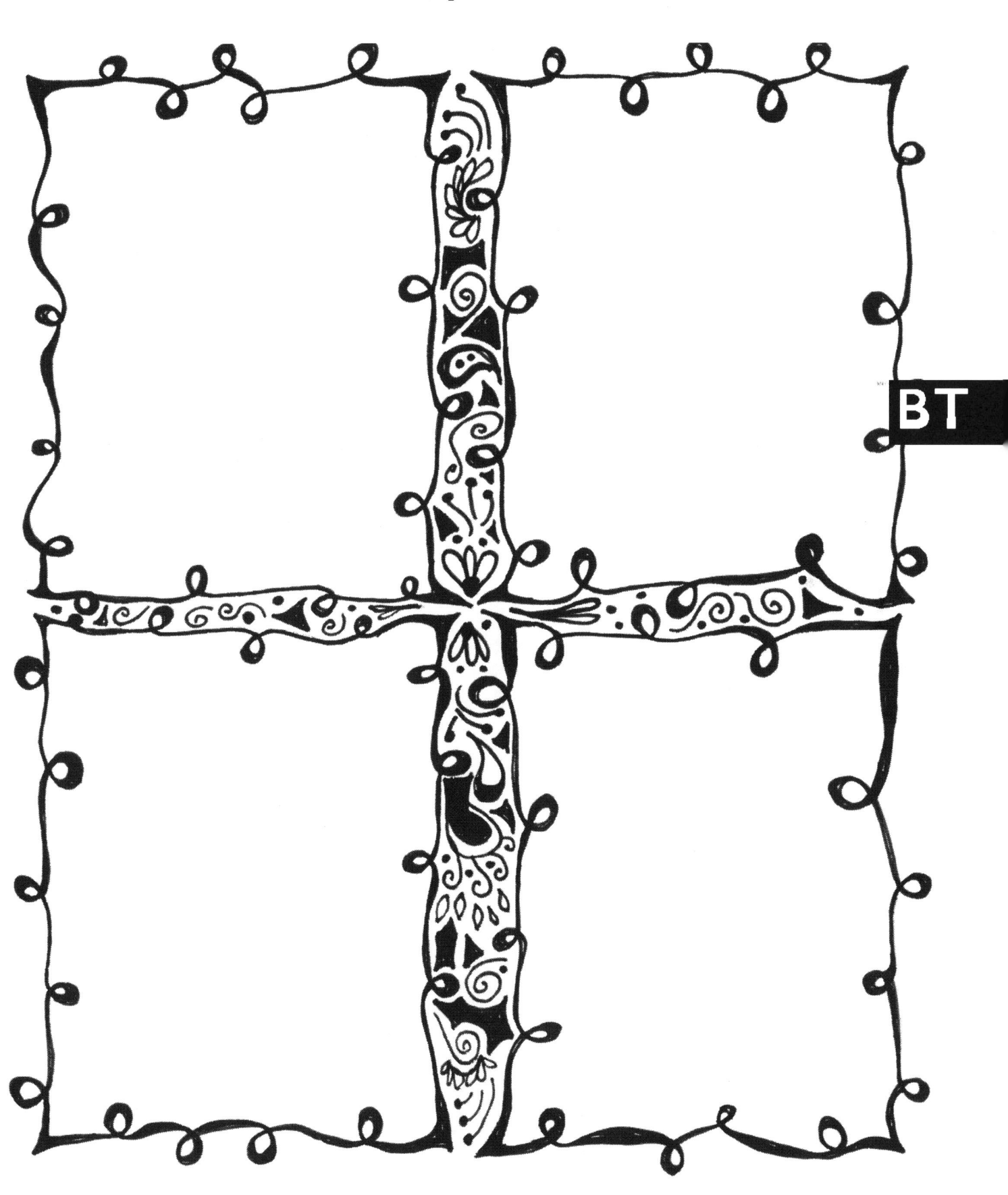

TITLE:_____

Date_____

Quotes, Tips and Ideas

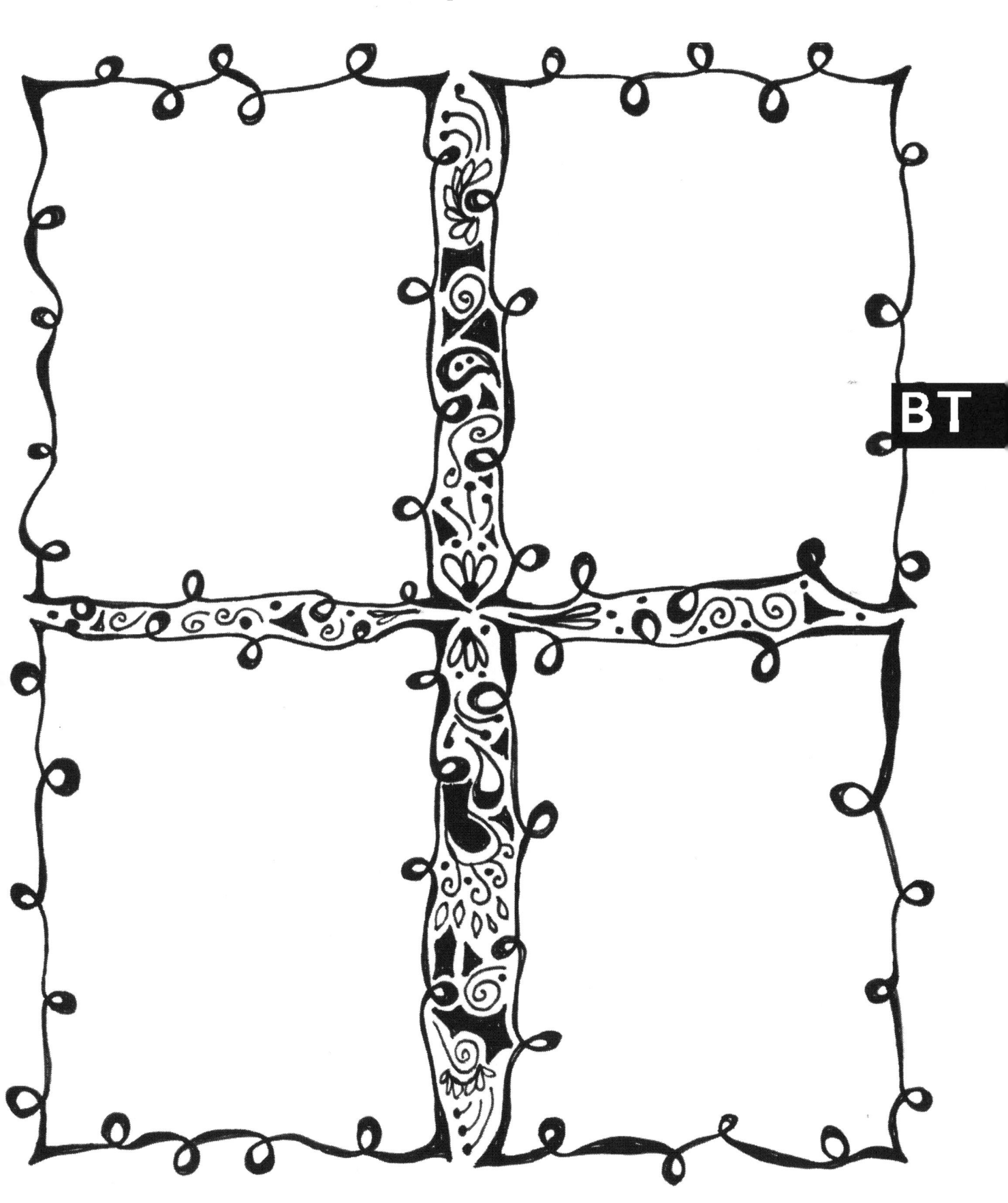

TITLE:_____

Date_____

Quotes, Tips and Ideas

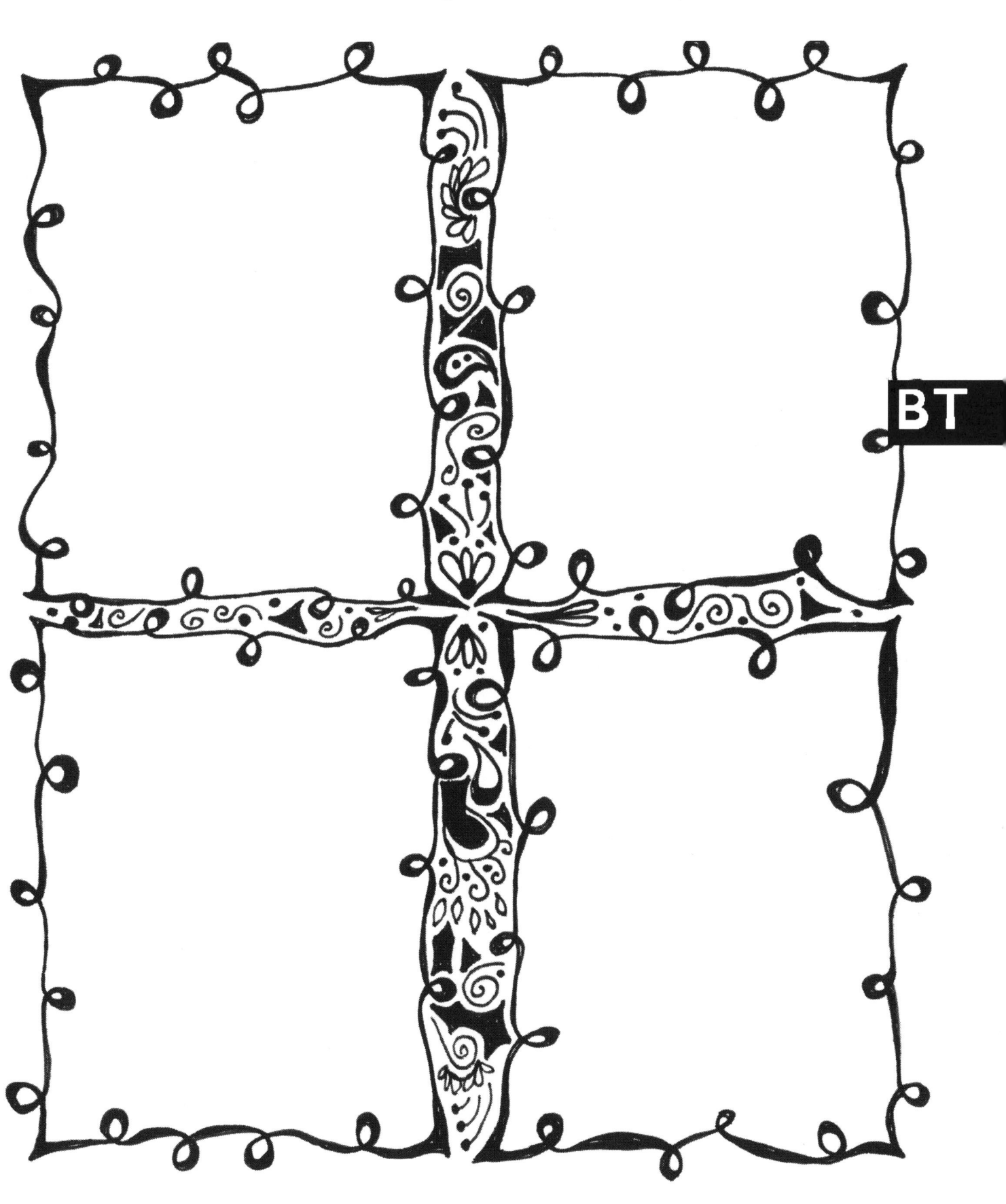

TITLE:_____

Date_____

Quotes, Tips and Ideas

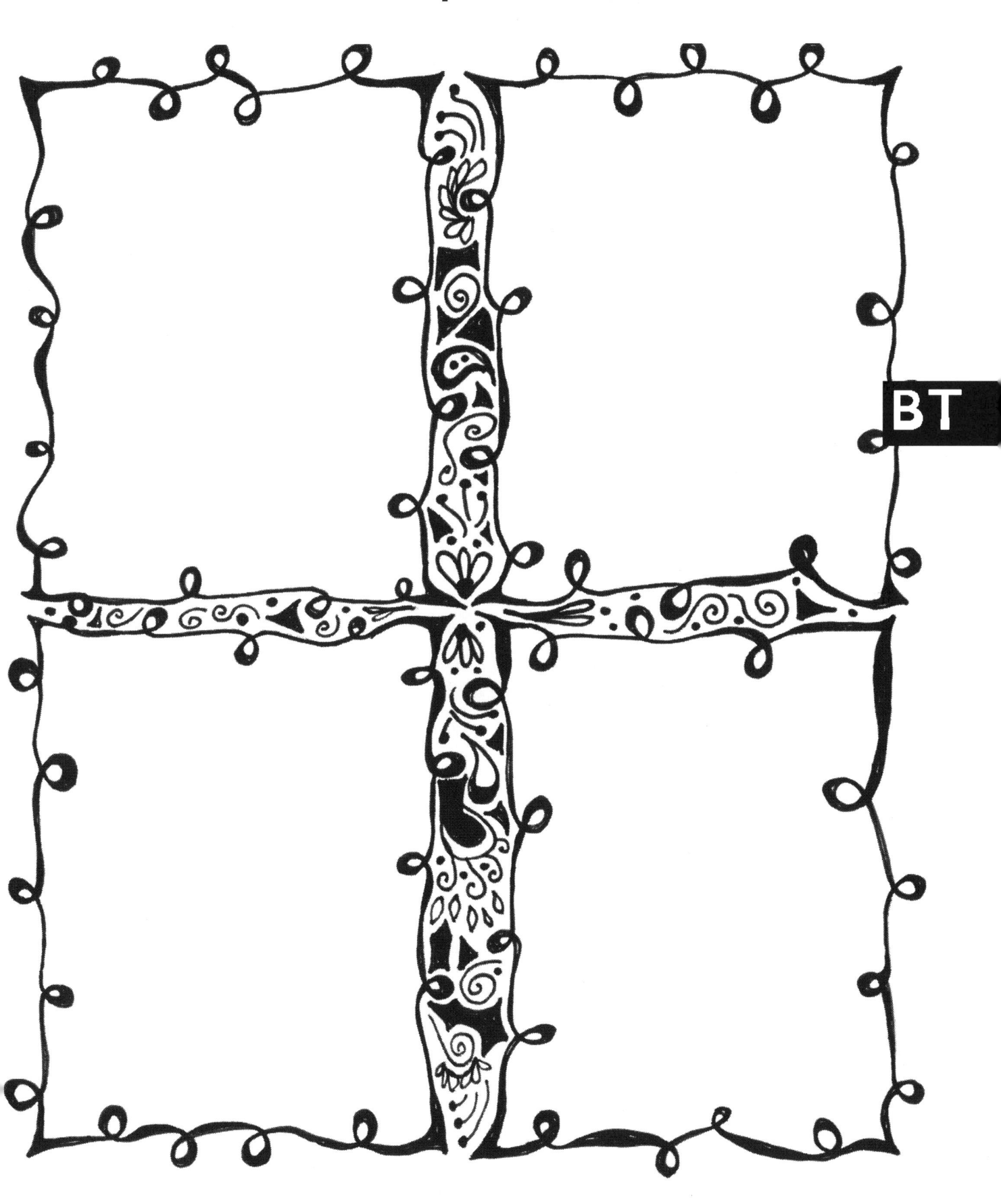

TITLE:_____

Date_____

Quotes, Tips and Ideas

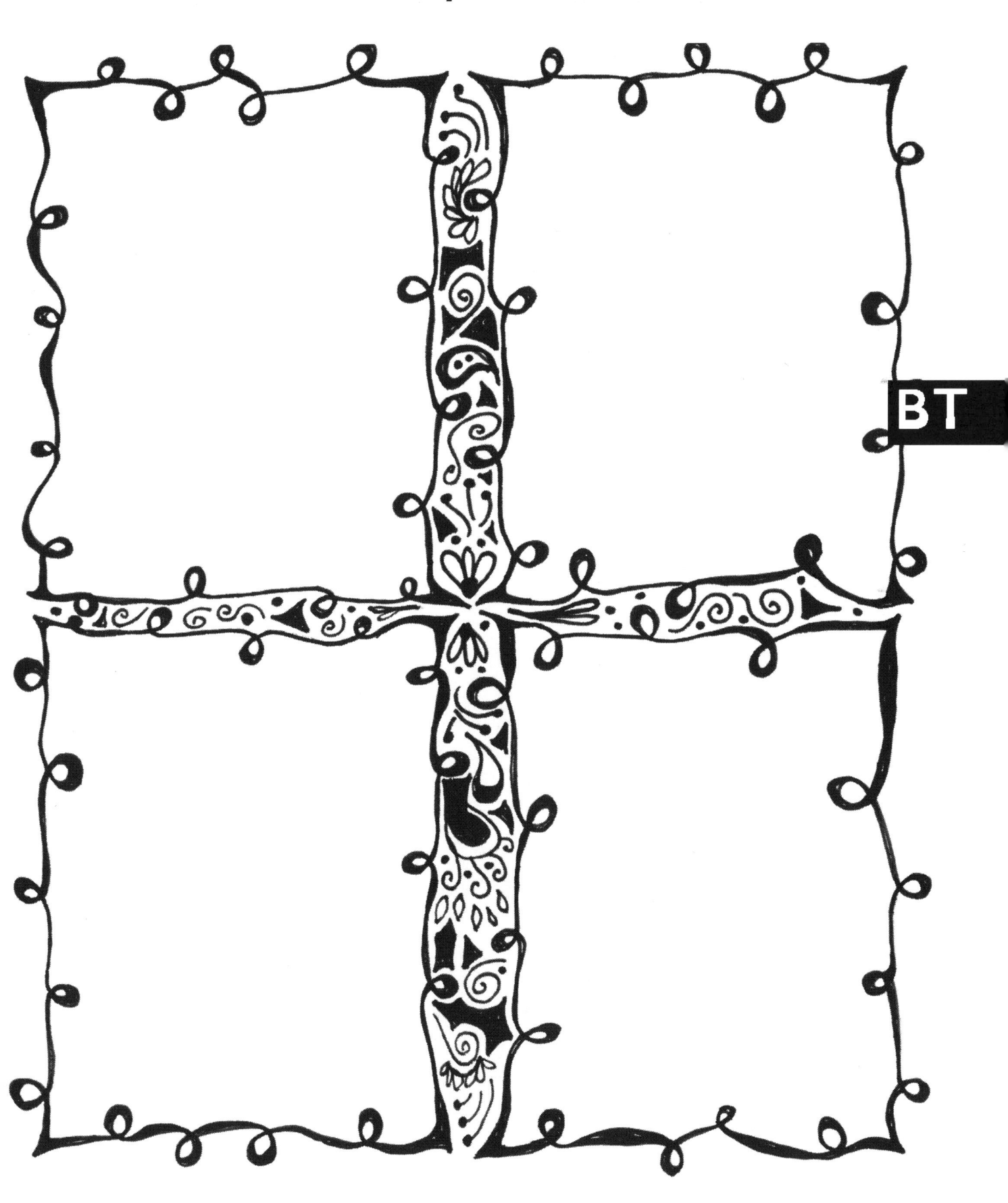

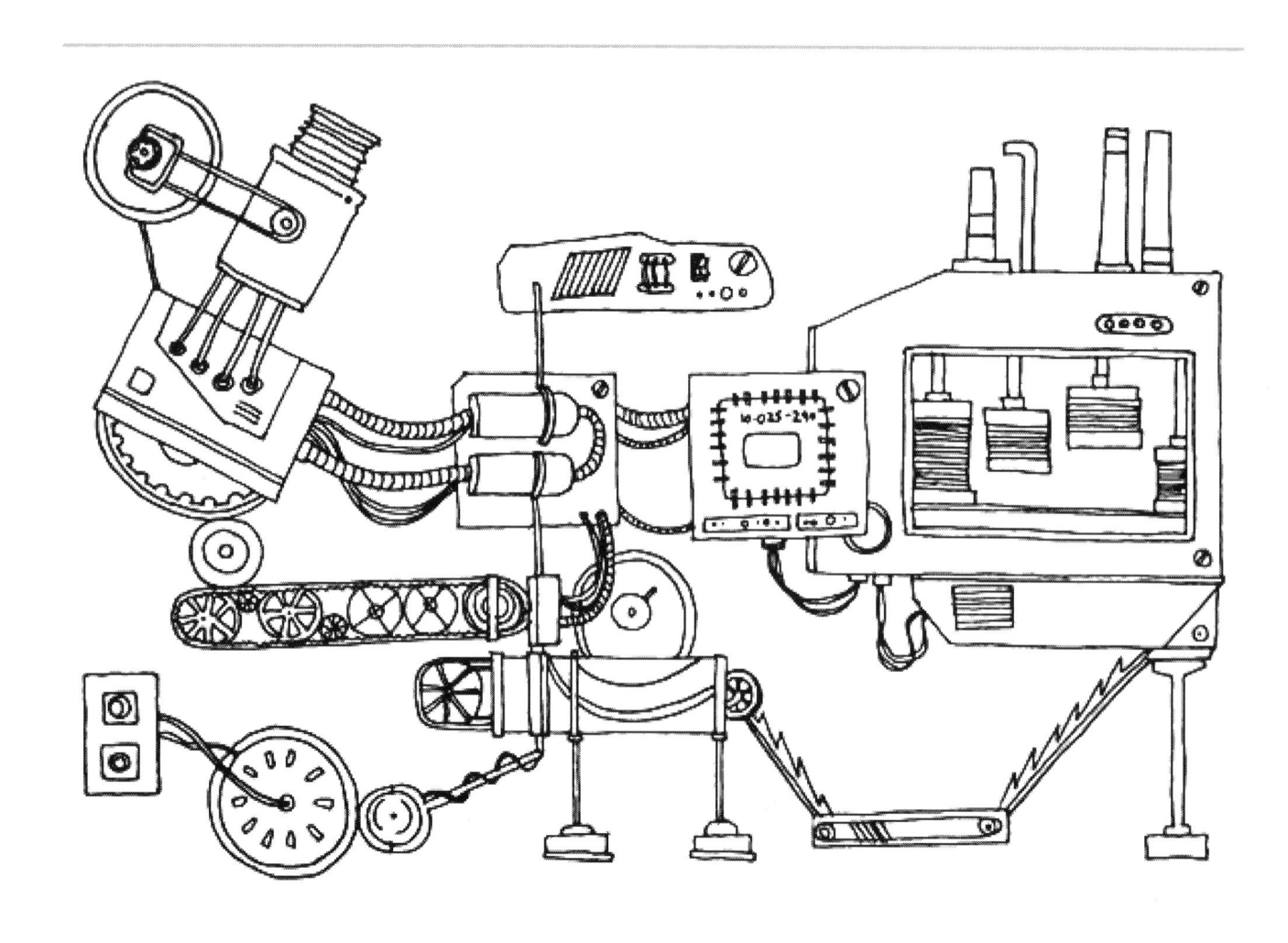

TITLE:_____

Date_____

Quotes, Tips and Ideas

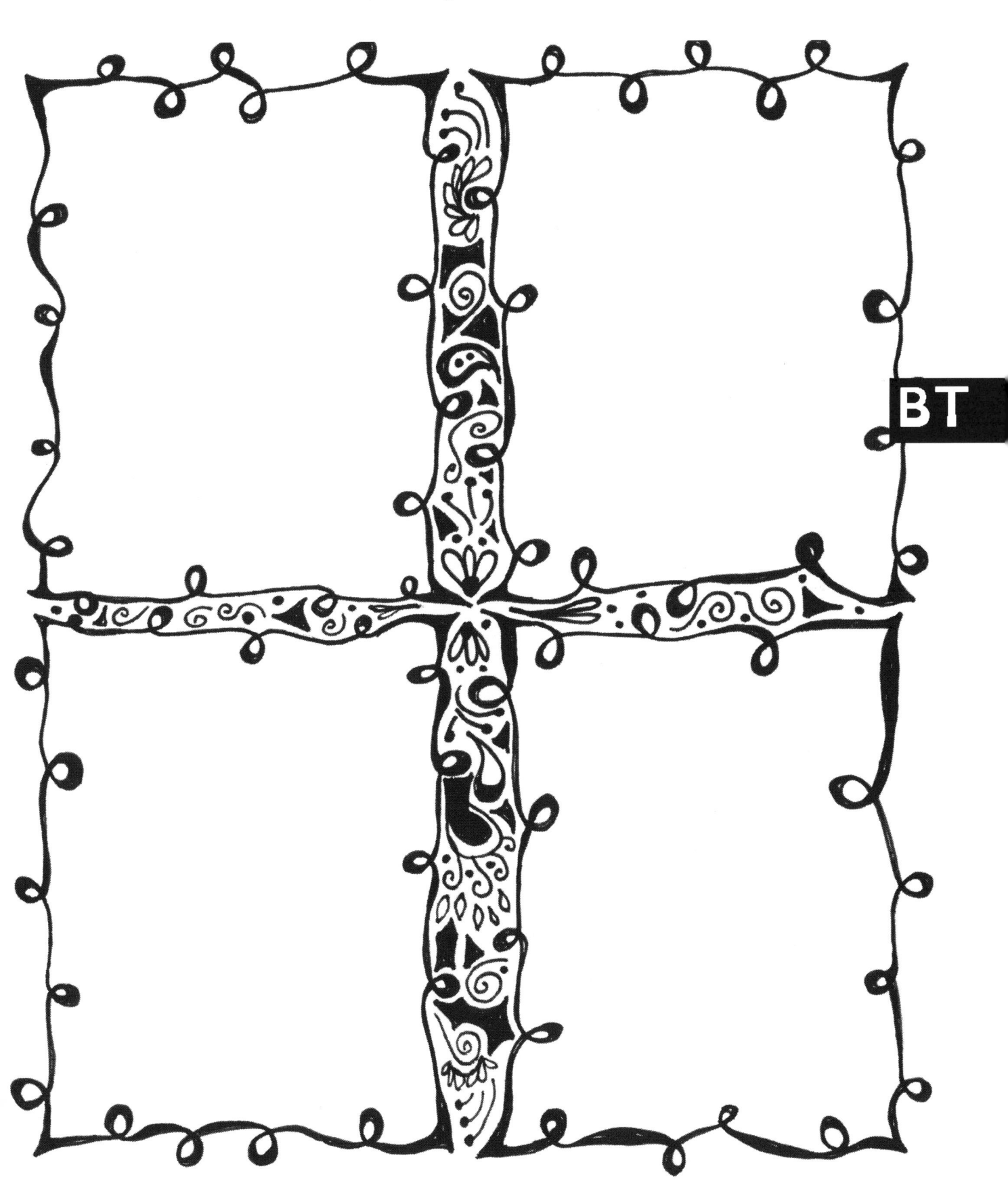

TITLE:_____

Date_____

Quotes, Tips and Ideas

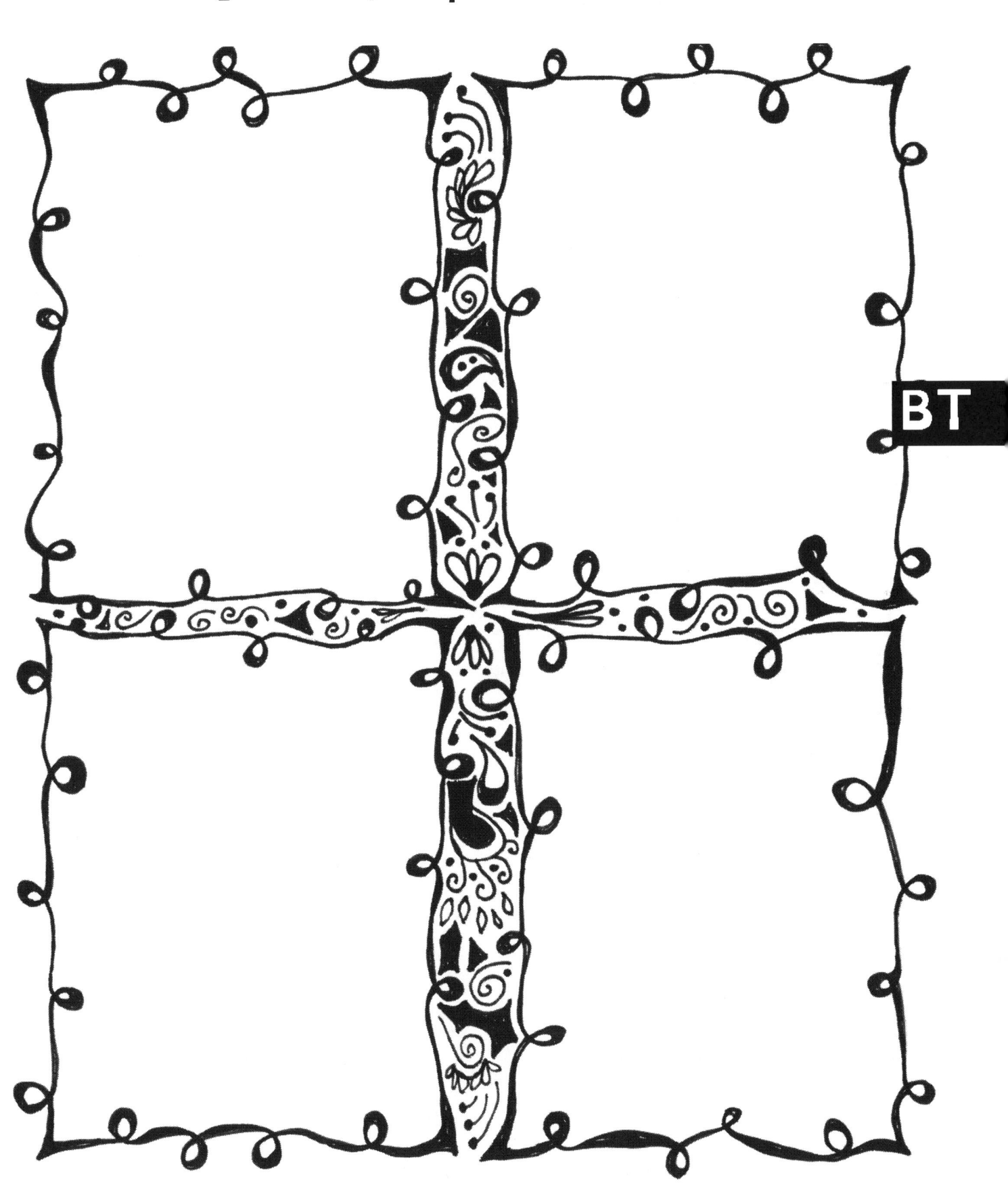

TITLE:_____

Date_____

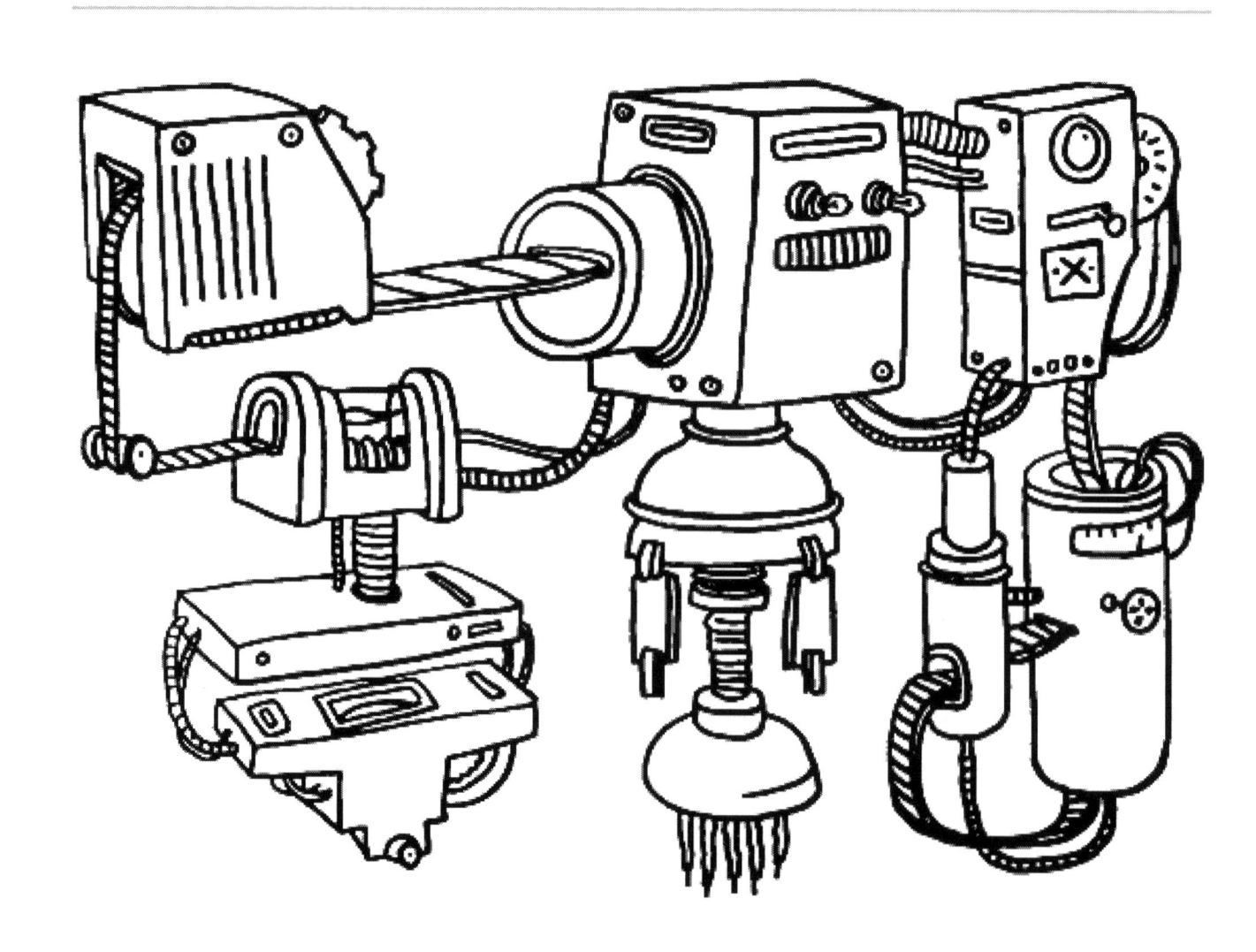

Quotes, Tips and Ideas

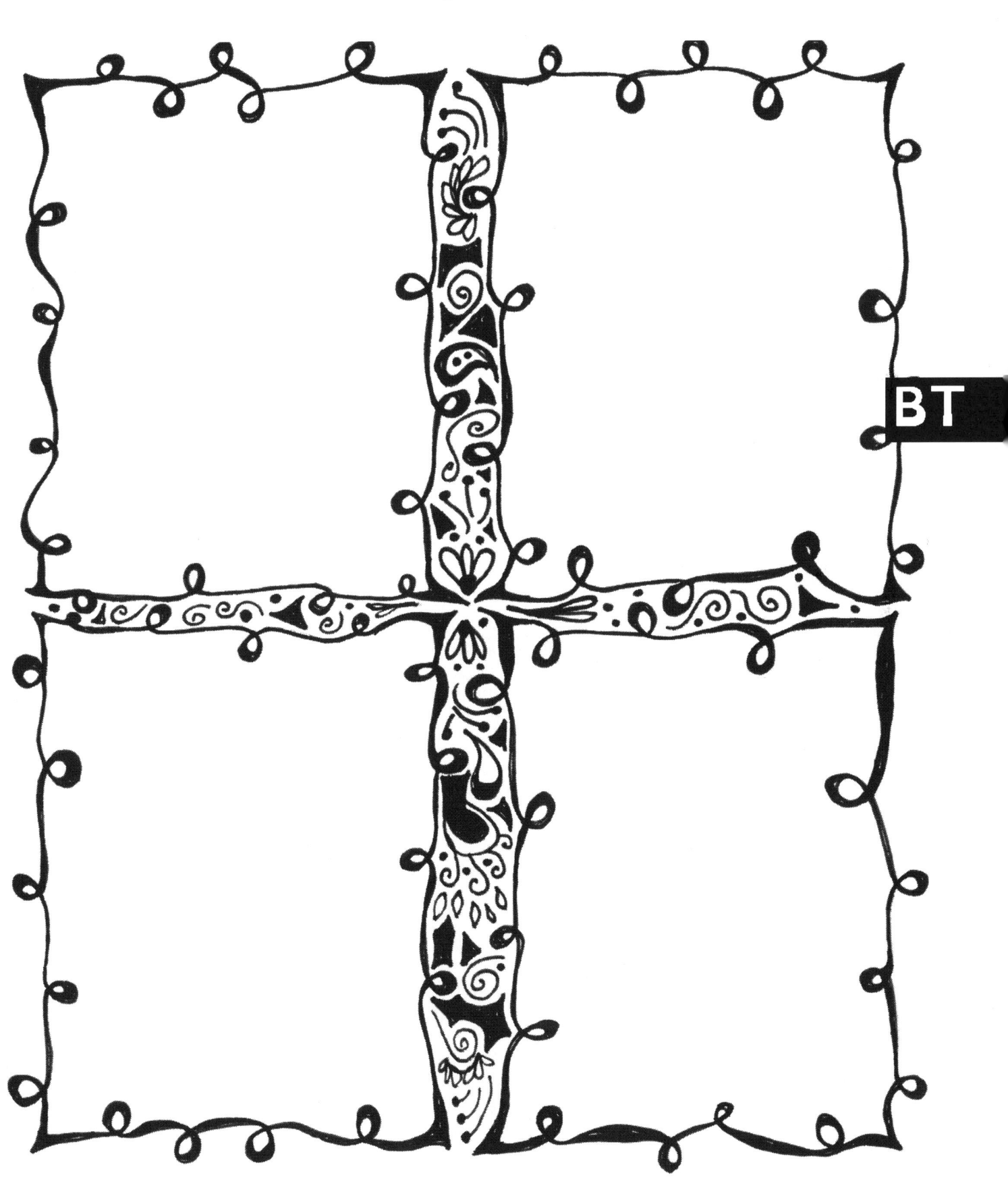

TITLE:_____

Date_____

Quotes, Tips and Ideas

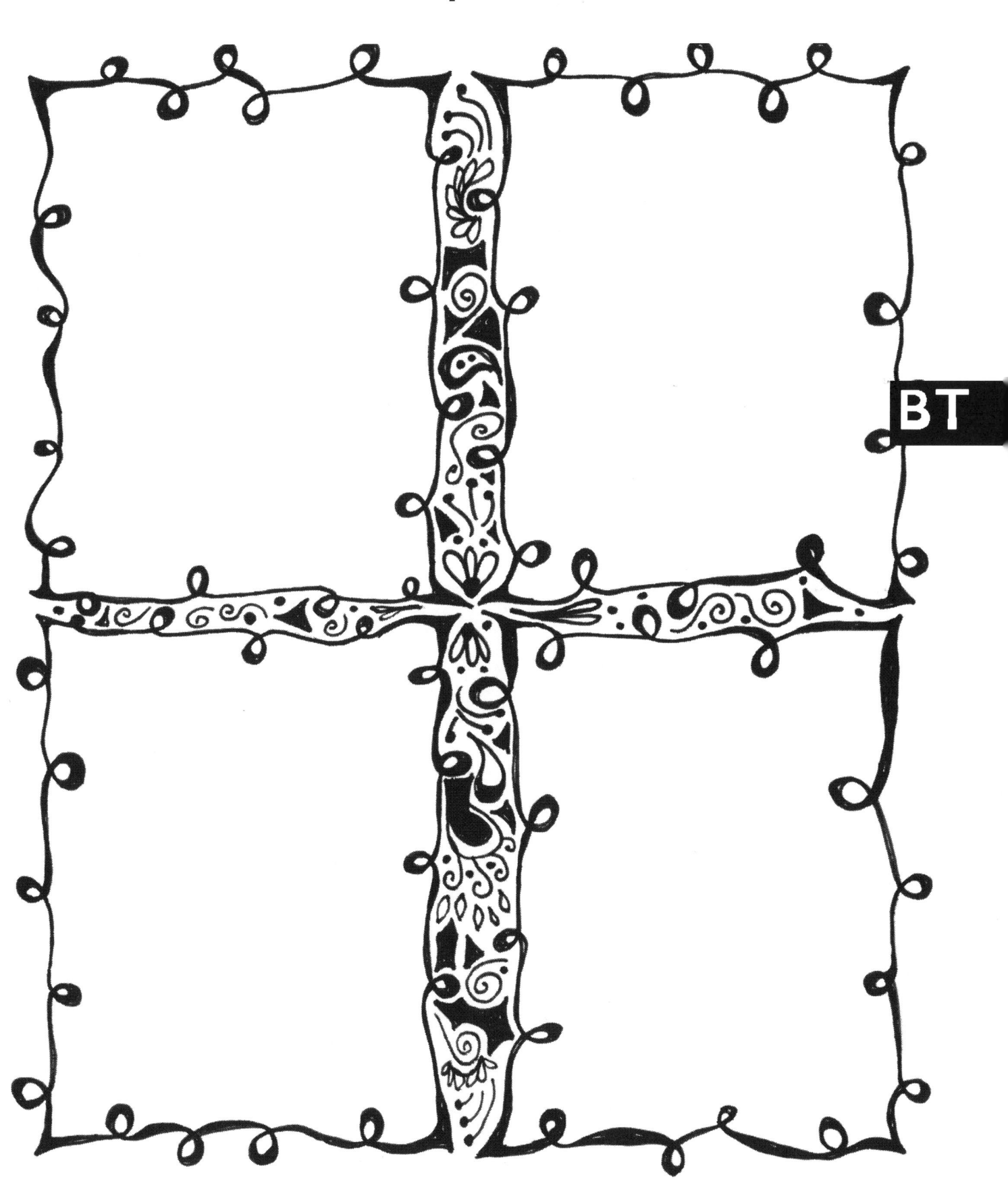

TITLE:_____

Date_____

Quotes, Tips and Ideas

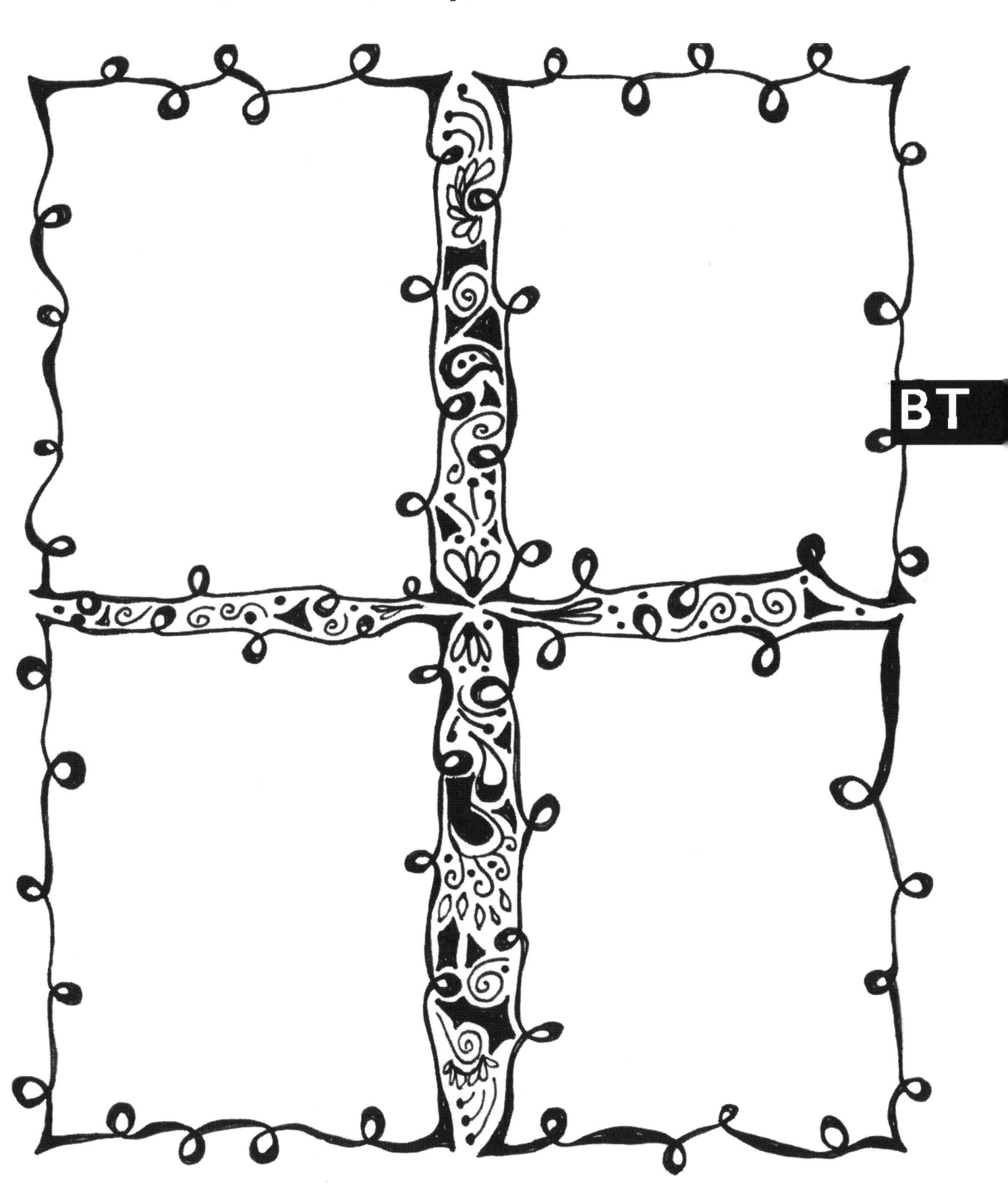

TITLE:_____

Date_____

Quotes, Tips and Ideas

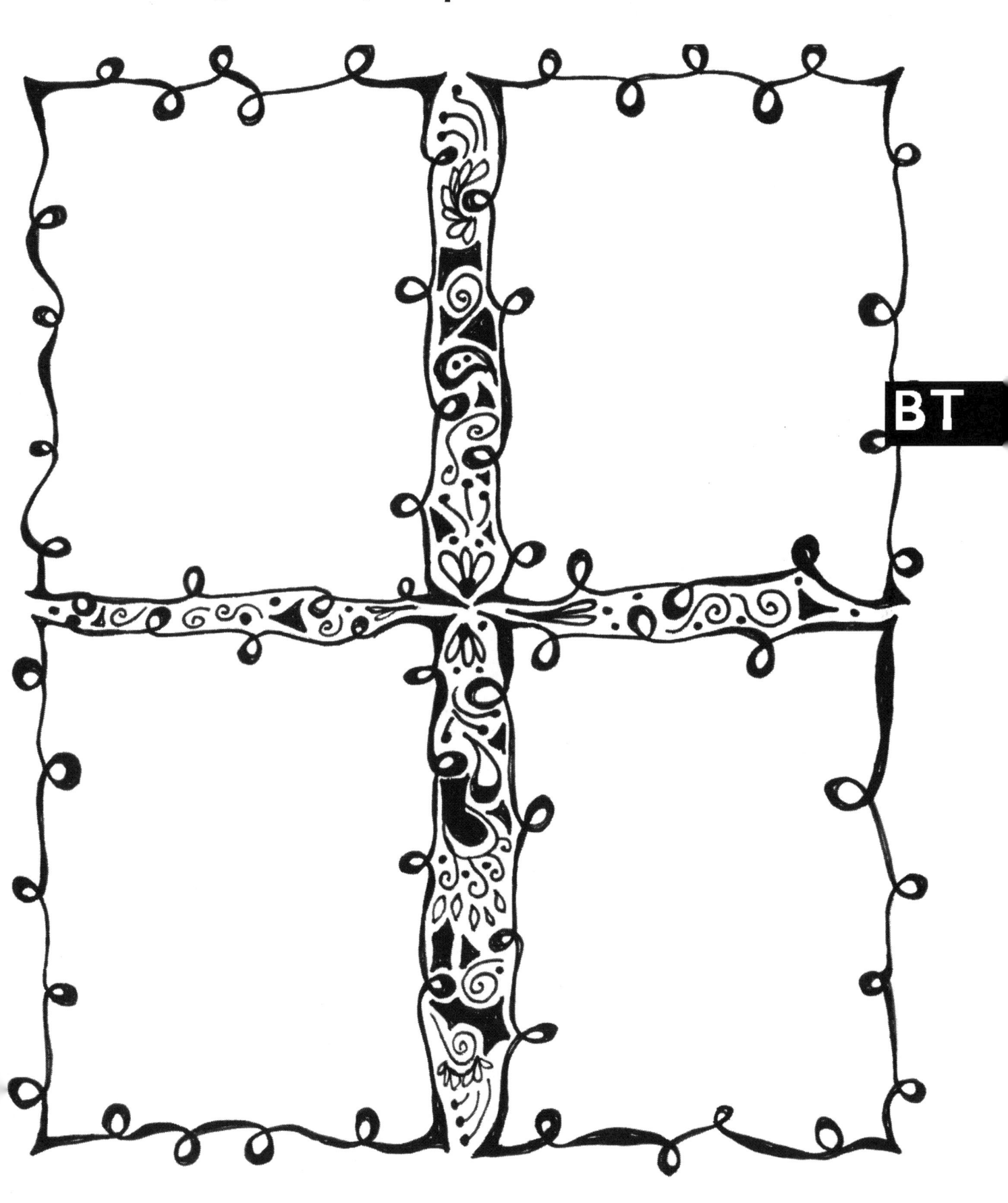

TITLE:_____

Date_____

Quotes, Tips and Ideas

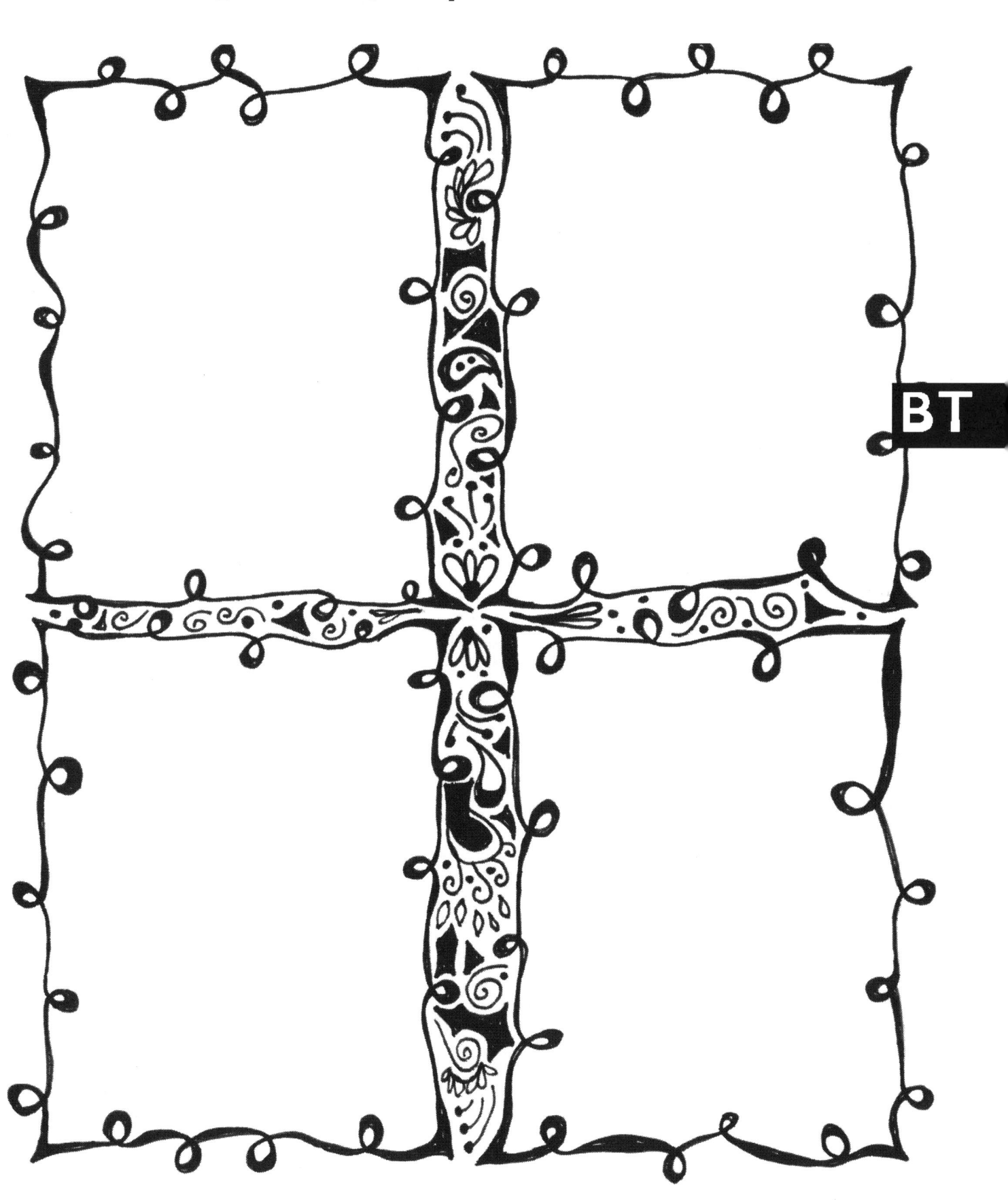

TITLE:_____

Date_____

Quotes, Tips and Ideas

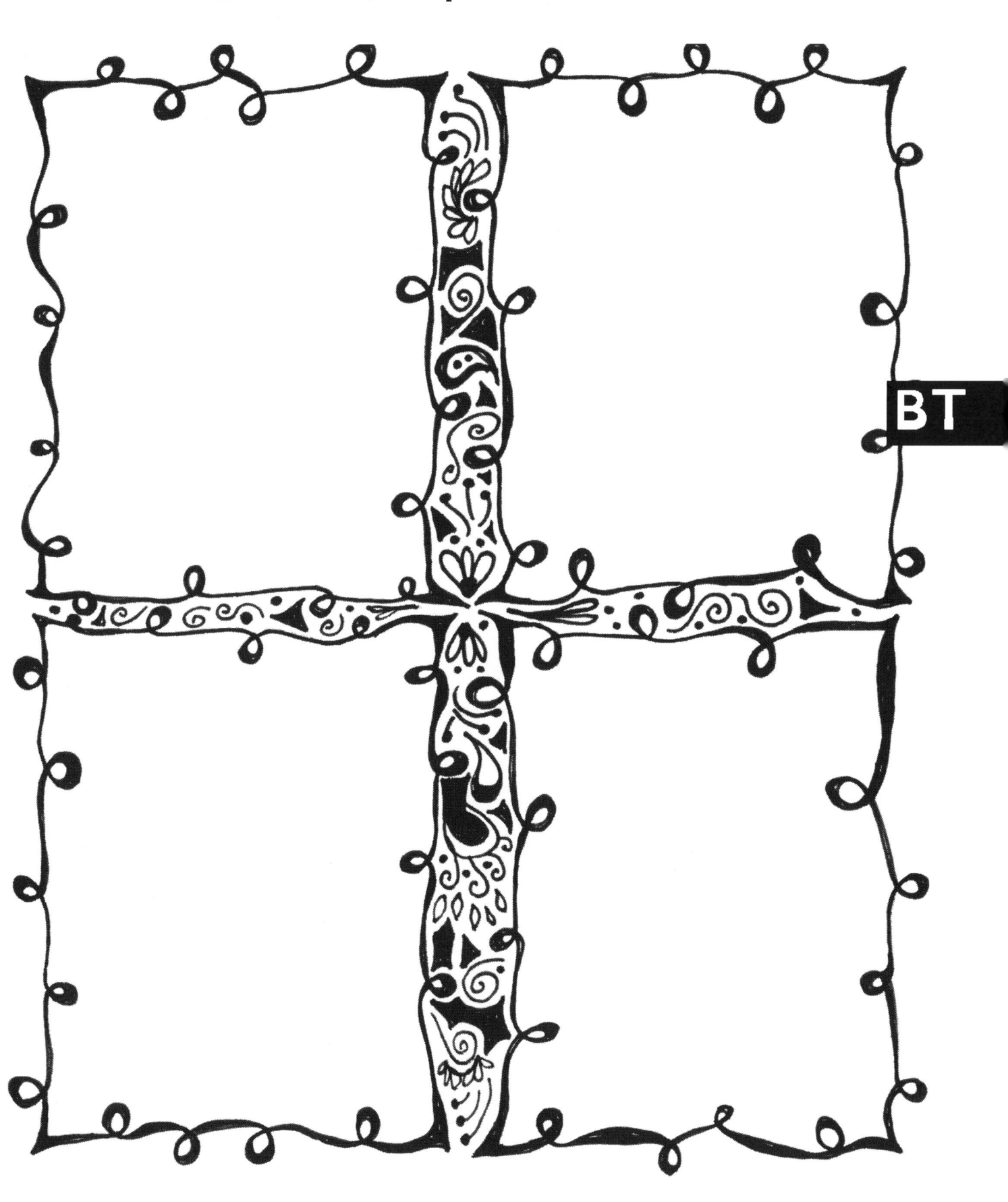

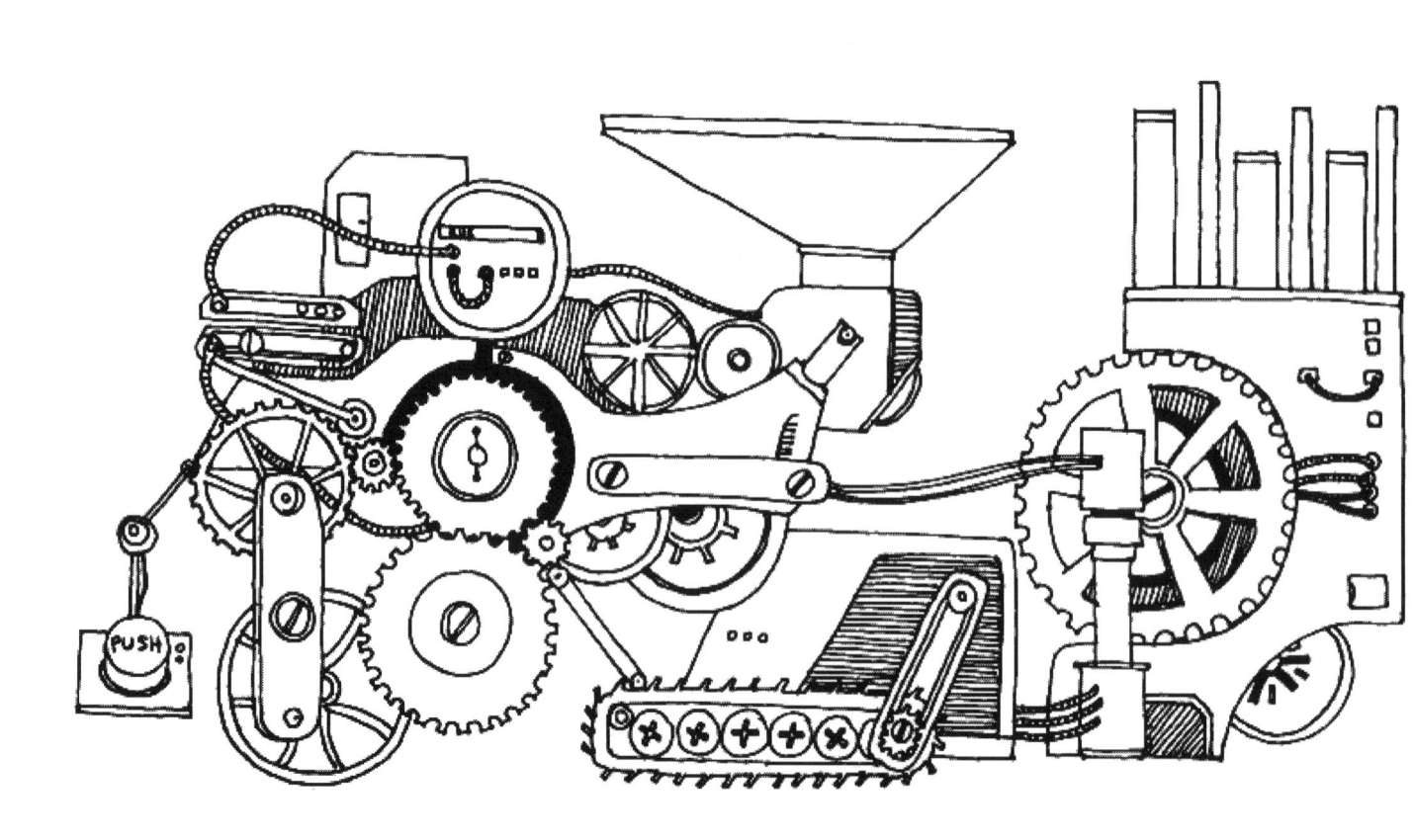

TITLE:_____

Date_____

Quotes, Tips and Ideas

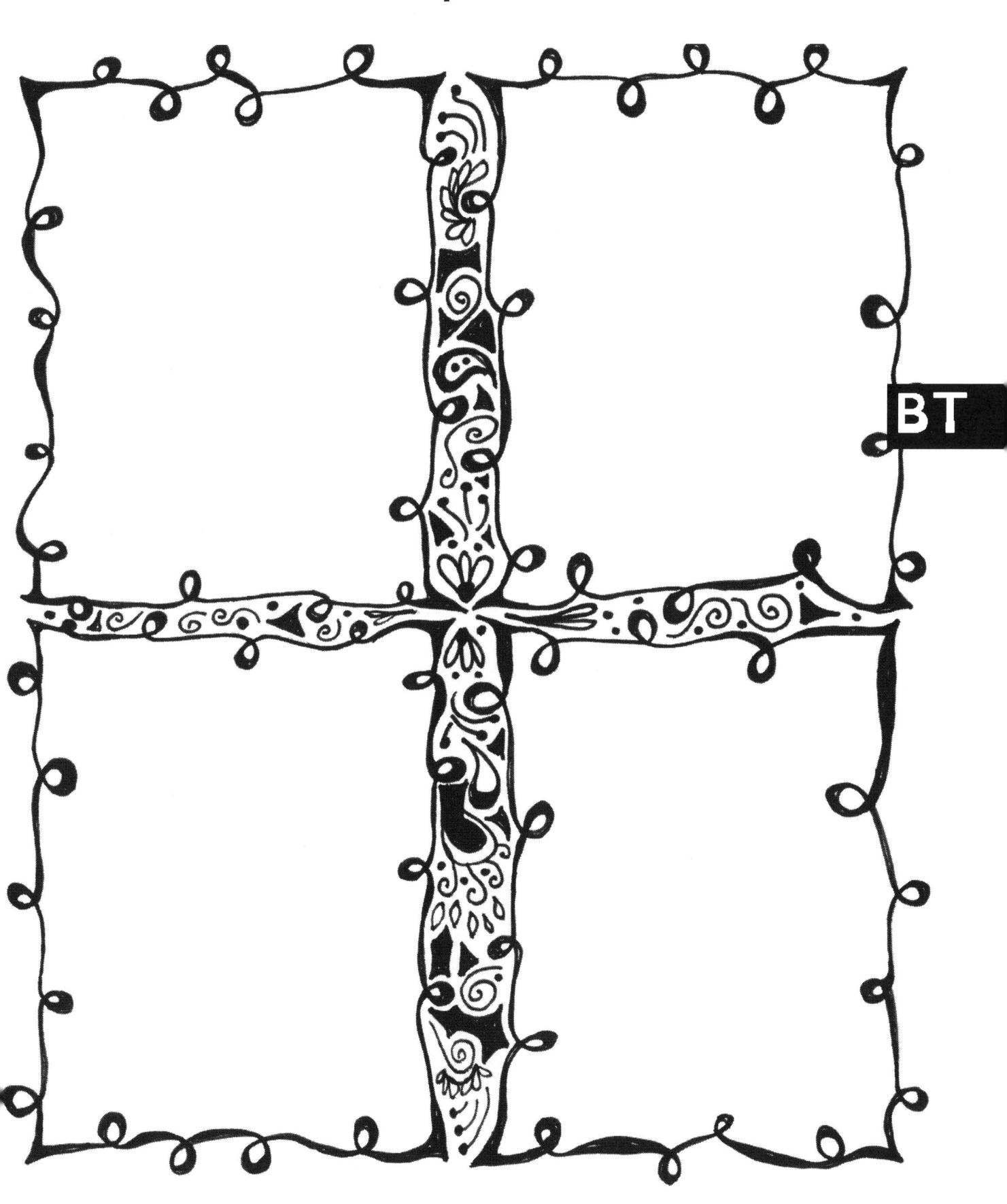

TITLE:_____

Date_____

Quotes, Tips and Ideas

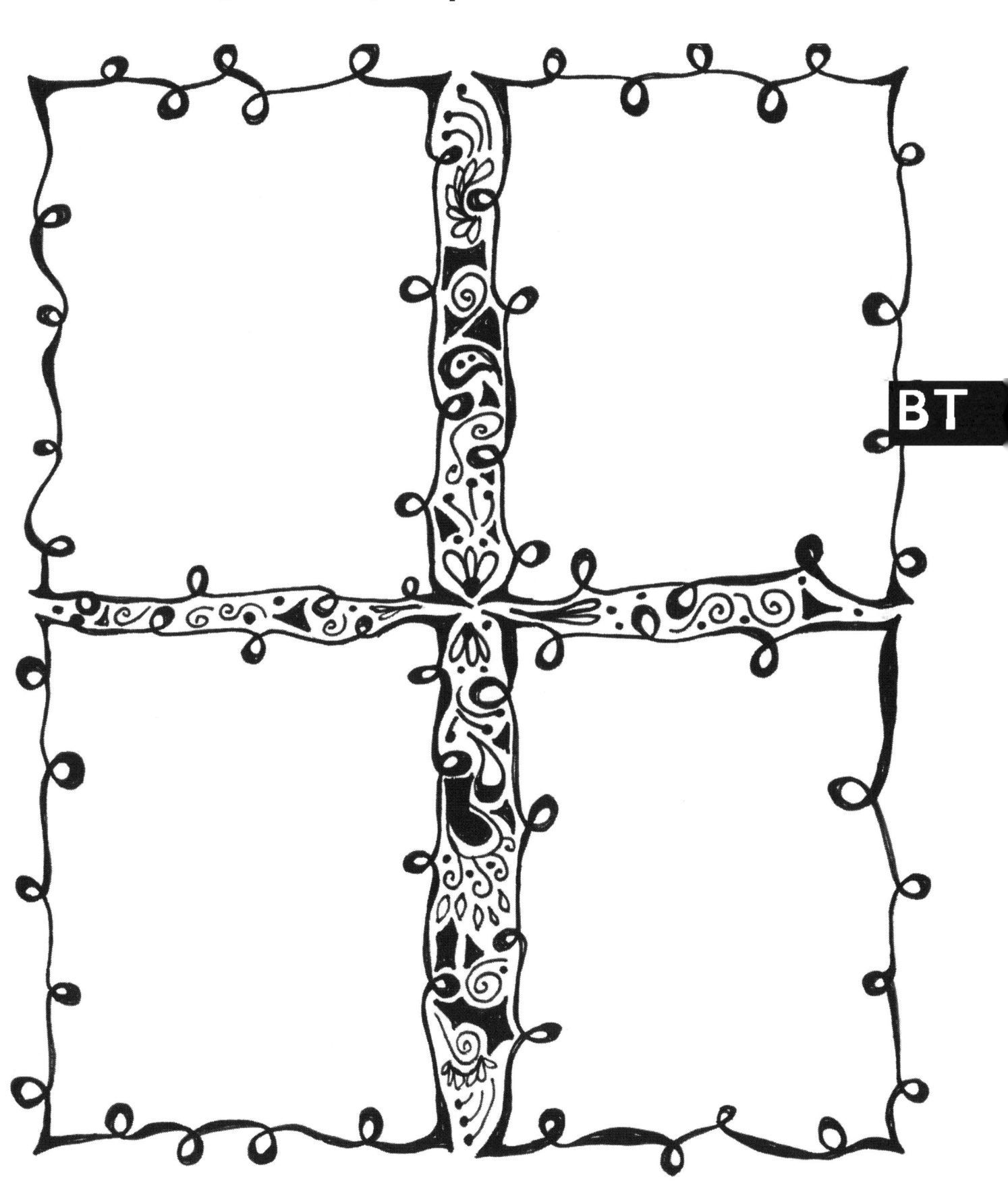

Language Arts

What do you want to learn about language arts?

Vocabulary, Grammar, Spelling, Journalism, Writing, Poetry...

1.

2.

3.

4.

5.

Action Steps:

1. Go to the library or bookstore.

2. Bring home a stack of at least FOUR interesting books about this subject. Choose some that have diagrams, instructions and illustrations.

Supplies Needed:

You will need pencils, black drawing pens, colored pencils, gel pens and markers.

NOTES:

Choose FOUR Books About Laungage Arts To Use As School Books! Draw the Covers.

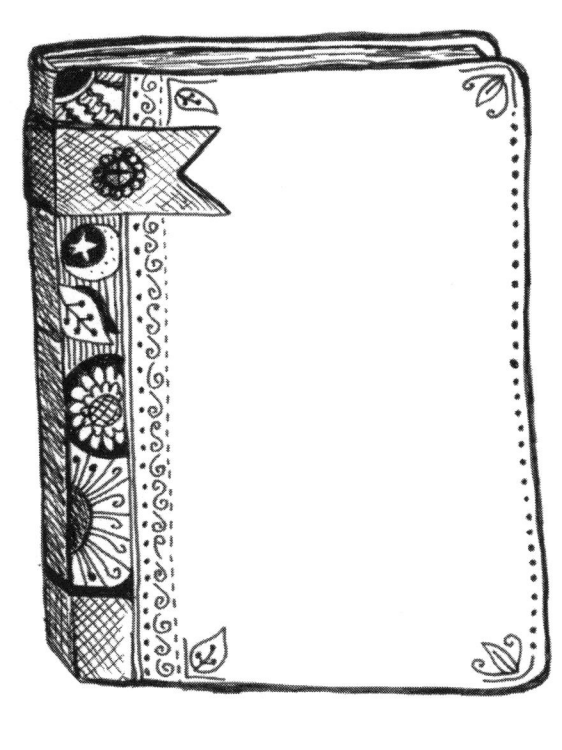

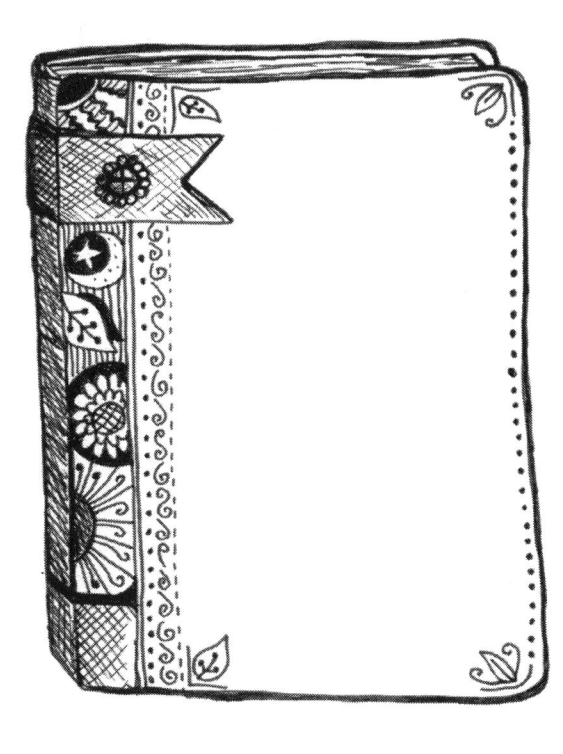

LA

Things I Want to Remember:

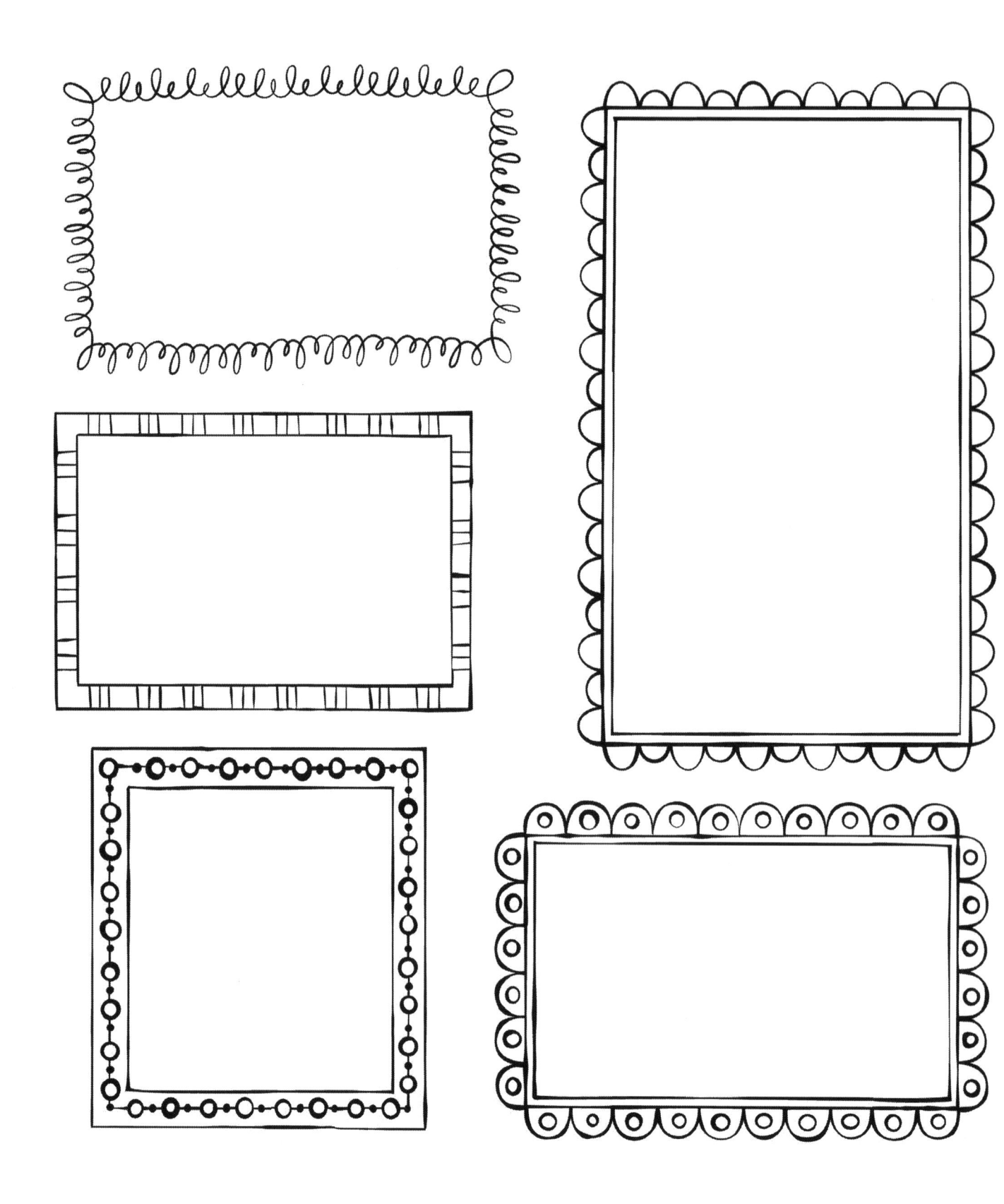

10 Vocabulary & Spelling Words:
Search for words with 8 Letters

1_____

2_____

3_____

4_____

5_____

6_____

7_____

8_____

9_____

10_____

LA

Language Arts

Date:_____ Topic:_____

10 Vocabulary & Spelling Words:
Search for words with 9 Letters

1_____

2_____

3_____

4_____

5_____

6_____

7_____

8_____

9_____

10_____

LA

Grammar Tips

Date:_____ Topic:_____

10 Vocabulary & Spelling Words:
Search for words with 10 Letters

1. _____
2. _____
3. _____
4. _____
5. _____
6. _____
7. _____
8. _____
9. _____
10. _____

LA

Copy a Poem or Song

10 Vocabulary & Spelling Words:
Search for words with 10 Letters

1 _____

2 _____

3 _____

4 _____

5 _____

6 _____

7 _____

8 _____

9 _____

10 _____

LA

Things I Want to Remember:

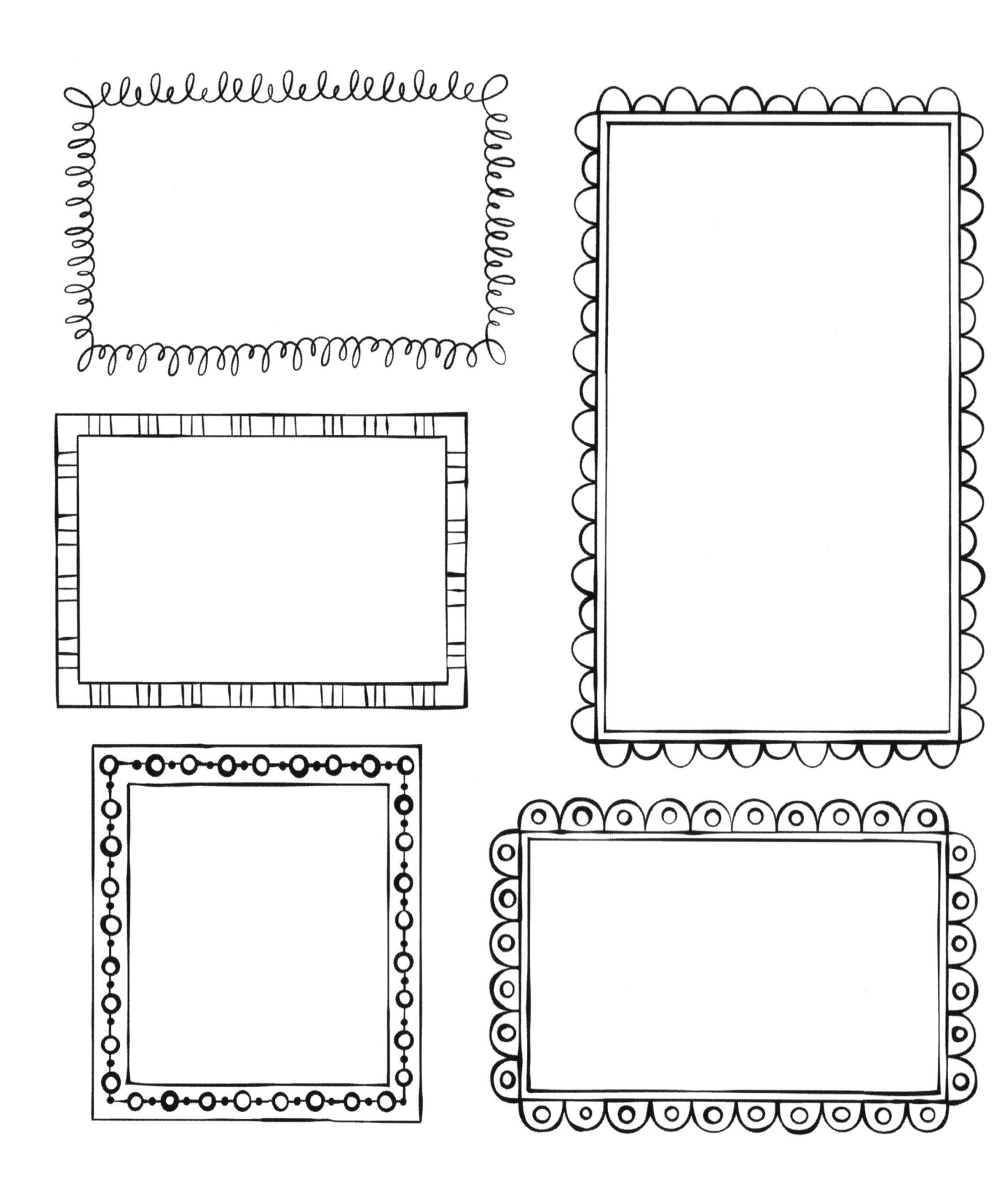

10 Vocabulary & Spelling Words:

Search for words with 11 Letters

1_____

2_____

3_____

4_____

5_____

6_____

7_____

8_____

9_____

10_____

LA

Creative Writing

Date:____ Topic:_____

10 Vocabulary & Spelling Words:
Search for words with 12 Letters

1_____

2_____

3_____

4_____

5_____

6_____

7_____

8_____

9_____

10_____

LA

Grammar Tips

Date:_____ Topic:_____

10 Vocabulary & Spelling Words:

Search for words that start with the Letter E, and have at least 8 letters.

1 _____

2 _____

3 _____

4 _____

5 _____

6 _____

7 _____

8 _____

9 _____

LA

Copy a Poem or Song

____   _____

10 Vocabulary & Spelling Words:

Search for words that start with the Letter O, and have at least 8 letters.

1_____

2_____

3_____

4_____

5_____

6_____

7_____

8_____

9_____

LA

Things I Want to Remember:

10 Vocabulary & Spelling Words:

Search for words that start with the Letter U, and have at least 8 letters.

1_____

2_____

3_____

4_____

5_____

6_____

7_____

8_____

9_____

LA

Creative Writing

Date:____   Topic:_____

10 Vocabulary & Spelling Words:

Search for words that start with the Letter K, and have at least 8 letters.

1_____

2_____

3_____

4_____

5_____

6_____

7_____

8_____

9_____

Grammar Tips

Date:____ Topic:_____

10 Vocabulary & Spelling Words:

Search for words that start with the Letter **Q**, and have at least 8 letters.

1_____

2_____

3_____

4_____

5_____

6_____

7_____

8_____

9_____

LA

Copy a Poem or Song

10 Vocabulary & Spelling Words:

Search for words that start with the Letter V, and have at least 8 letters.

1_____

2_____

3_____

4_____

5_____

6_____

7_____

8_____

9_____

LA

Things I Want to Remember:

10 Vocabulary & Spelling Words:

Search for words that start with the Letter P, and have at least 8 letters.

1_____

2_____

3_____

4_____

5_____

6_____

7_____

8_____

9_____

LA

Literature & Copywork

What great works of Literature do you want to read?

1.

2.

3.

4.

5.

Action Steps:

1. Go to the library or bookstore.

2. Bring home a great book to read, when you finish it, get another. Choose some that have diagrams, instructions and illustrations.

3. Choose 4 Audio Books, and then draw, doodle and take notes while listening.

Supplies Needed:

You will need pencils, black drawing pens, colored pencils, gel pens and markers.

Book List

Title & Author:

Choose SIX Books to Read & Copy

1. Write down the titles on each cover below.
2. Copy a paragraph from your current book each day.
3. when you read a word you don't know, look it up.

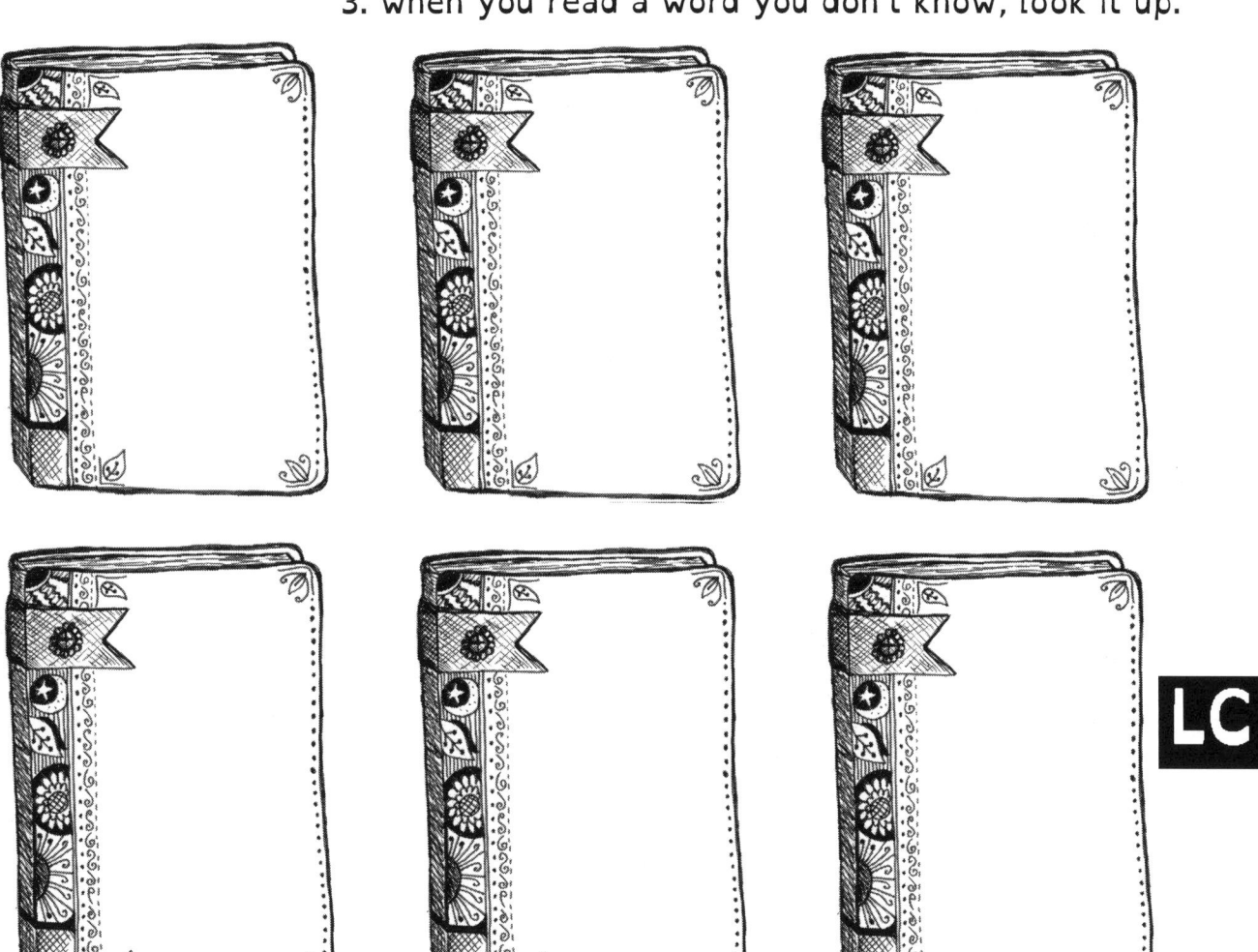

Audio Books

1.
2.
3.
4.

TITLE:_____

Date_____

Copy a Paragraph from Your Book. Page #_____

Tell the Story with Words & Pictures:

TITLE:_____

Date_____

Copy a Paragraph from Your Book. Page #_____

Tell the Story with Words & Pictures:

TITLE:_____

Date_____

Copy a Paragraph from Your Book. Page #_____

Tell the Story with Words & Pictures:

TITLE:_____

Date_____

Copy a Paragraph from Your Book. Page #_____

Tell the Story with Words & Pictures:

TITLE:_____

Date_____

Copy a Paragraph from Your Book. Page #_____

Tell the Story with Words & Pictures:

TITLE:_____

Date_____

Copy a Paragraph from Your Book. Page #_____

Tell the Story with Words & Pictures:

TITLE:_____

Date_____

Copy a Paragraph from Your Book. Page #_____

Tell the Story with Words & Pictures:

TITLE:_____

Date_____

Copy a Paragraph from Your Book. Page #_____

Tell the Story with Words & Pictures:

TITLE:_____

Date_____

Copy a Paragraph from Your Book. Page #_____

Tell the Story with Words & Pictures:

TITLE:_____

Date_____

Copy a Paragraph from Your Book. Page #_____

Tell the Story with Words & Pictures:

TITLE:_____

Date_____

Copy a Paragraph from Your Book. Page #_____

Tell the Story with Words & Pictures:

TITLE:_____

Date_____

Copy a Paragraph from Your Book. Page #_____

Tell the Story with Words & Pictures:

TITLE:_____

Date_____

Copy a Paragraph from Your Book. Page #_____

Tell the Story with Words & Pictures:

TITLE:_____

Date_____

Copy a Paragraph from Your Book. Page #_____

Tell the Story with Words & Pictures:

The ARTS

Art, Music, Drama, Drawing, Dance, Photography...

What do you want to study?

1.

2.

3.

4.

5.

Action Steps:

1. Go to the library or bookstore.

2. Bring home a six books to read and study.

Choose some that have diagrams, instructions and illustrations.

3. Watch at least ten tutorials on these topics to learn more!

Supplies Needed:

You will need pencils, black drawing pens, colored pencils, gel pens and markers.

Projects:

Choose THREE Books about the Arts to Study

1. Write down the titles on each cover below.

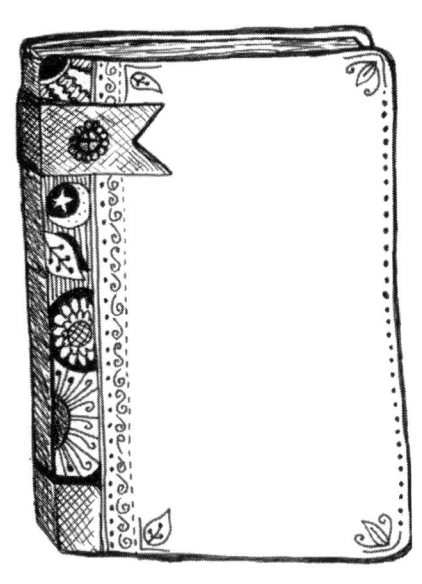

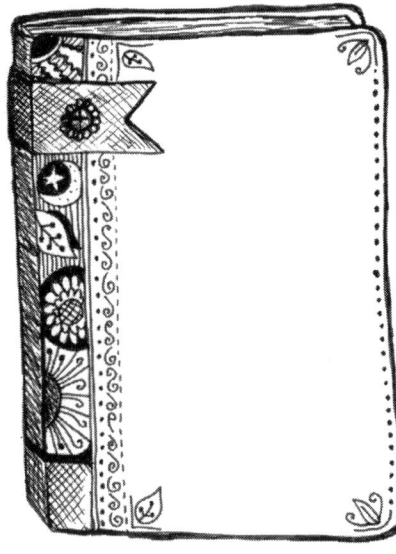

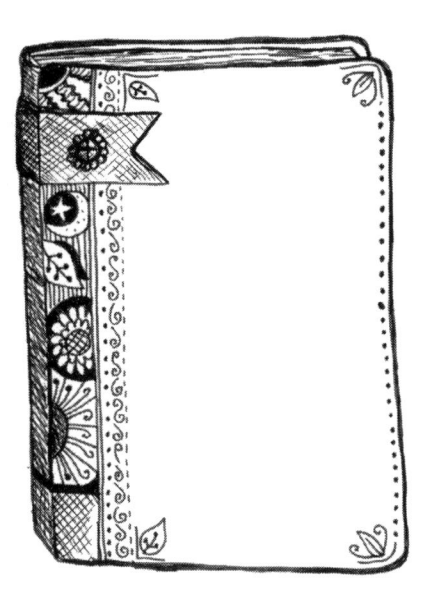

Tutorials

1.
2.
3.
4.
5.
6.
7.
8.
9.
10.

TA

TITLE:_____

Date_____

TA

TITLE:_____

Date_____

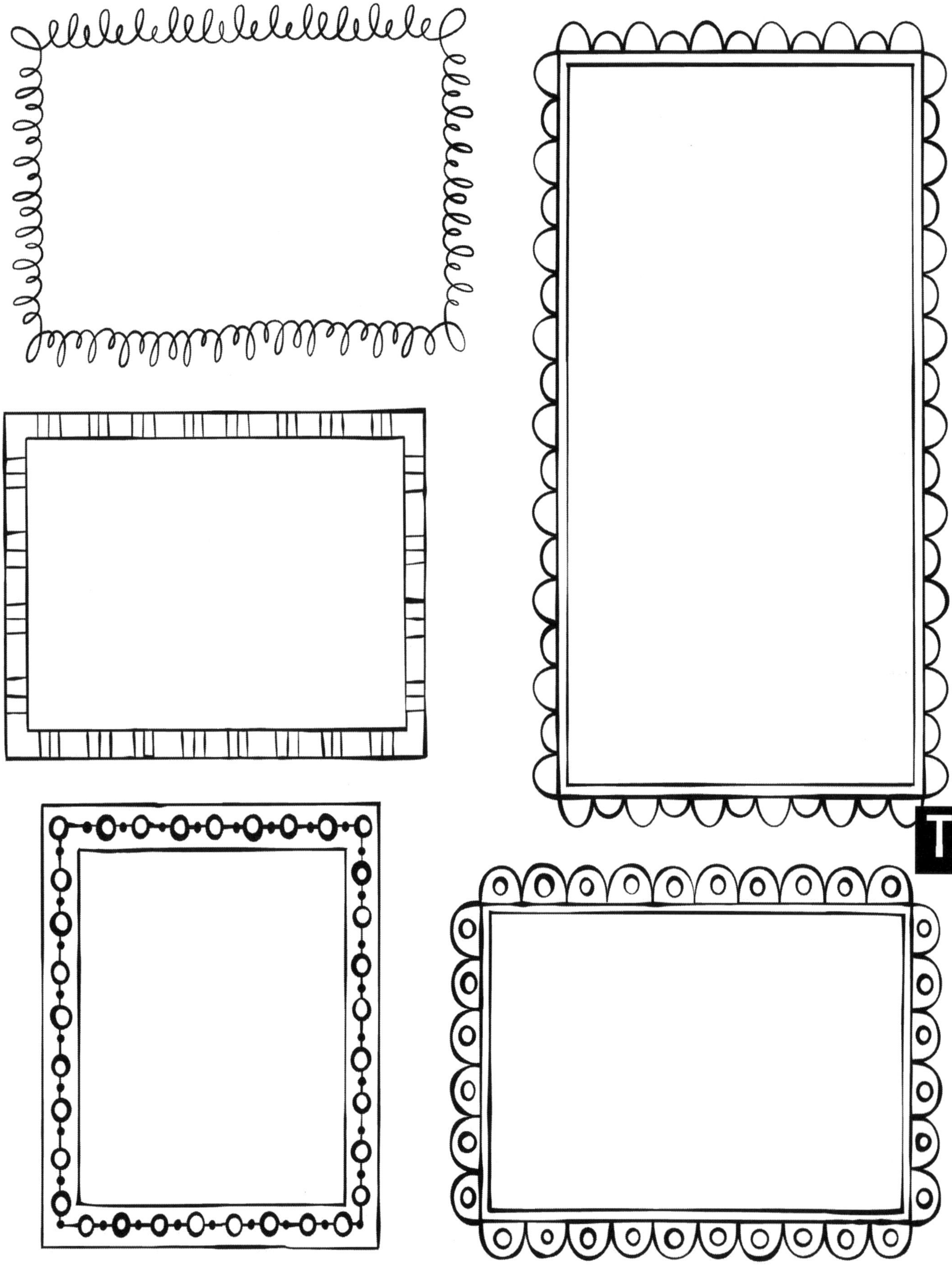

TITLE:_____

Date_____

Drawings, Photos & Images:

TA

TITLE:_____

Date_____

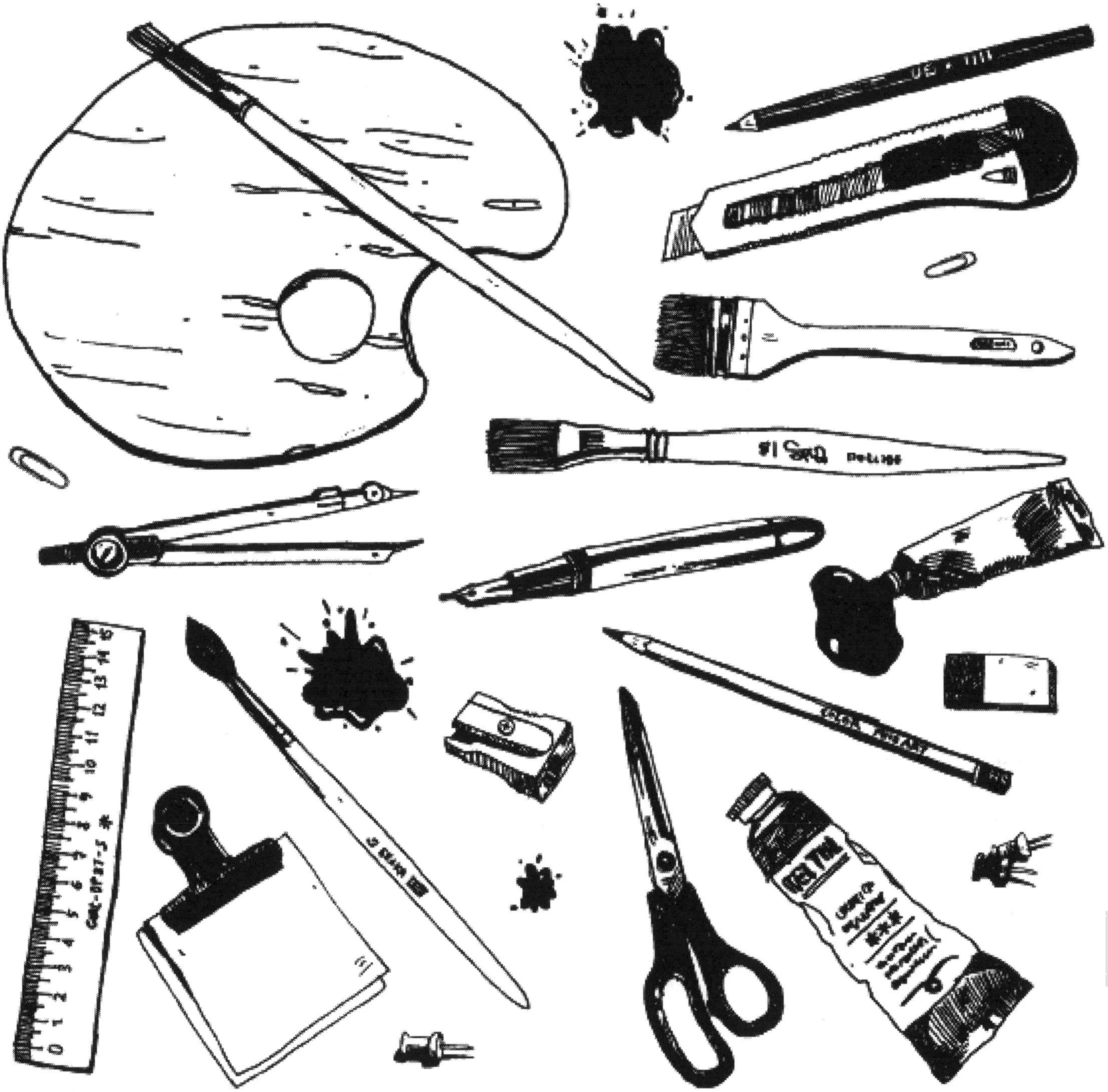

TITLE:_____

Date_____

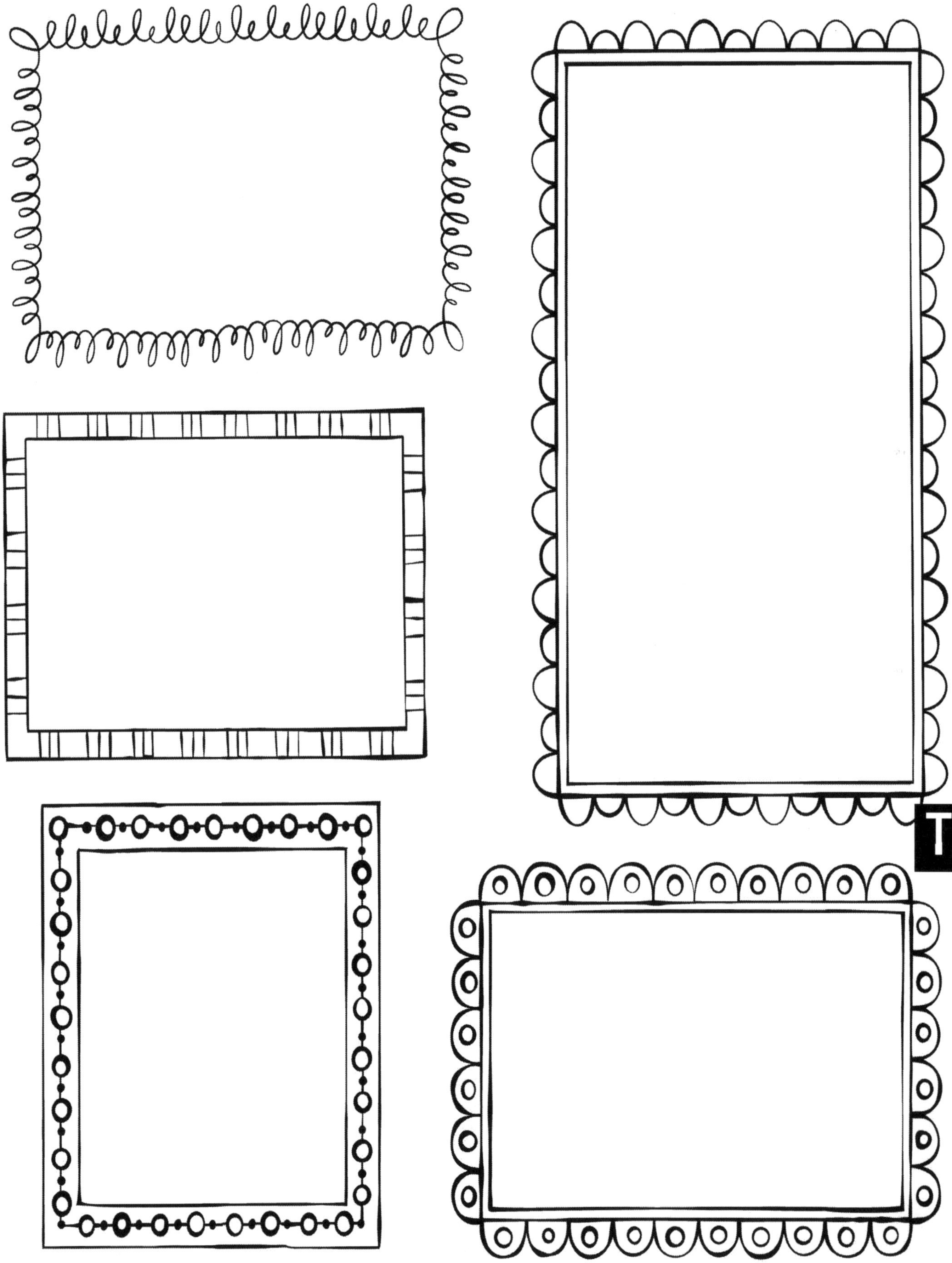

TA

TITLE:_____

Date_____

Drawings, Photos & Images:

TA

TITLE:_____

Date_____

Drawings, Photos & Images:

TITLE:_____

Date_____

TA

TITLE:_____

Date_____

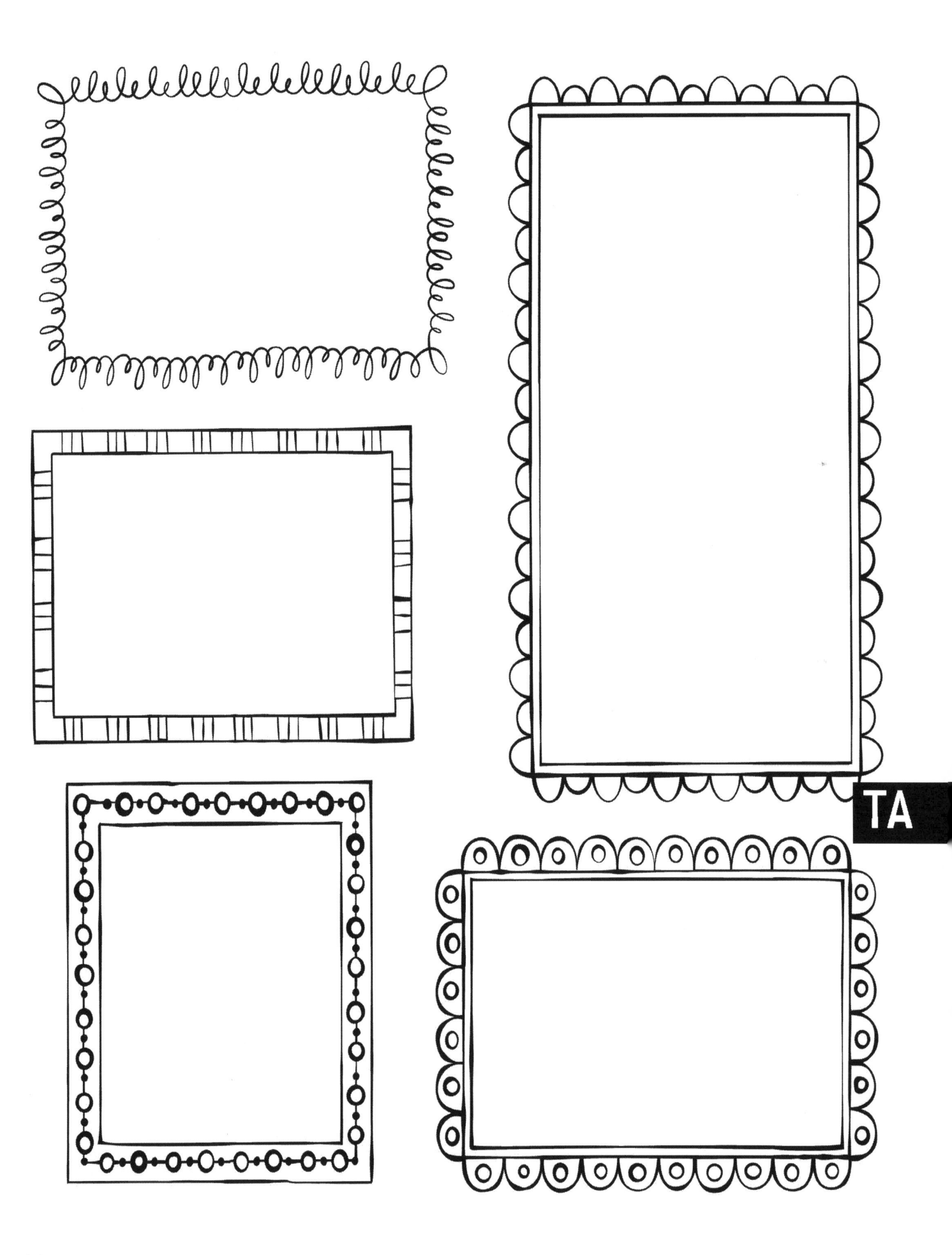

TA

TITLE:_____

Date_____

Drawings, Photos & Images:

TA

TITLE:_____

Date_____

Drawings, Photos & Images:

TA

TITLE:_____

Date_____

TA

TITLE:_____

Date_____

TA

TITLE:_____

Date_____

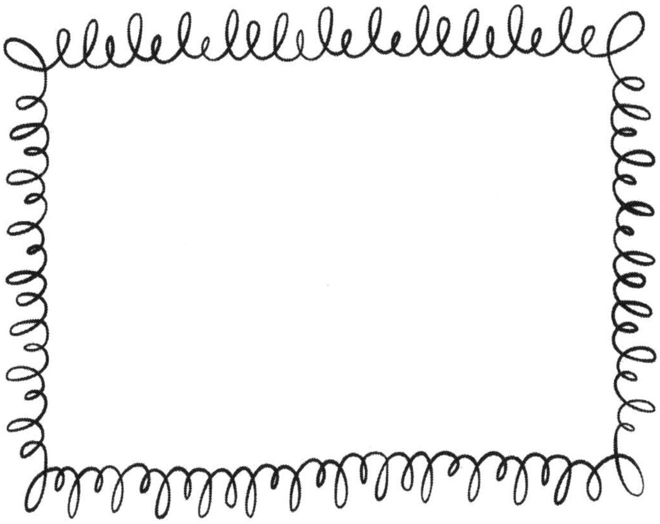

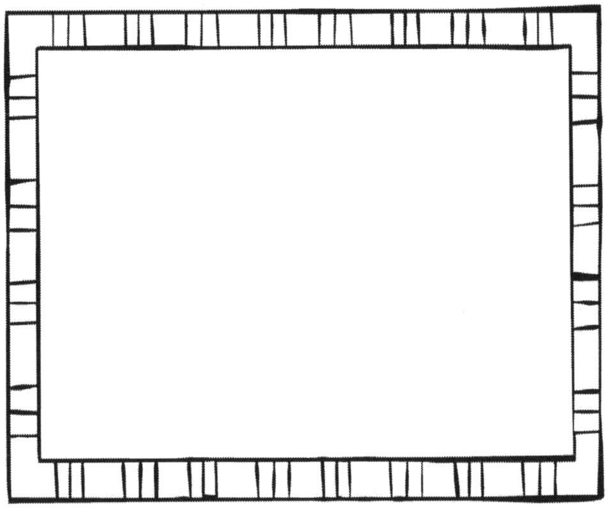

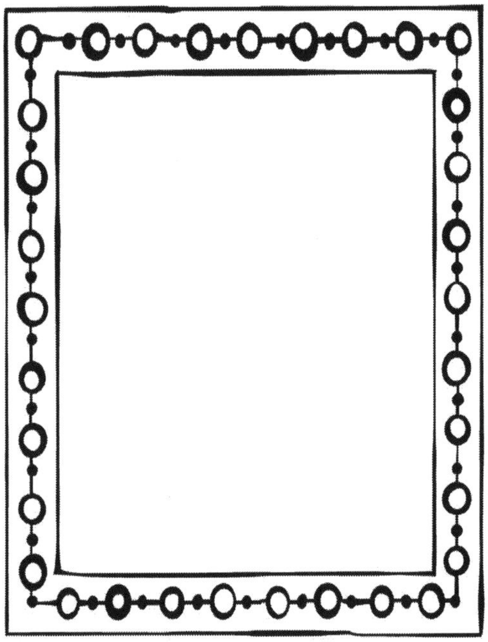

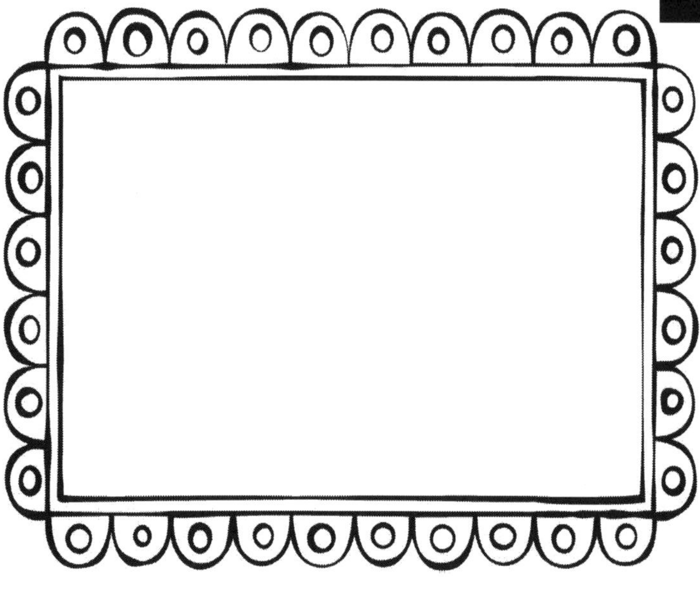

TITLE:_____

Date_____

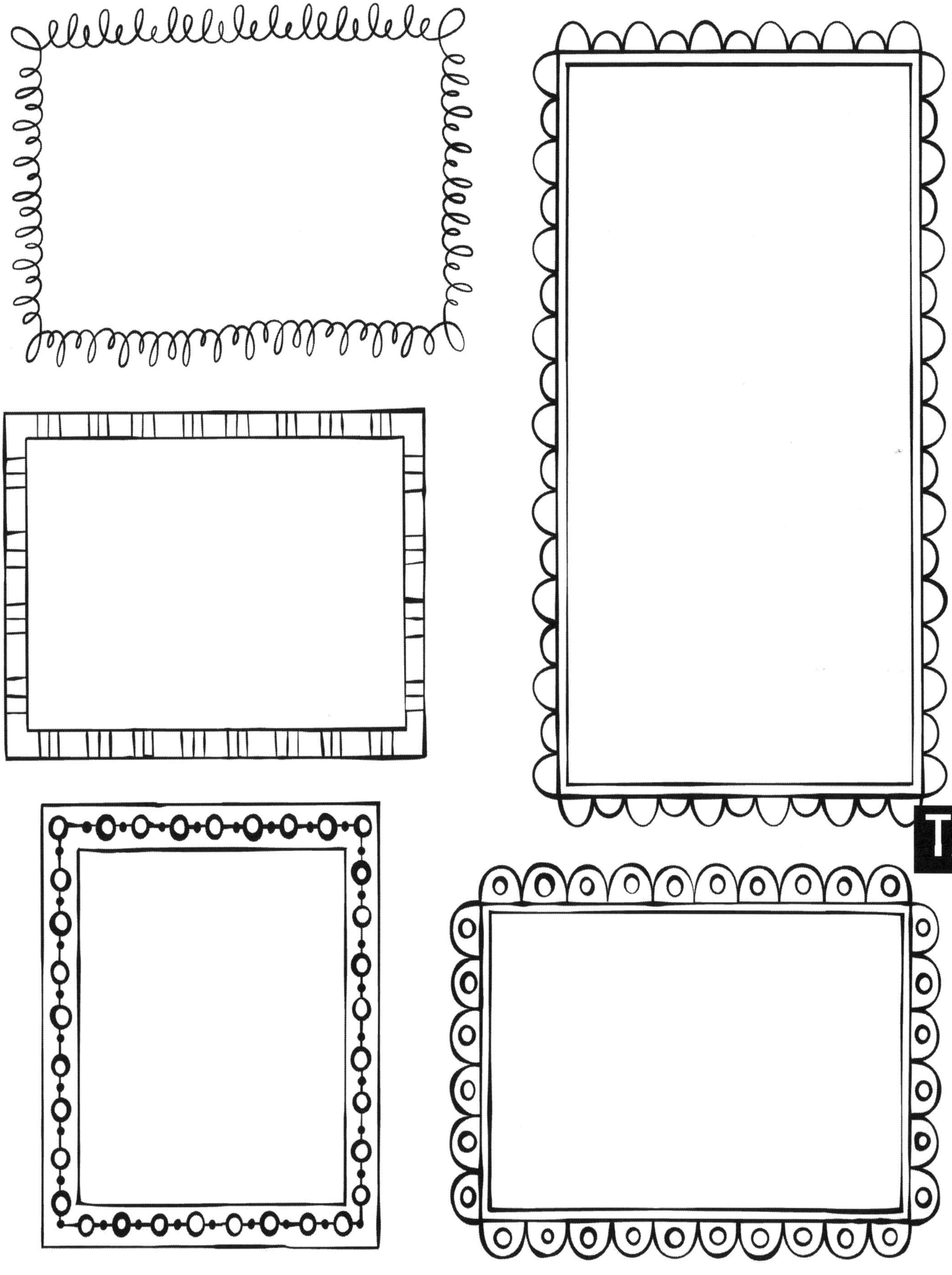

TA

TITLE:_____

Date_____

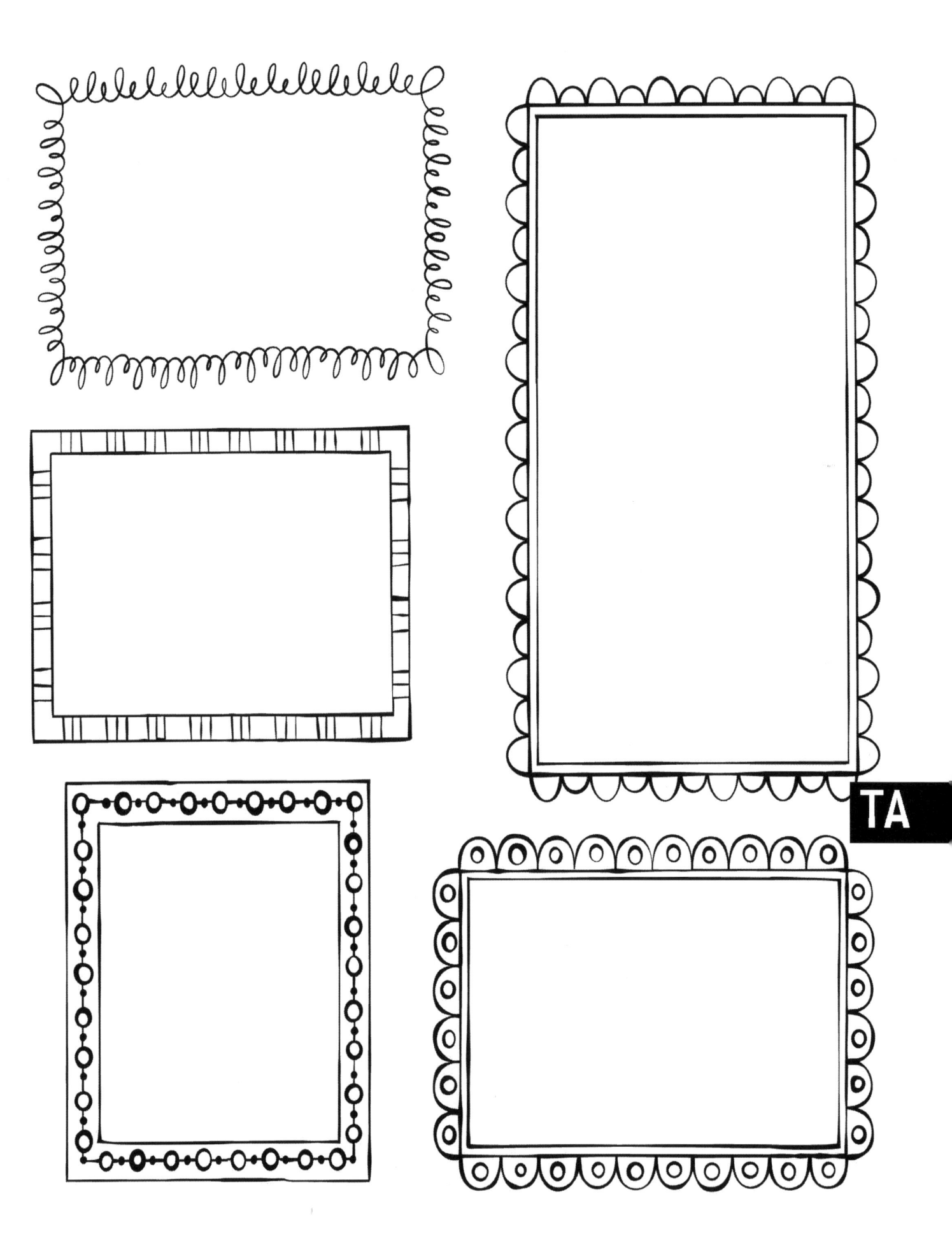

TA

TITLE:_____

Date_____

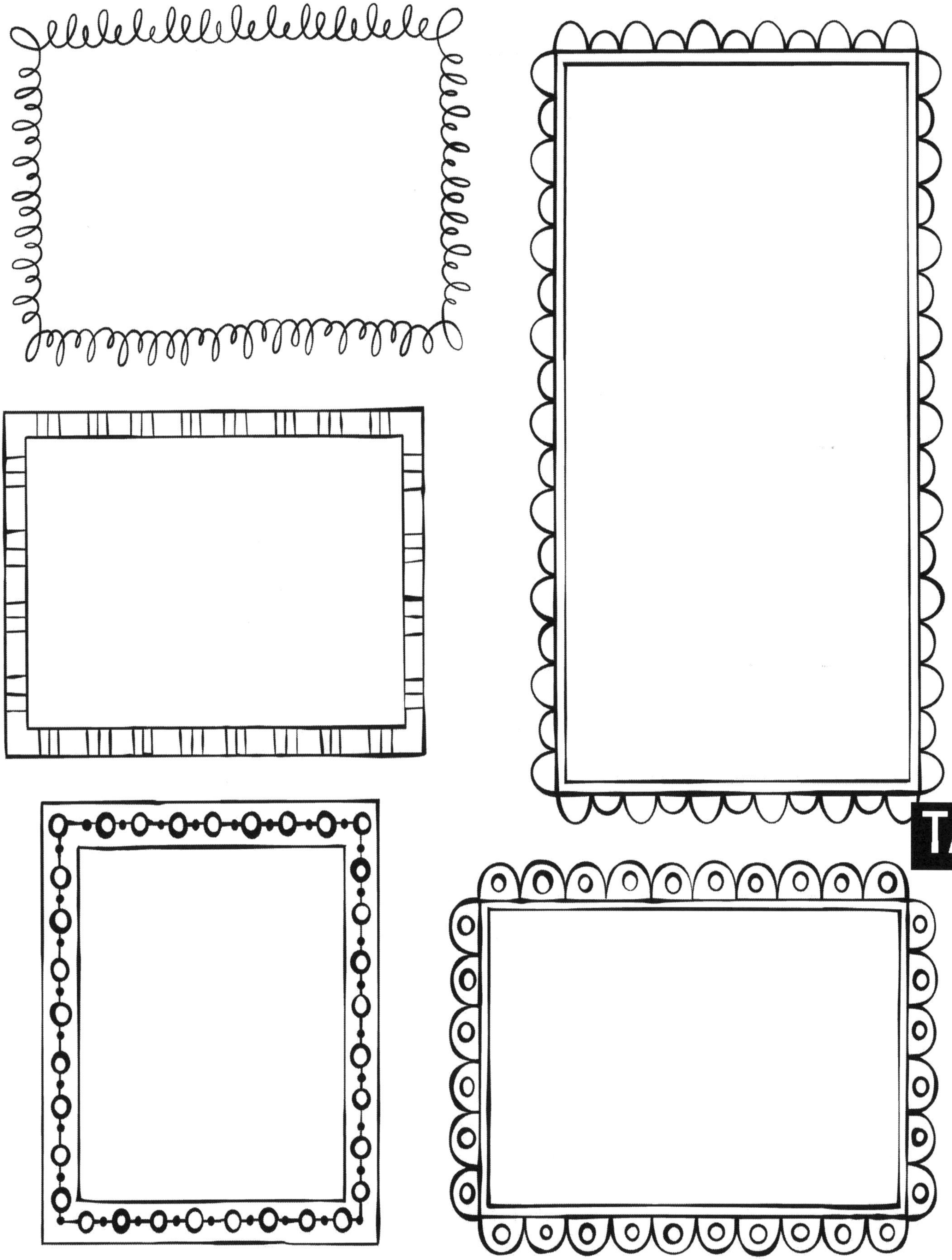

Social Studies

Find interesting Books about Culture, Politics, Economics, Ethnic Foods, Communities, Journalism, Entertainment, Media, Human Behavior, Social Networking, World Records, and other Hot Topics!

1.

2.

3.

4.

5.

Action Steps:

1. Go to the library or bookstore.
2. Bring home a stack of at least FOUR interesting books about social studies. Choose some that have diagrams, instructions and illustrations.
3. Plan to watch documentaries too, these are often about social topics.

Supplies Needed:

You will need pencils, black drawing pens, colored pencils, gel pens and markers.

Documentaries:

_____
_____
_____
_____
_____

Choose FOUR Books About Social Studies To Use As School Books!

1. Write down the titles on each cover below.
2. You may also choose Videos, Tutorials and Documenteries to help you learn about these topics.

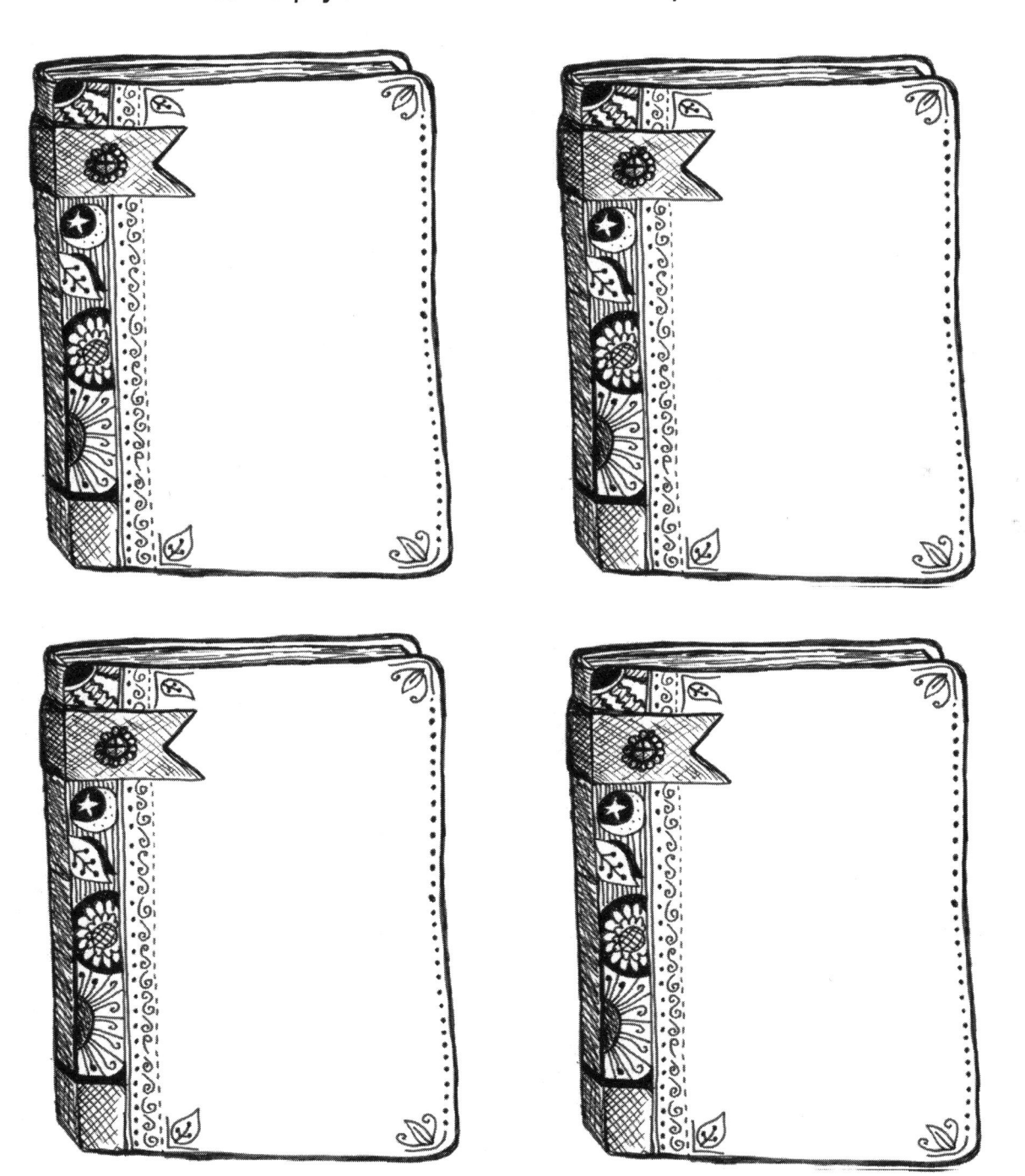

SS

TITLE:_____

Date_____

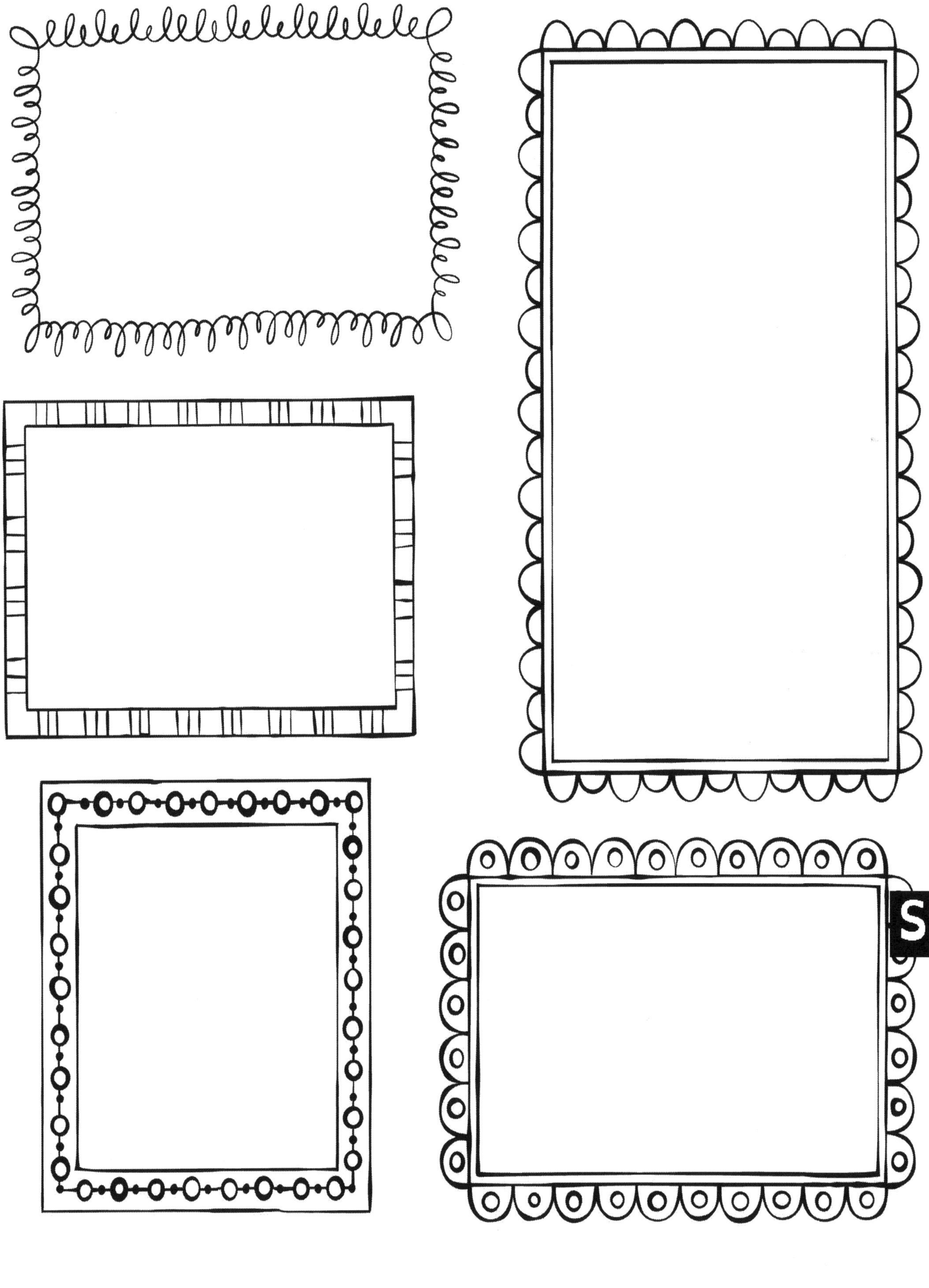

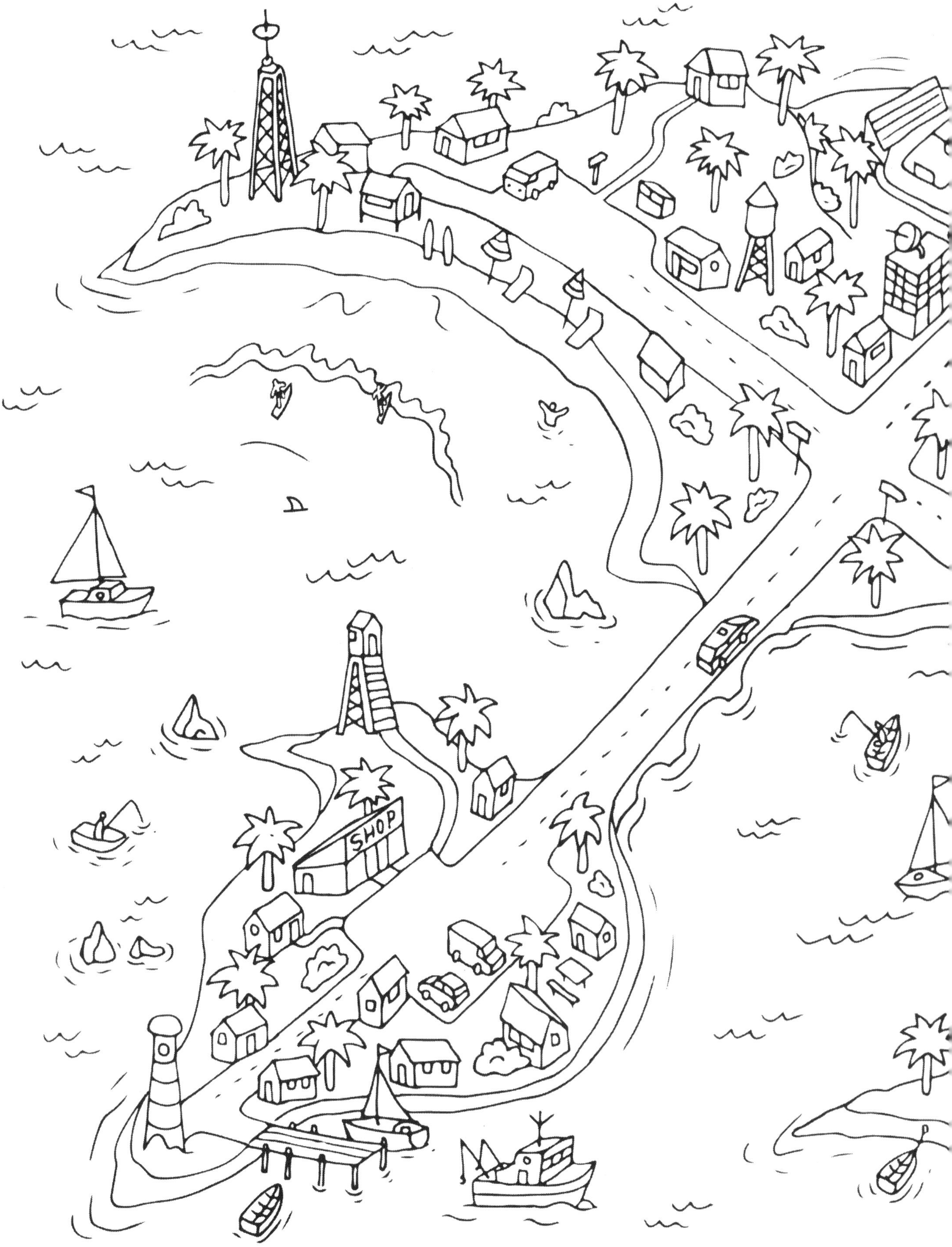
SHOP

SS

TITLE:_____

Date_____

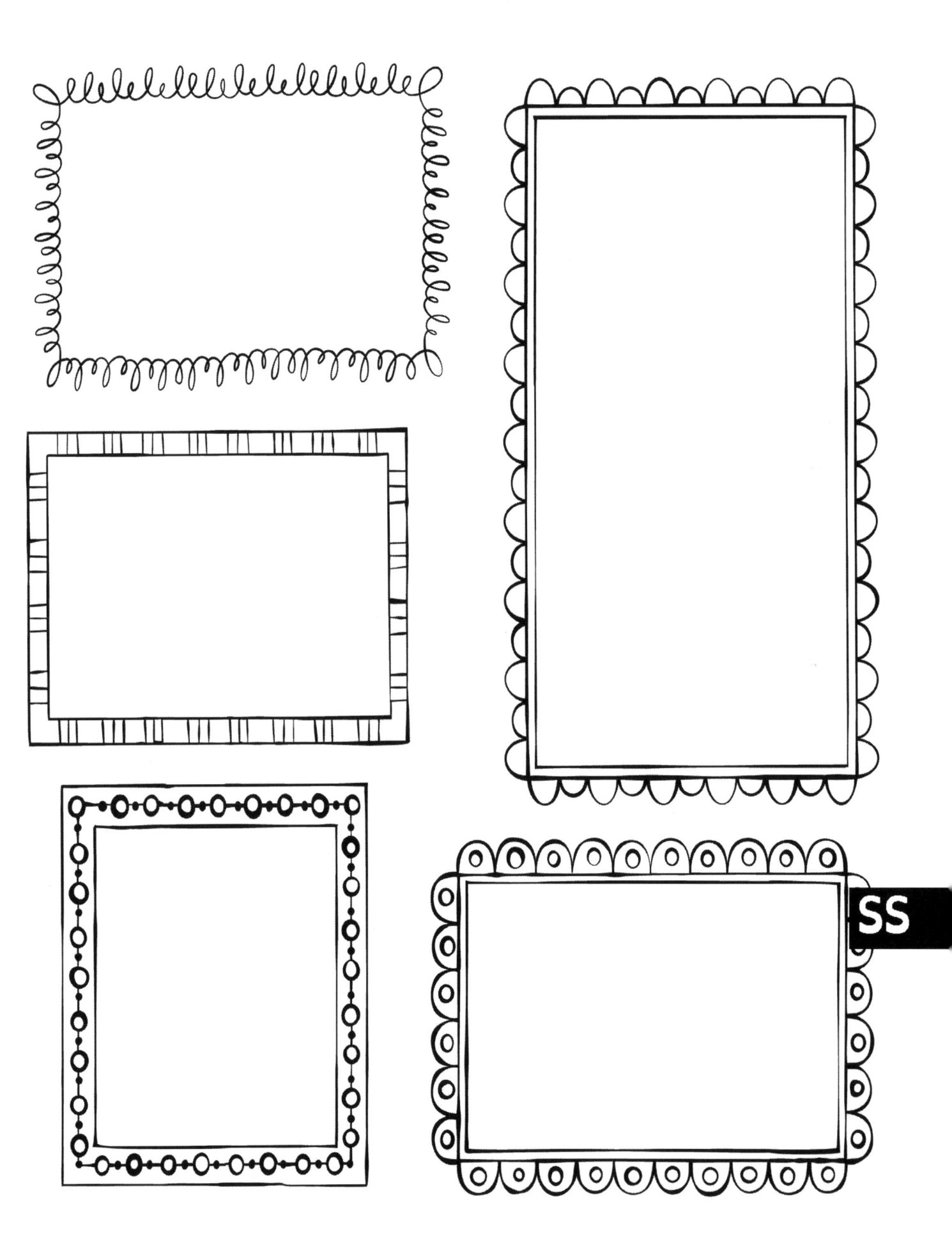

SS

TITLE:_____

Date_____

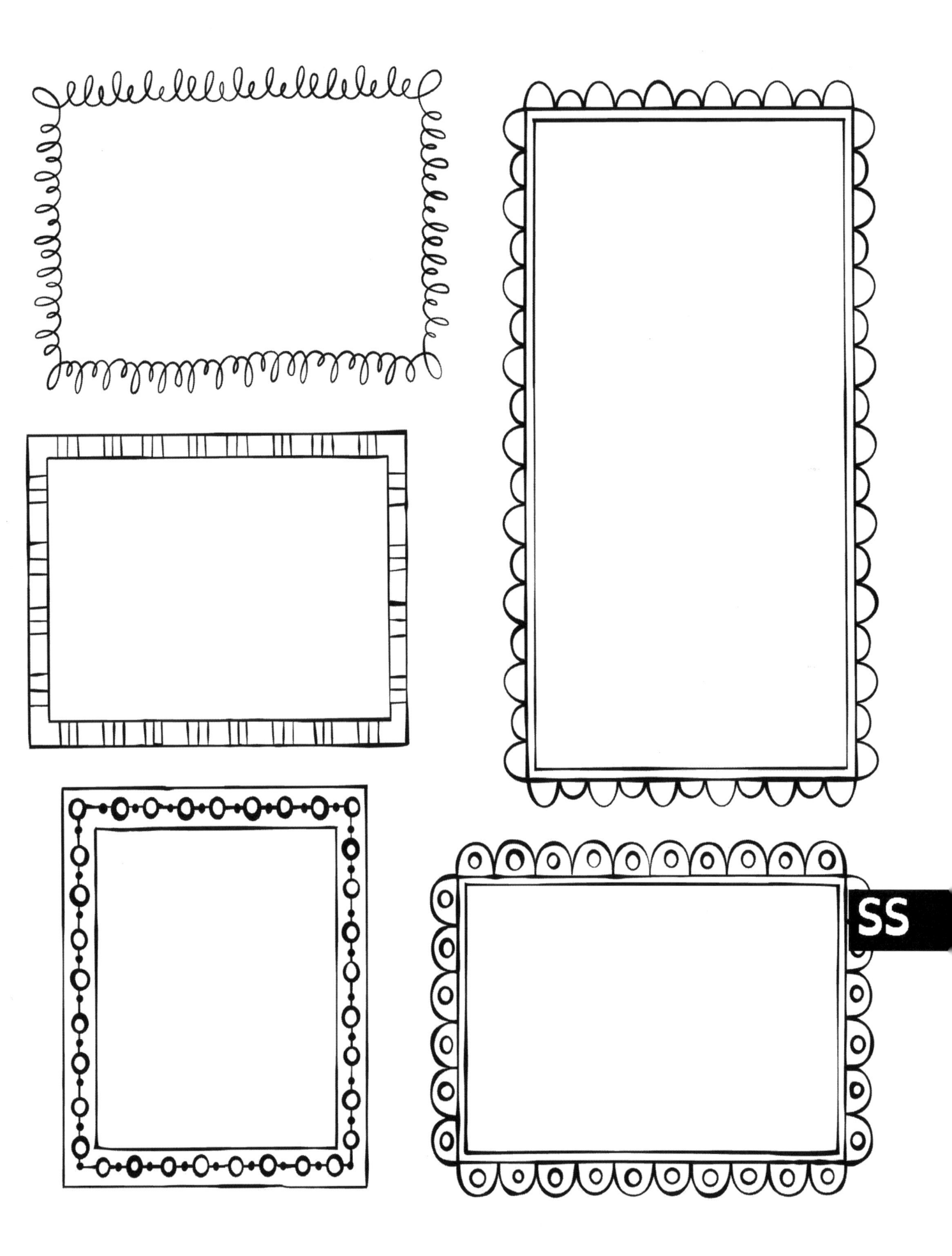

SS

TITLE:_____

Date_____

SS

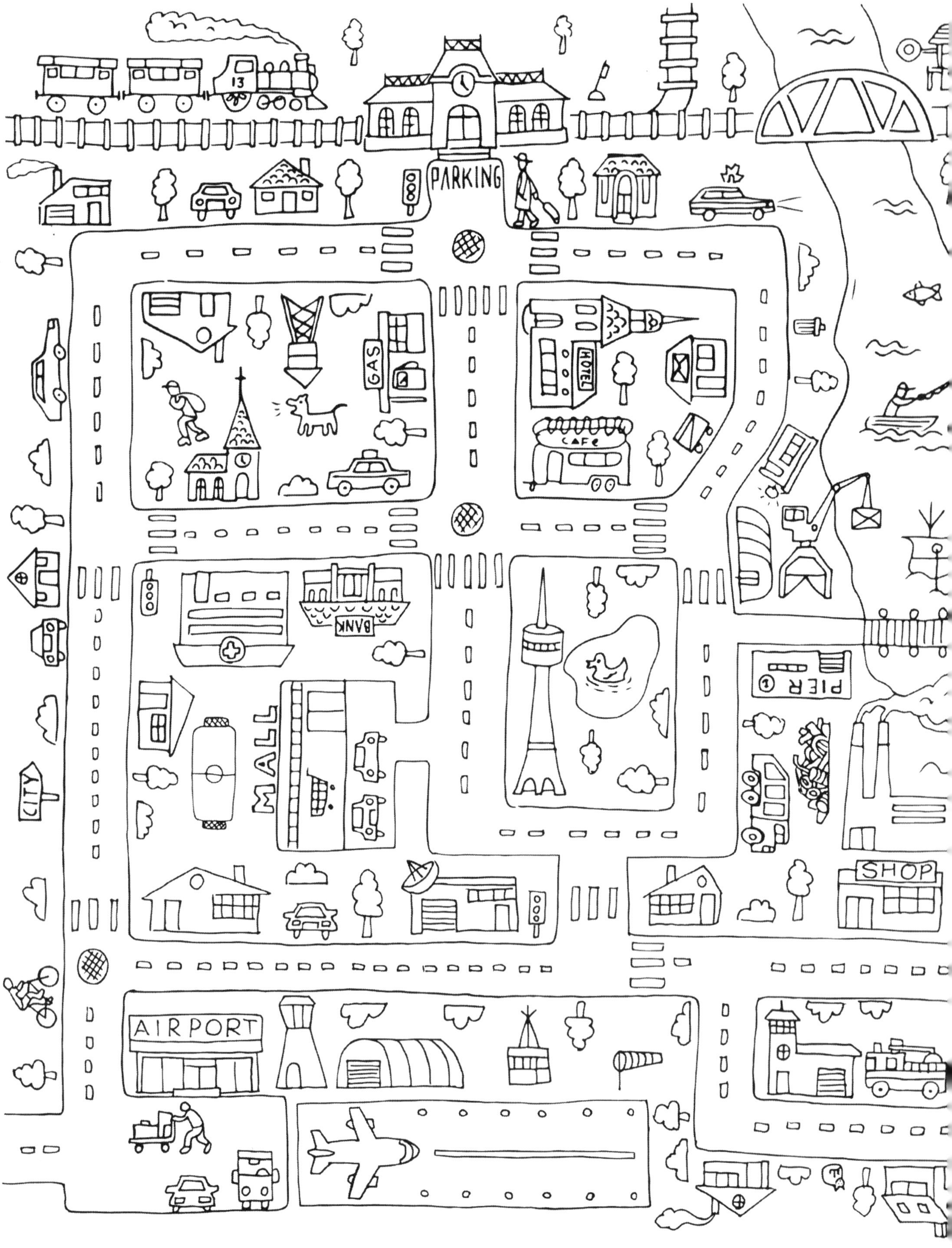

13
PARKING
GAS
HOTEL
CAFE
BANK
MALL
PIER
CITY
SHOP
AIRPORT

SS

TITLE:_____

Date_____

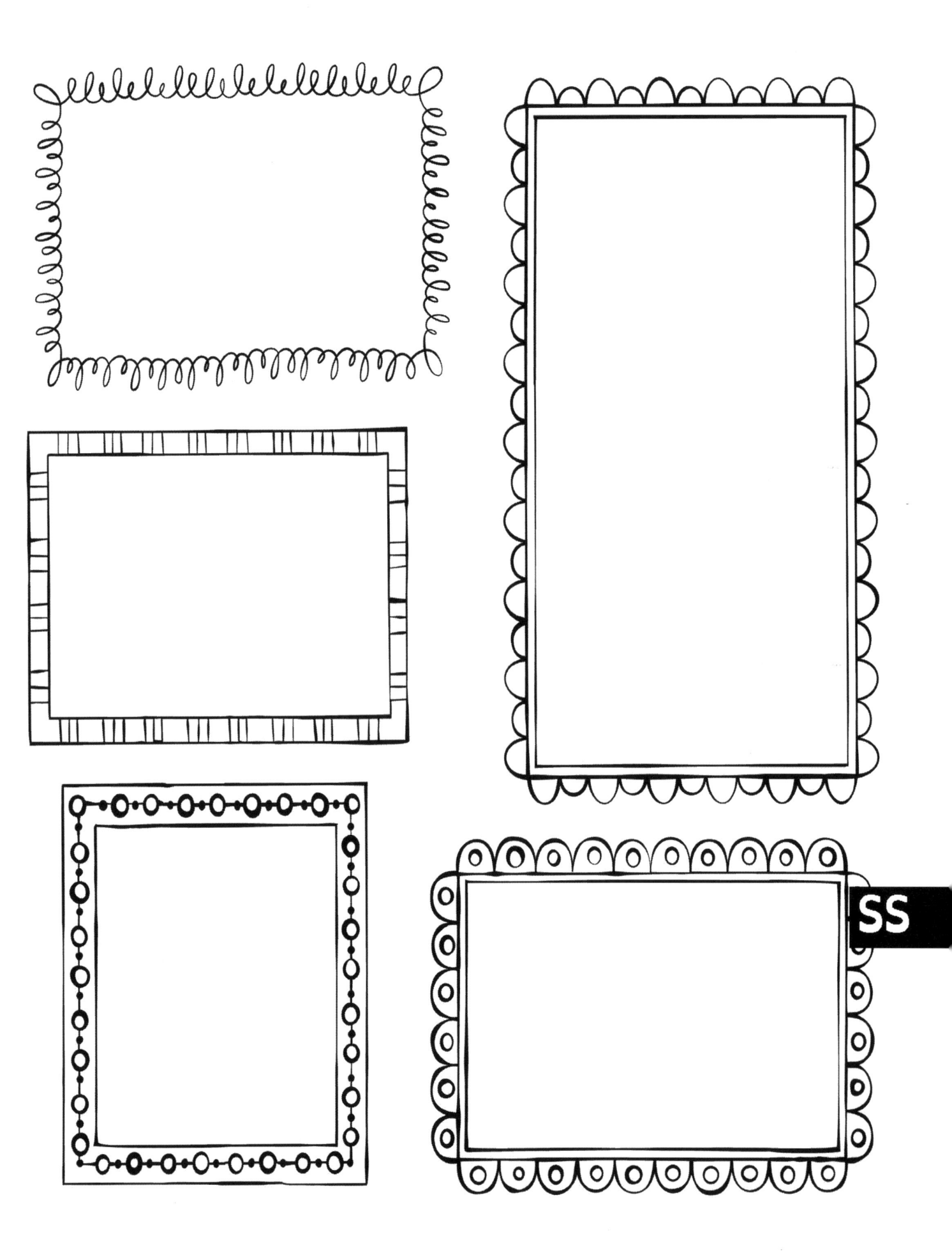

SS

TITLE:_____

Date_____

SS

TITLE:_____

Date_____

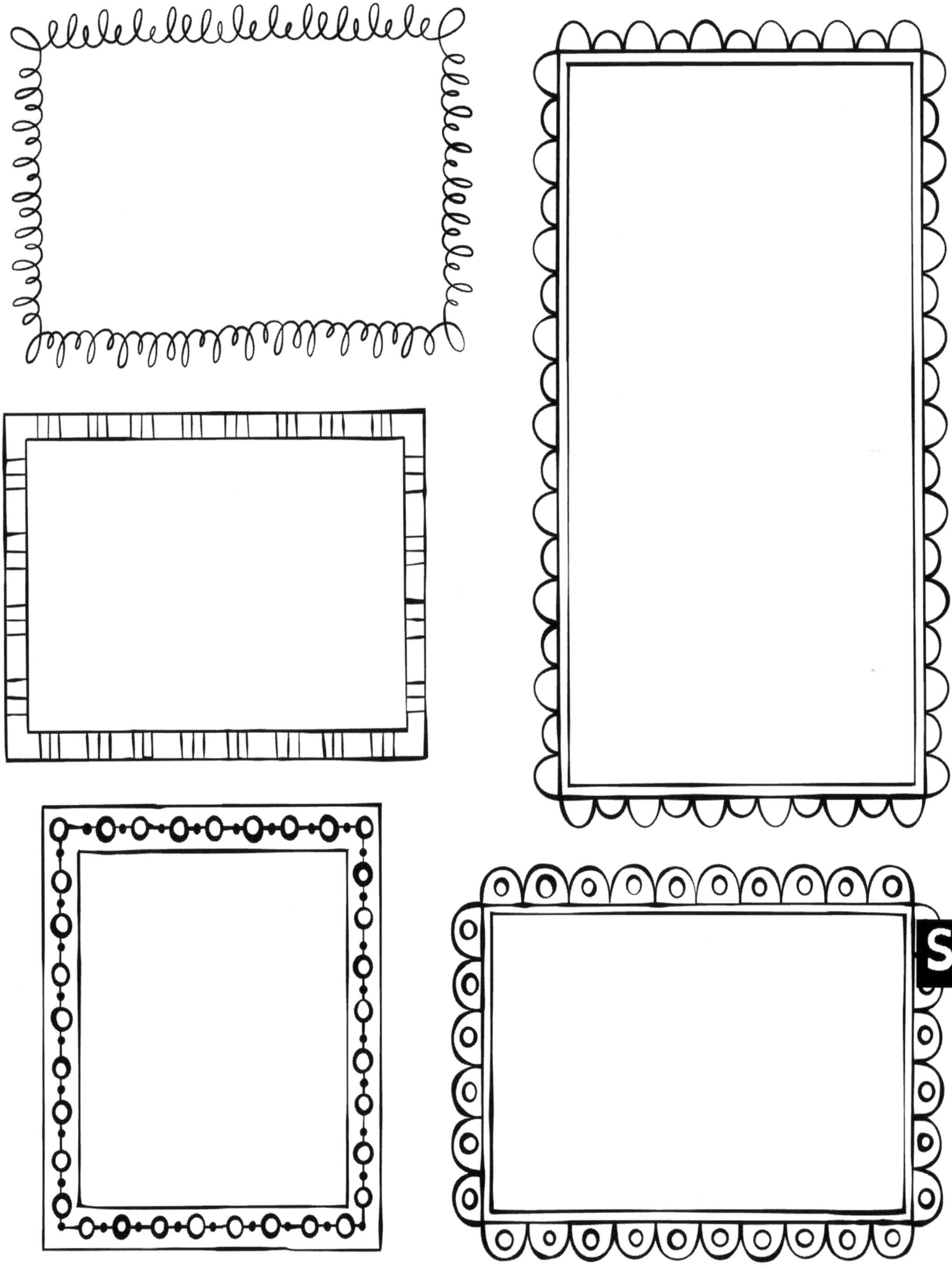

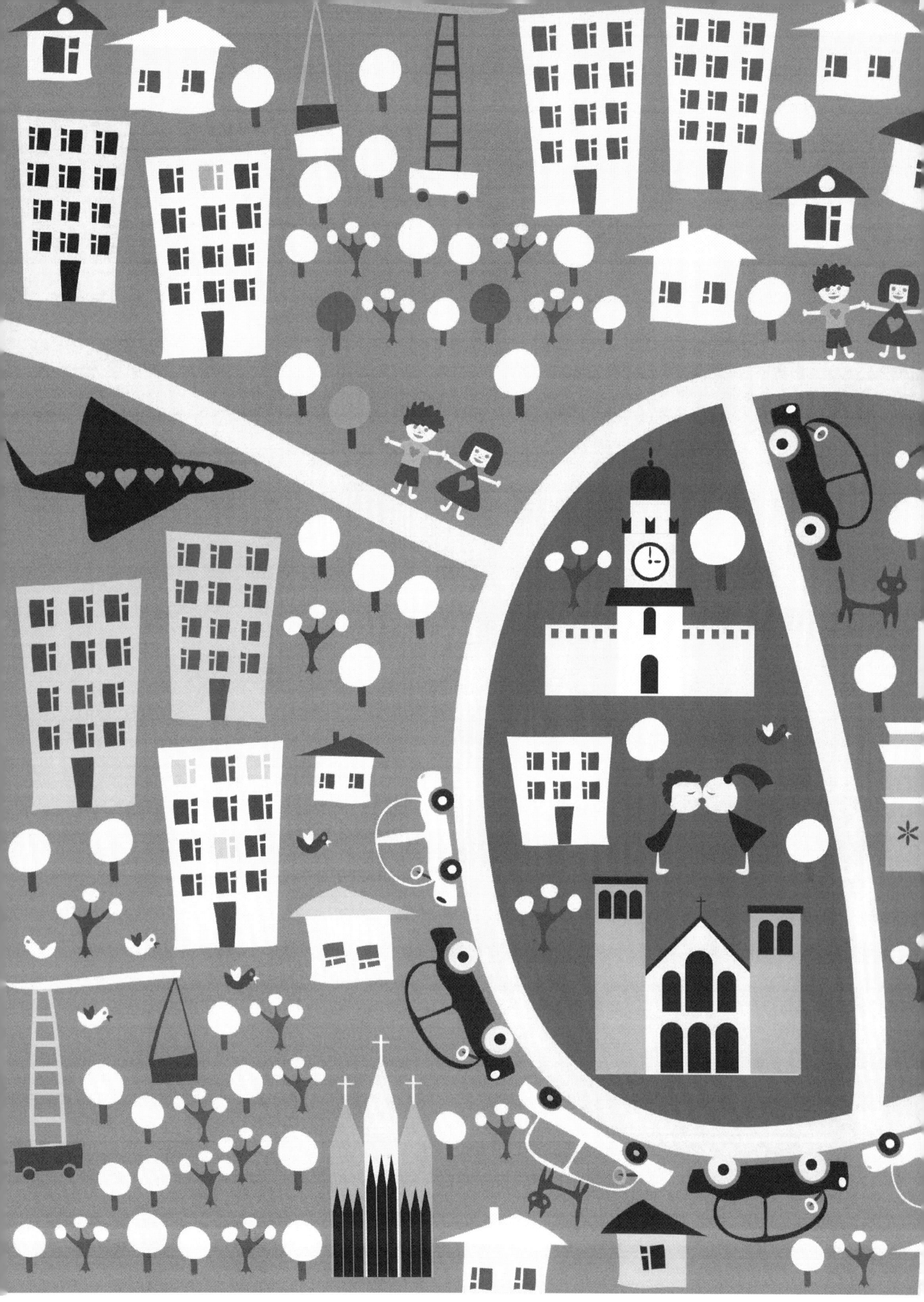

SS

TITLE:_____

Date_____

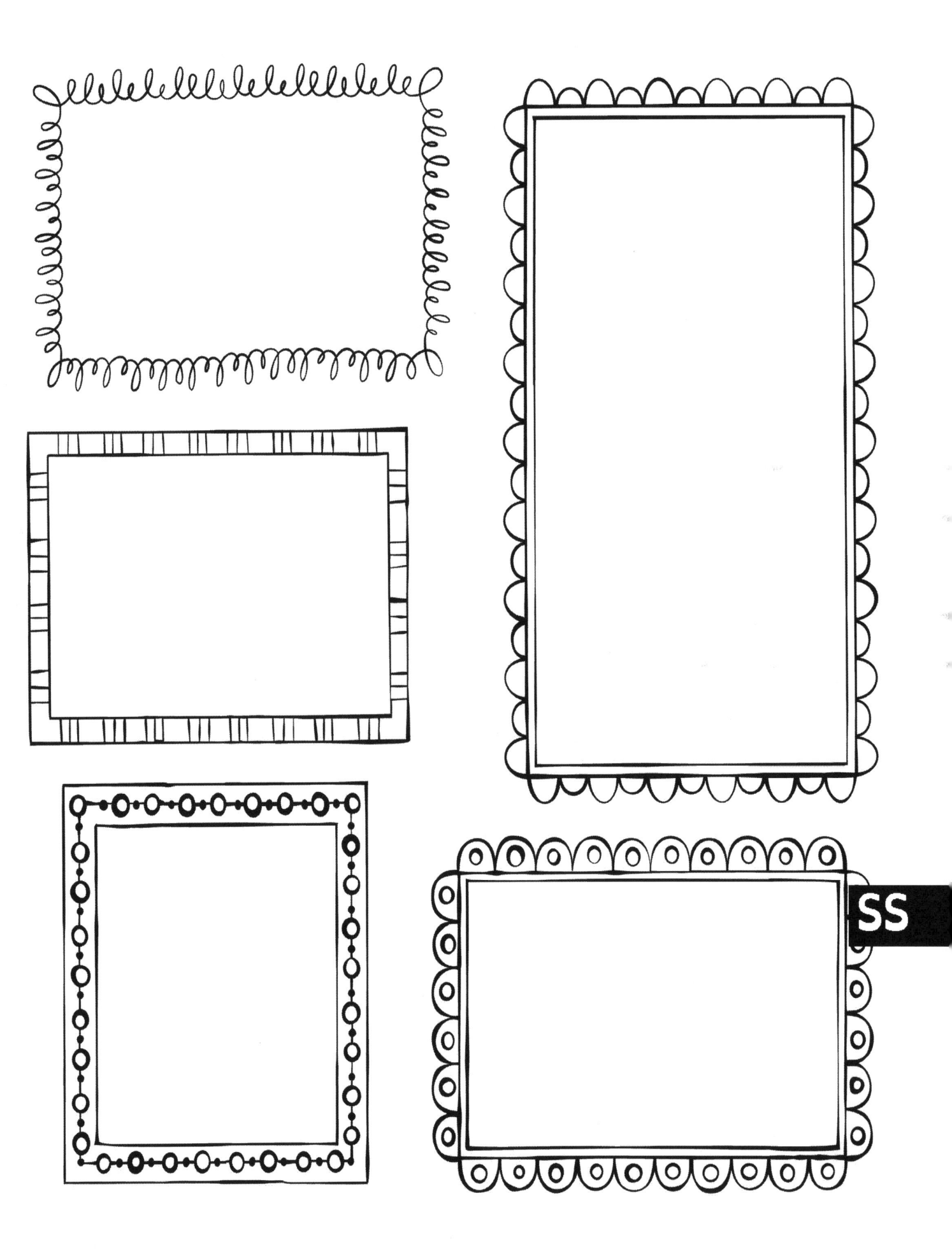

SS

TITLE:_____

Date_____

SS

TITLE:_____

Date_____

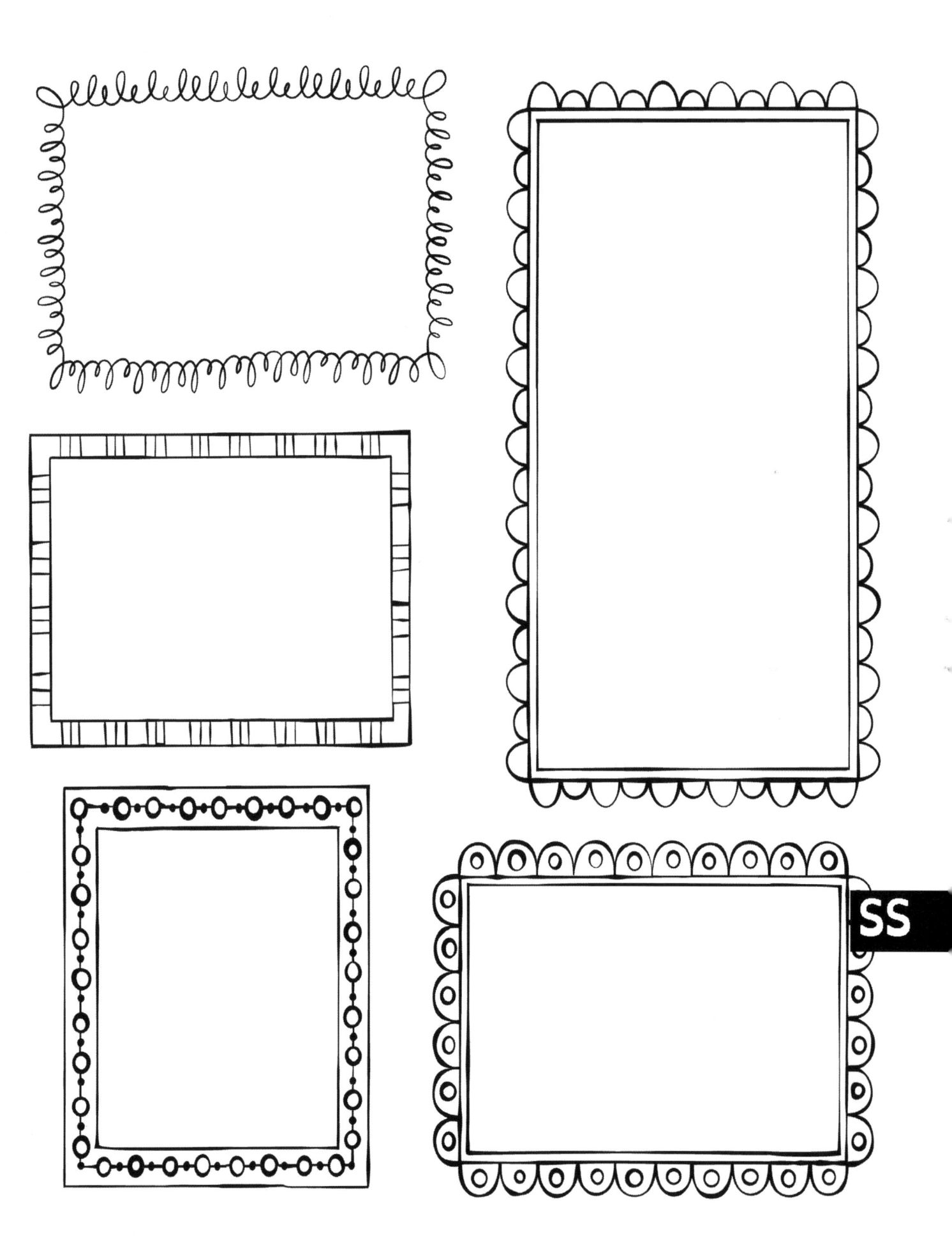

SS

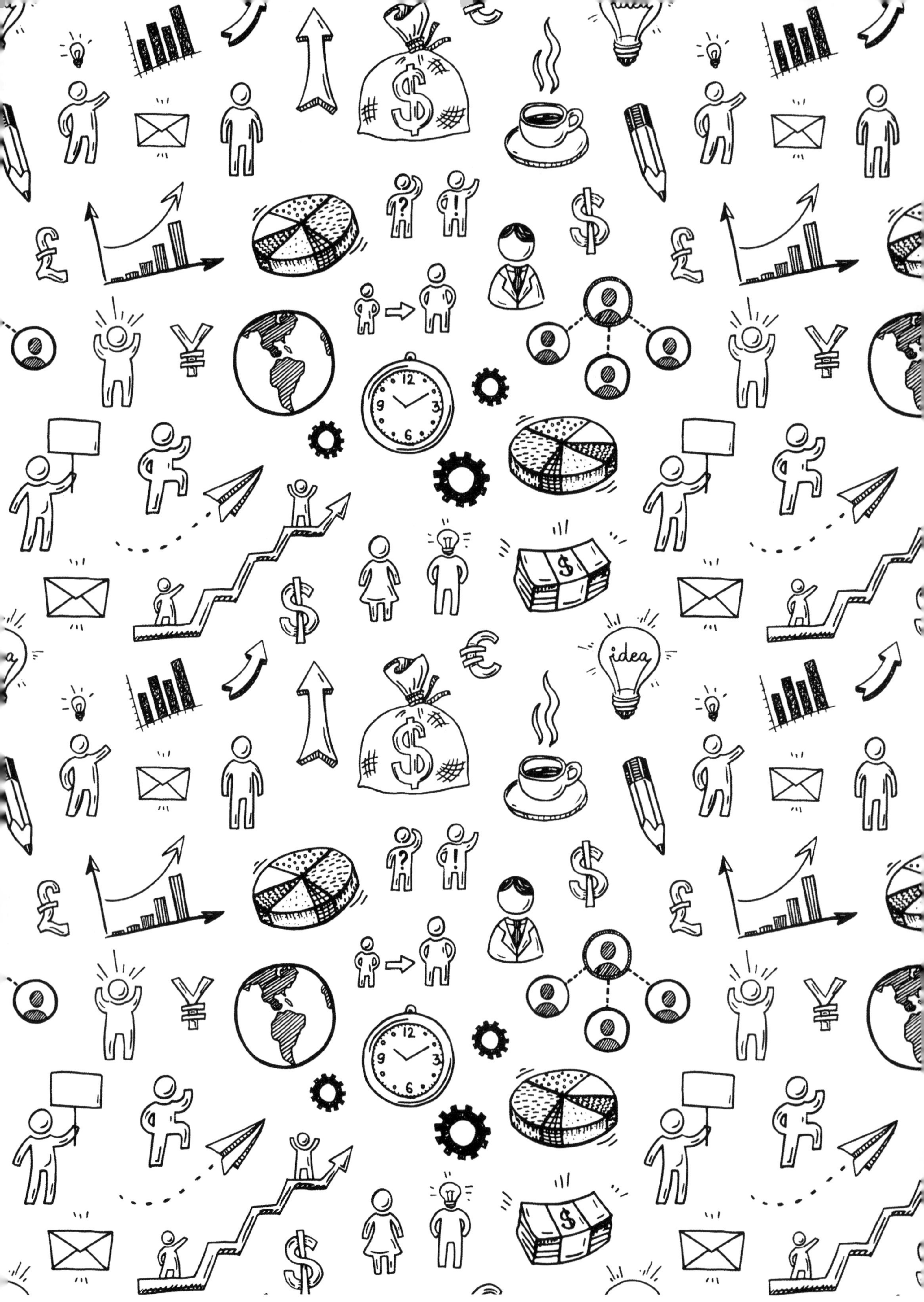
idea

SS

TITLE:_____

Date_____

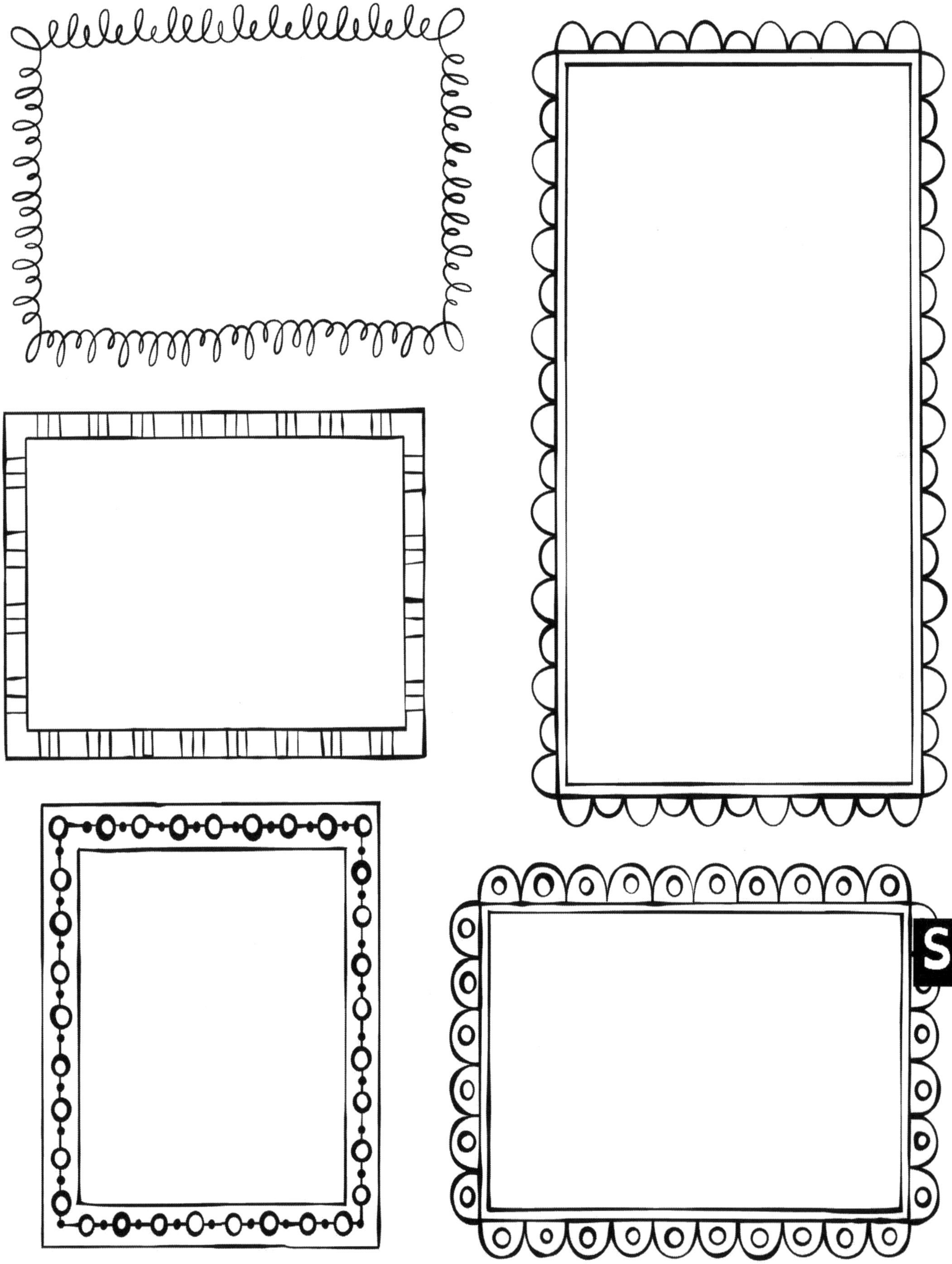

SS

TITLE:_____

Date_____

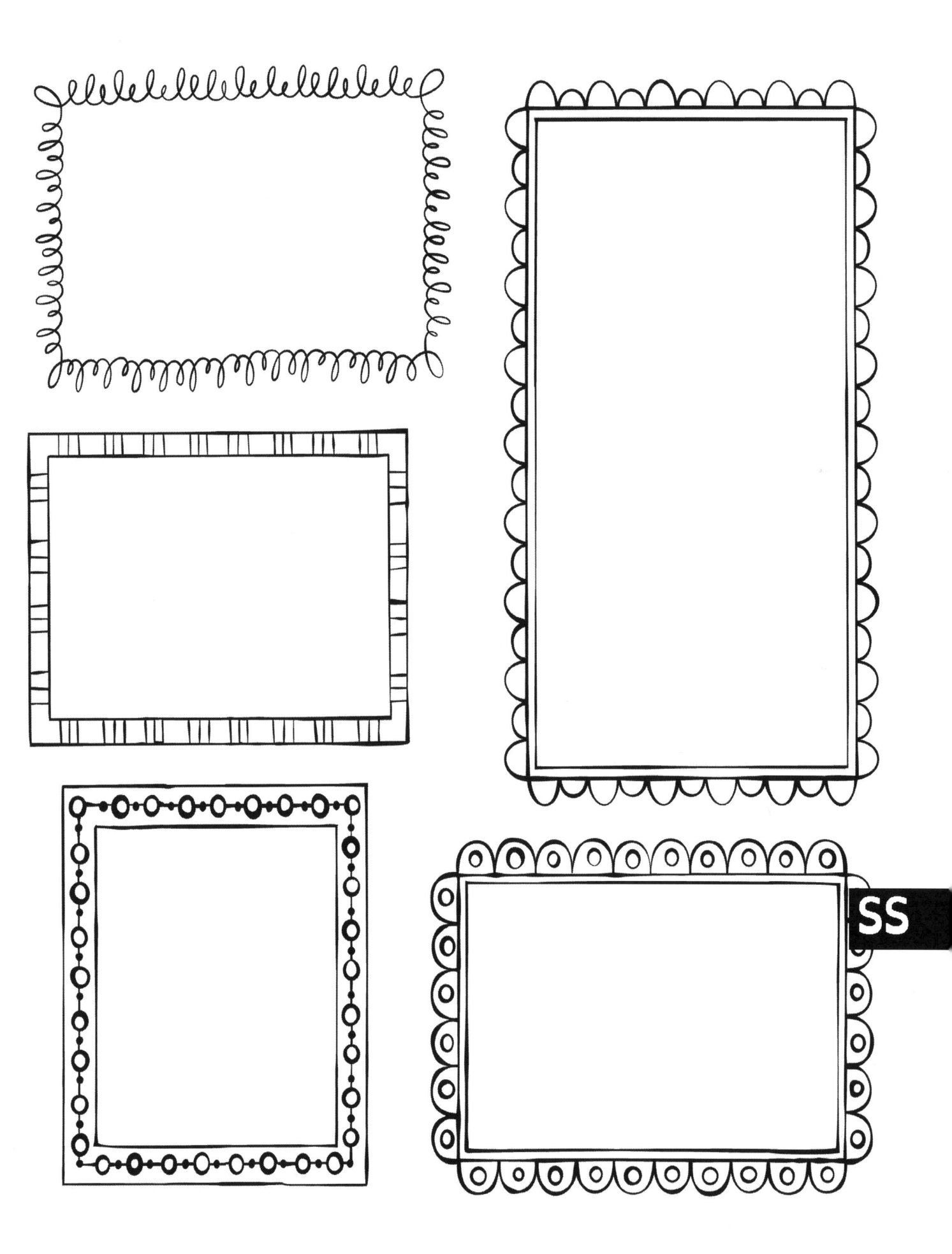

SS

TITLE:_____

Date_____

SS

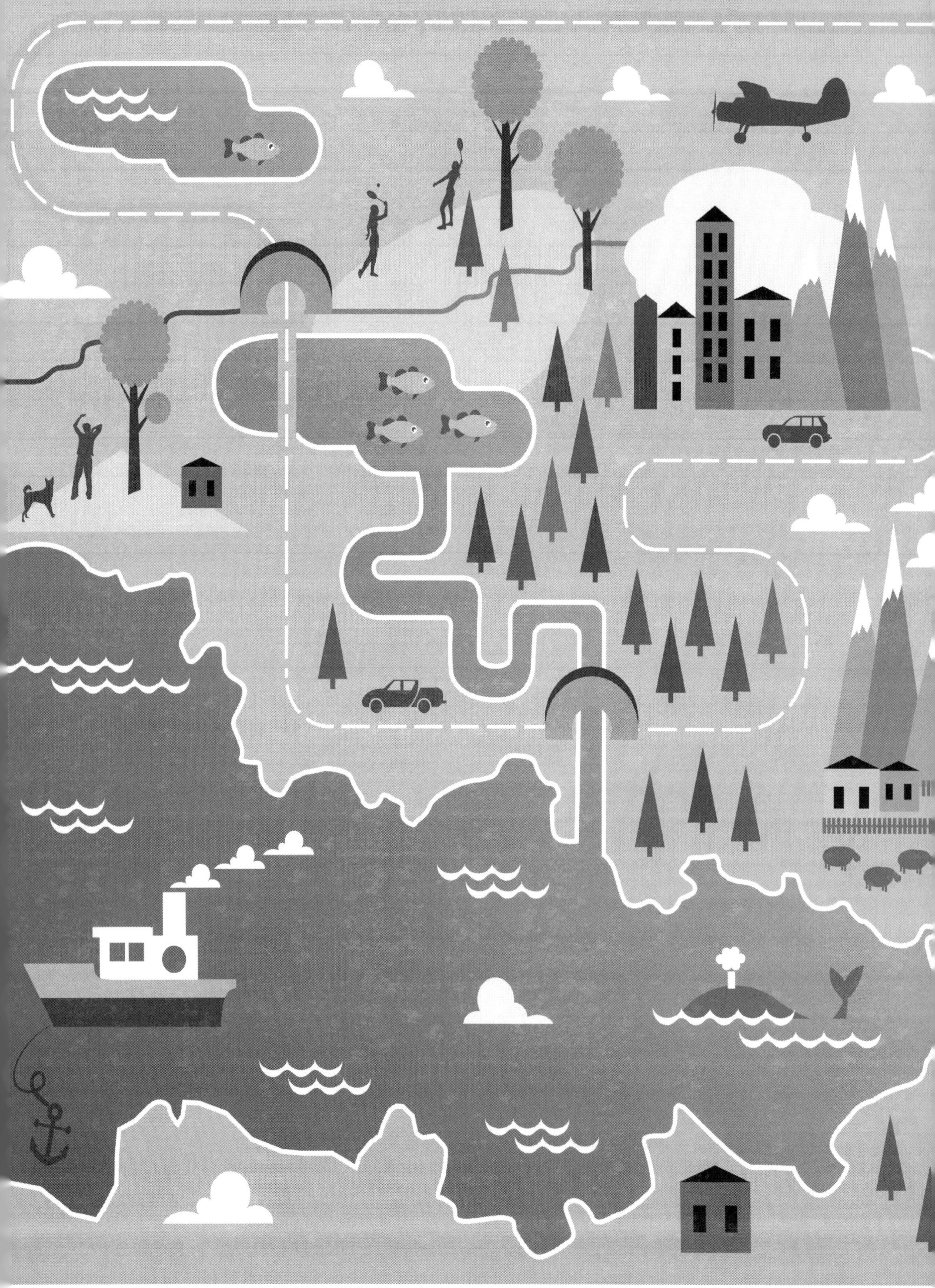

SS

TITLE:_____

Date_____

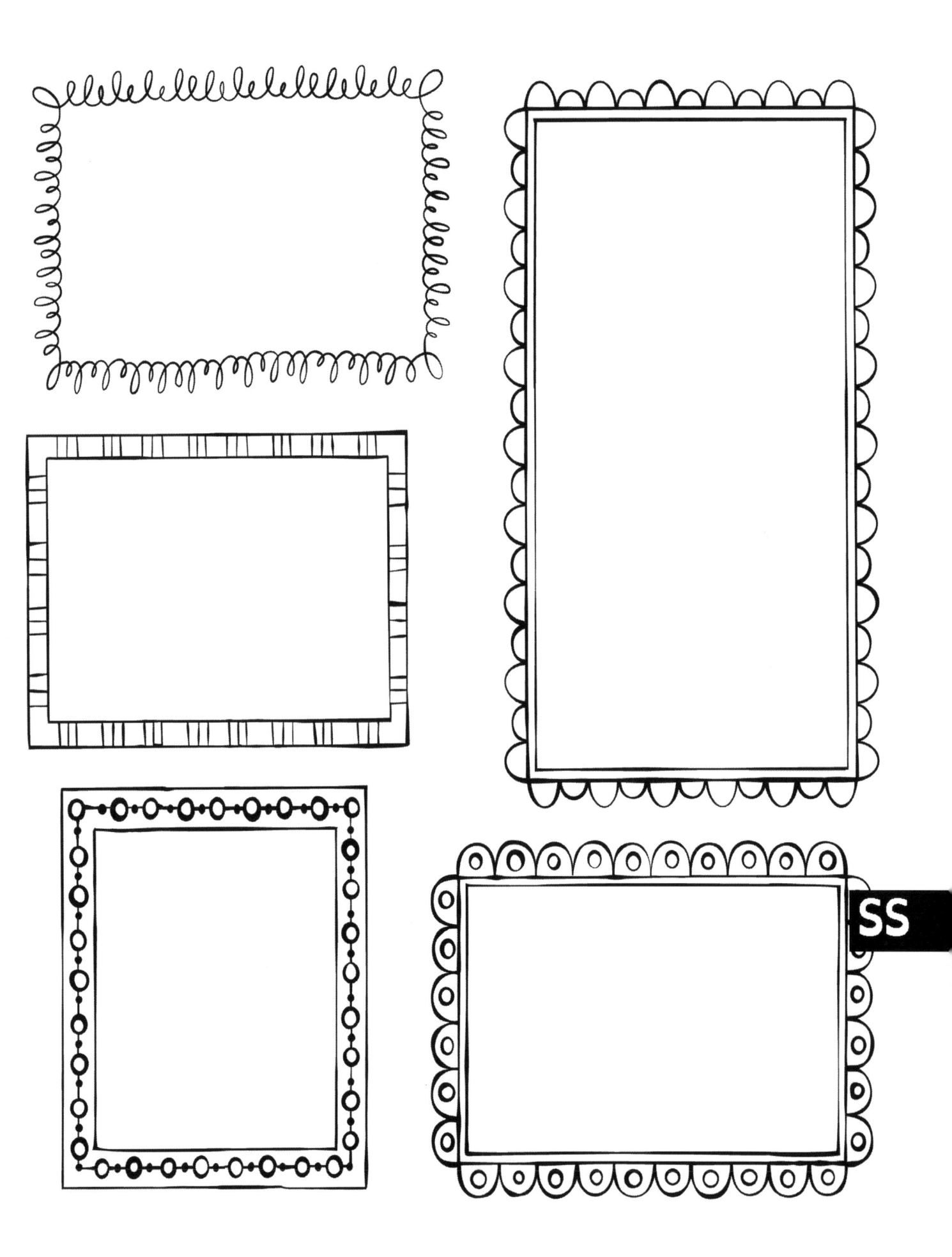

SS

TITLE:_____

Date_____

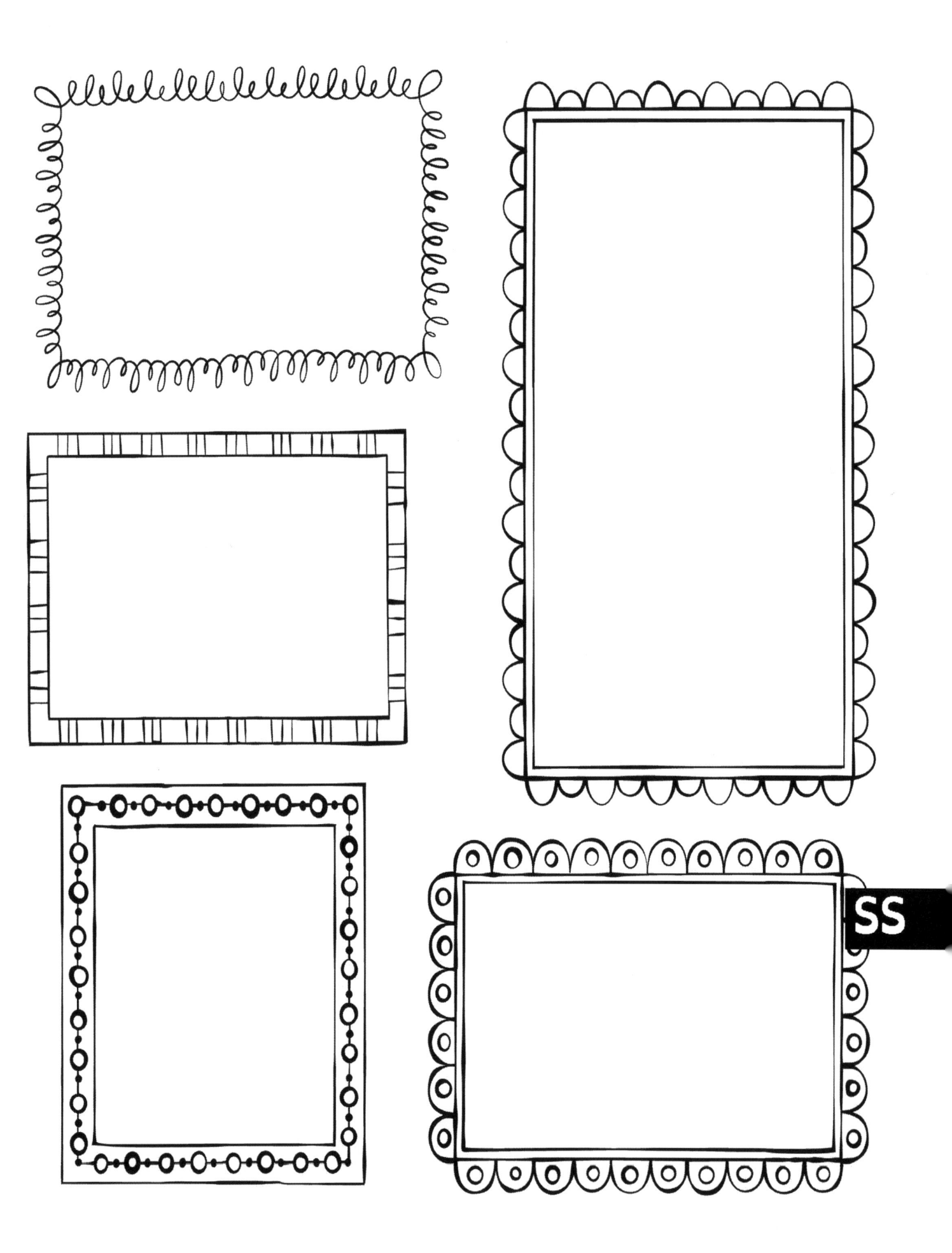

SS

Films & Tutorials

List all the Films, Tutorials & Documentaries

That you are using for your research and training:

DATE: _____TITLE: _____

TOPIC:_____

_____

DATE: _____TITLE: _____

TOPIC:_____

_____

DATE: _____TITLE: _____

TOPIC:_____

_____

DATE: _____TITLE: _____

TOPIC:_____

_____

DATE: _____TITLE: _____

TOPIC:_____

_____

DATE: _____TITLE: _____

TOPIC:_____

_____

Favorite Character:

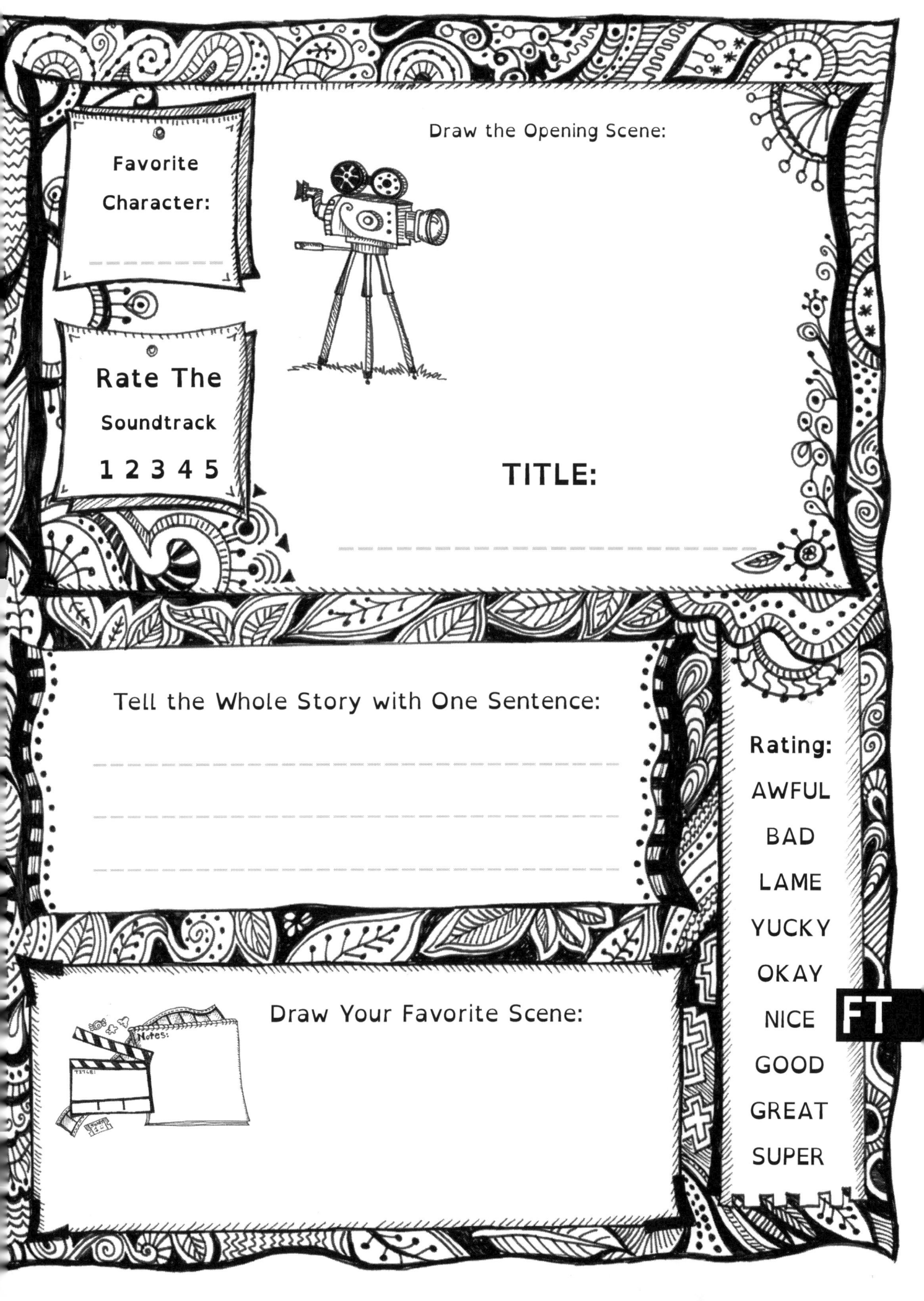

Rate The Soundtrack
1 2 3 4 5

Draw the Opening Scene:

TITLE:

Tell the Whole Story with One Sentence:

Rating:
AWFUL
BAD
LAME
YUCKY
OKAY
NICE
GOOD
GREAT
SUPER

Draw Your Favorite Scene:

Films & Tutorials

List all the Films, Tutorials & Documentaries
That you are using for your research and training:

DATE: _____TITLE: _____
TOPIC:_____
_____

DATE: _____TITLE: _____
TOPIC:_____
_____

DATE: _____TITLE: _____
TOPIC:_____
_____

DATE: _____TITLE: _____
TOPIC:_____
_____

DATE: _____TITLE: _____
TOPIC:_____
_____

DATE: _____TITLE: _____
TOPIC:_____
_____

Favorite Character:

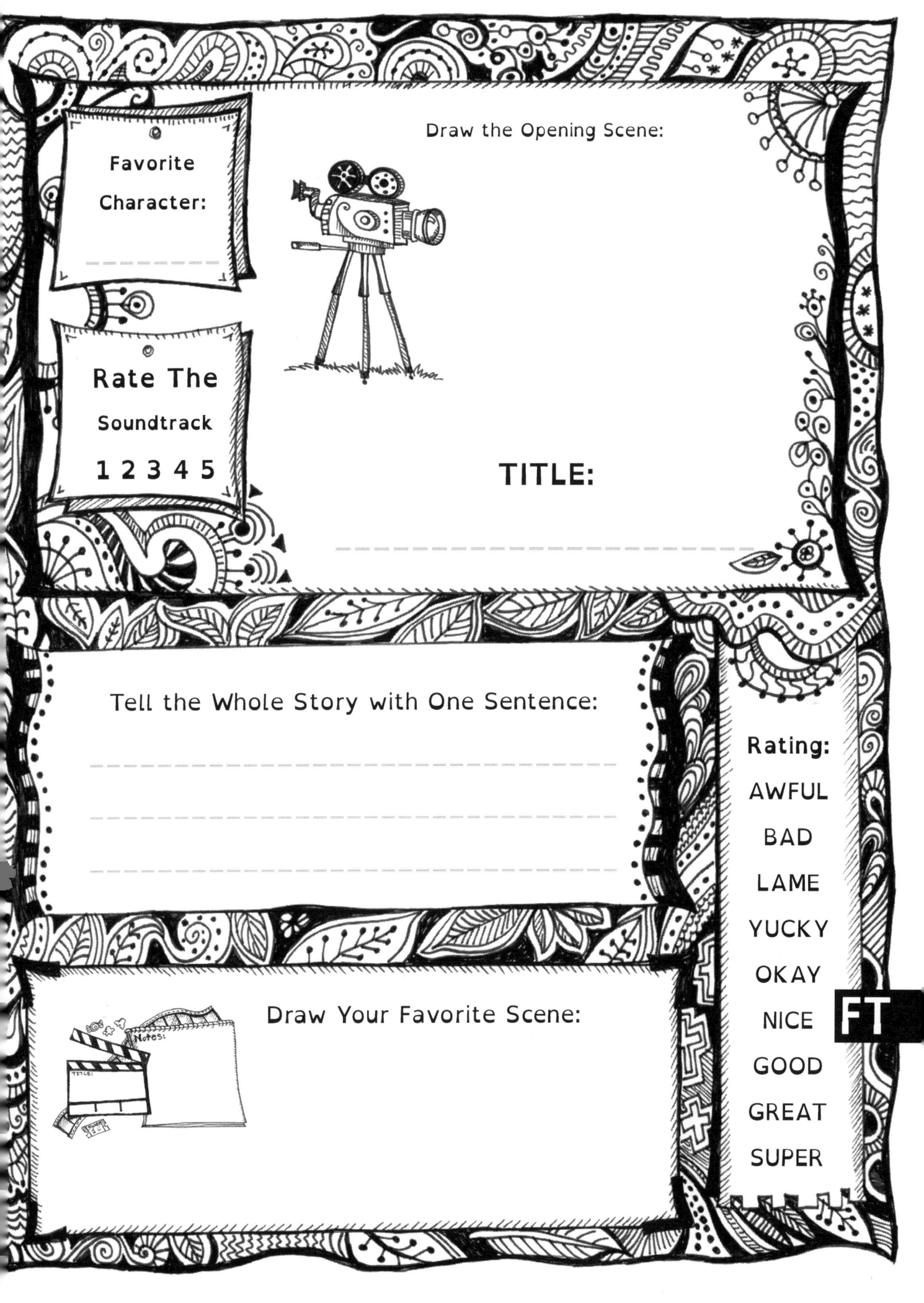

Rate The Soundtrack
1 2 3 4 5

Draw the Opening Scene:

TITLE:

Tell the Whole Story with One Sentence:

Rating:
AWFUL
BAD
LAME
YUCKY
OKAY
NICE
GOOD
GREAT
SUPER

Draw Your Favorite Scene:

FT

Films & Tutorials

List all the Films, Tutorials & Documentaries
That you are using for your research and training:

DATE: _____ TITLE: _____
TOPIC: _____
_____

DATE: _____ TITLE: _____
TOPIC: _____
_____

DATE: _____ TITLE: _____
TOPIC: _____
_____

DATE: _____ TITLE: _____
TOPIC: _____
_____

DATE: _____ TITLE: _____
TOPIC: _____
_____

DATE: _____ TITLE: _____
TOPIC: _____
_____

Favorite Character:

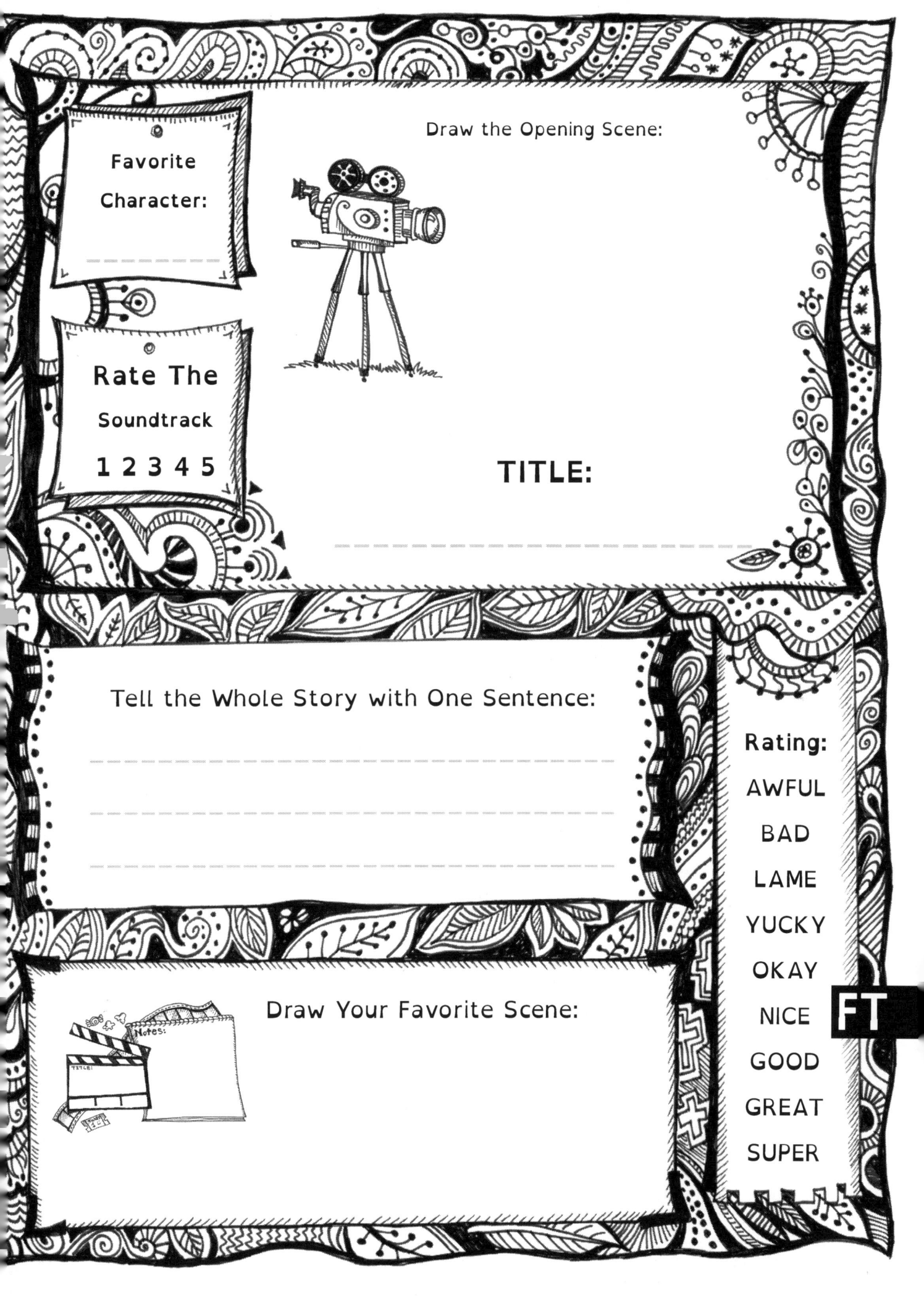

Rate The Soundtrack
1 2 3 4 5

Draw the Opening Scene:

TITLE:

Tell the Whole Story with One Sentence:

Rating:
AWFUL
BAD
LAME
YUCKY
OKAY
NICE
GOOD
GREAT
SUPER

Draw Your Favorite Scene:

FT

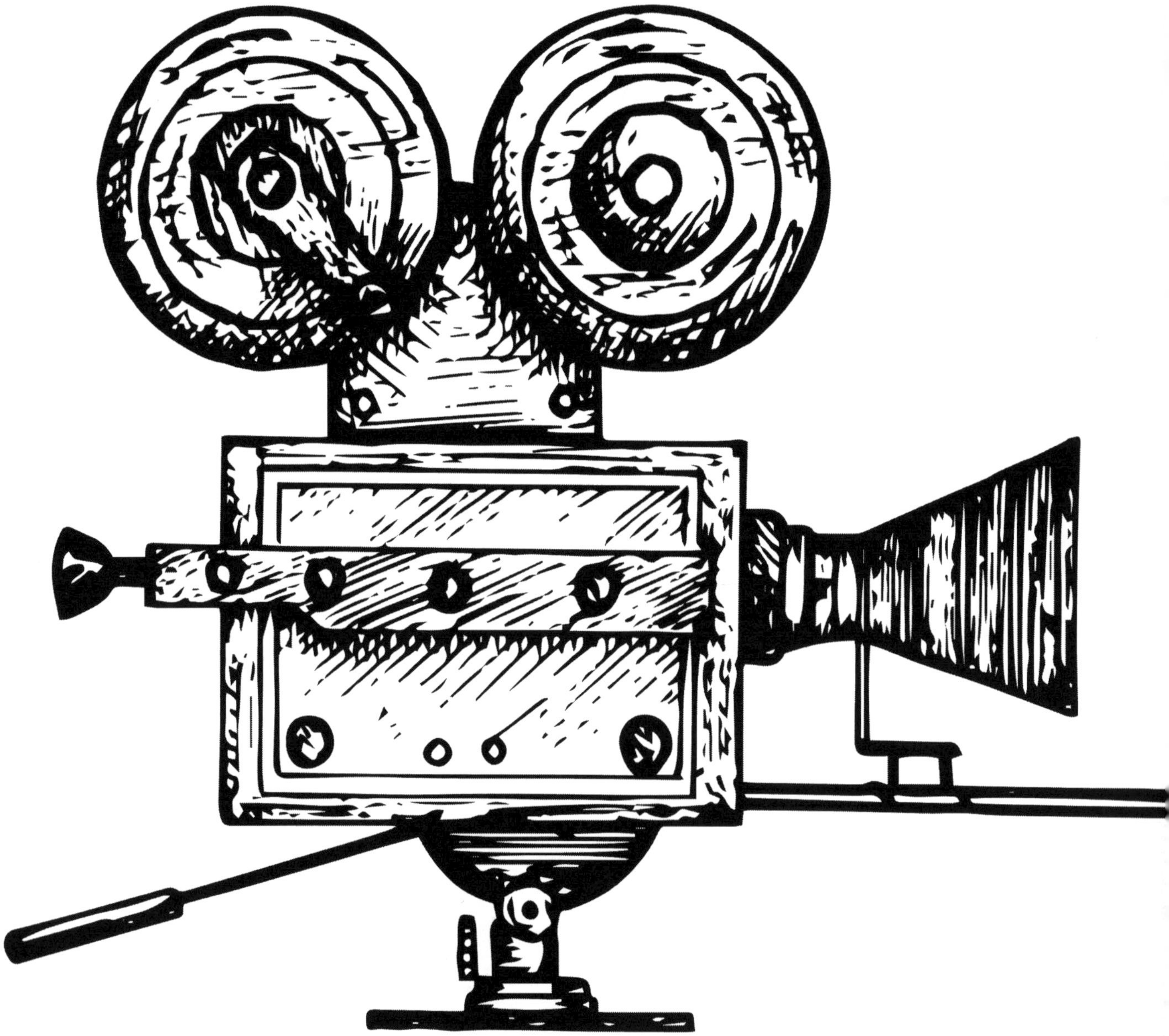

Favorite Character:

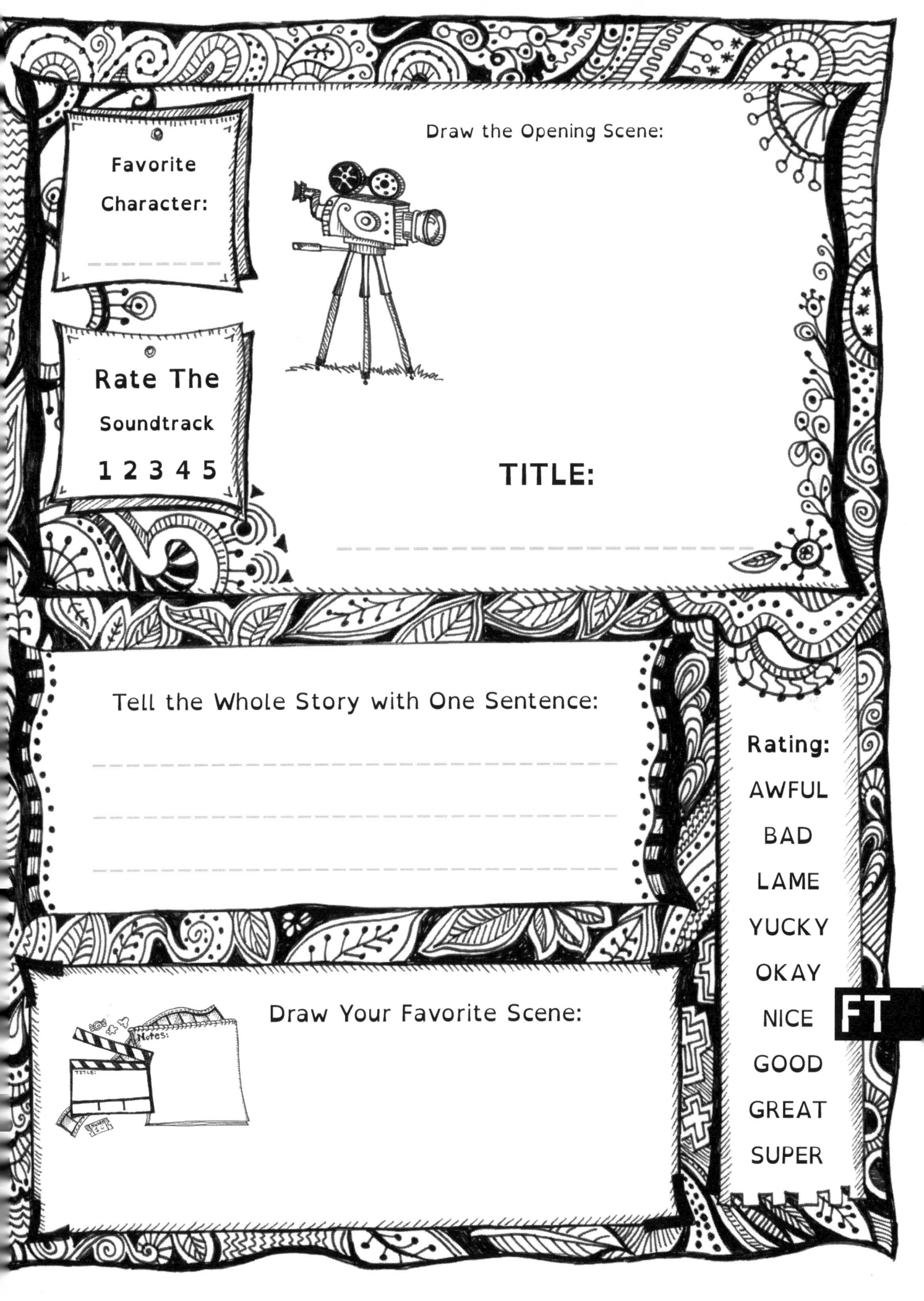

Rate The Soundtrack
1 2 3 4 5

Draw the Opening Scene:

TITLE:

Tell the Whole Story with One Sentence:

Draw Your Favorite Scene:

Rating:
AWFUL
BAD
LAME
YUCKY
OKAY
NICE
GOOD
GREAT
SUPER

Films & Tutorials

List all the Films, Tutorials & Documentaries
That you are using for your research and training:

DATE: _____ TITLE: _____
TOPIC: _____
_____

DATE: _____ TITLE: _____
TOPIC: _____
_____

DATE: _____ TITLE: _____
TOPIC: _____
_____

DATE: _____ TITLE: _____
TOPIC: _____
_____

DATE: _____ TITLE: _____
TOPIC: _____
_____

DATE: _____ TITLE: _____
TOPIC: _____
_____

Favorite Character:

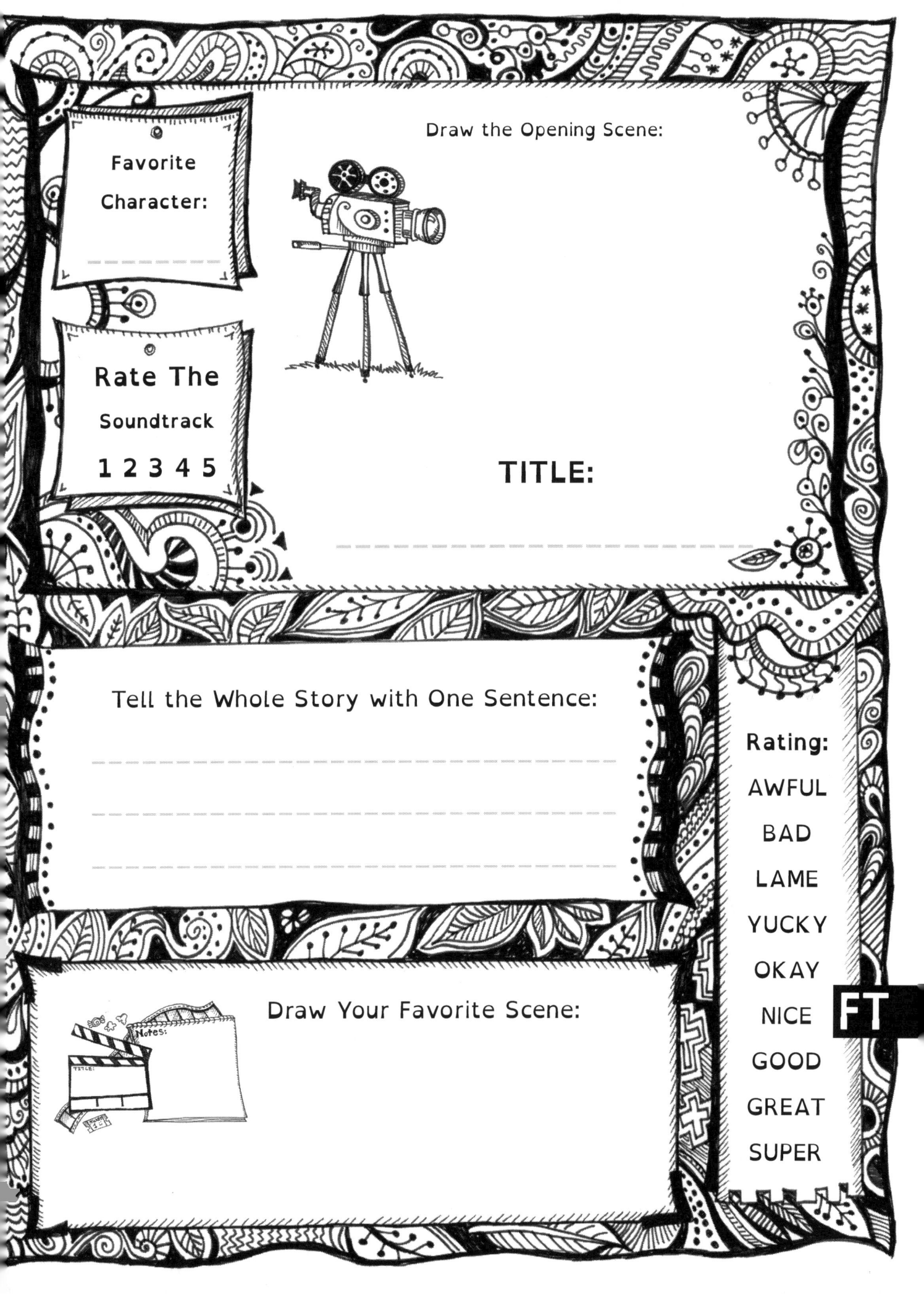

Rate The Soundtrack
1 2 3 4 5

Draw the Opening Scene:

TITLE:

Tell the Whole Story with One Sentence:

Draw Your Favorite Scene:

Rating:
AWFUL
BAD
LAME
YUCKY
OKAY
NICE
GOOD
GREAT
SUPER

Films & Tutorials

List all the Films, Tutorials & Documentaries
That you are using for your research and training:

DATE: _____ TITLE: _____
TOPIC:_____
_____

DATE: _____ TITLE: _____
TOPIC:_____
_____

DATE: _____ TITLE: _____
TOPIC:_____
_____

DATE: _____ TITLE: _____
TOPIC:_____
_____

DATE: _____ TITLE: _____
TOPIC:_____
_____

DATE: _____ TITLE: _____
TOPIC:_____
_____

Favorite Character:

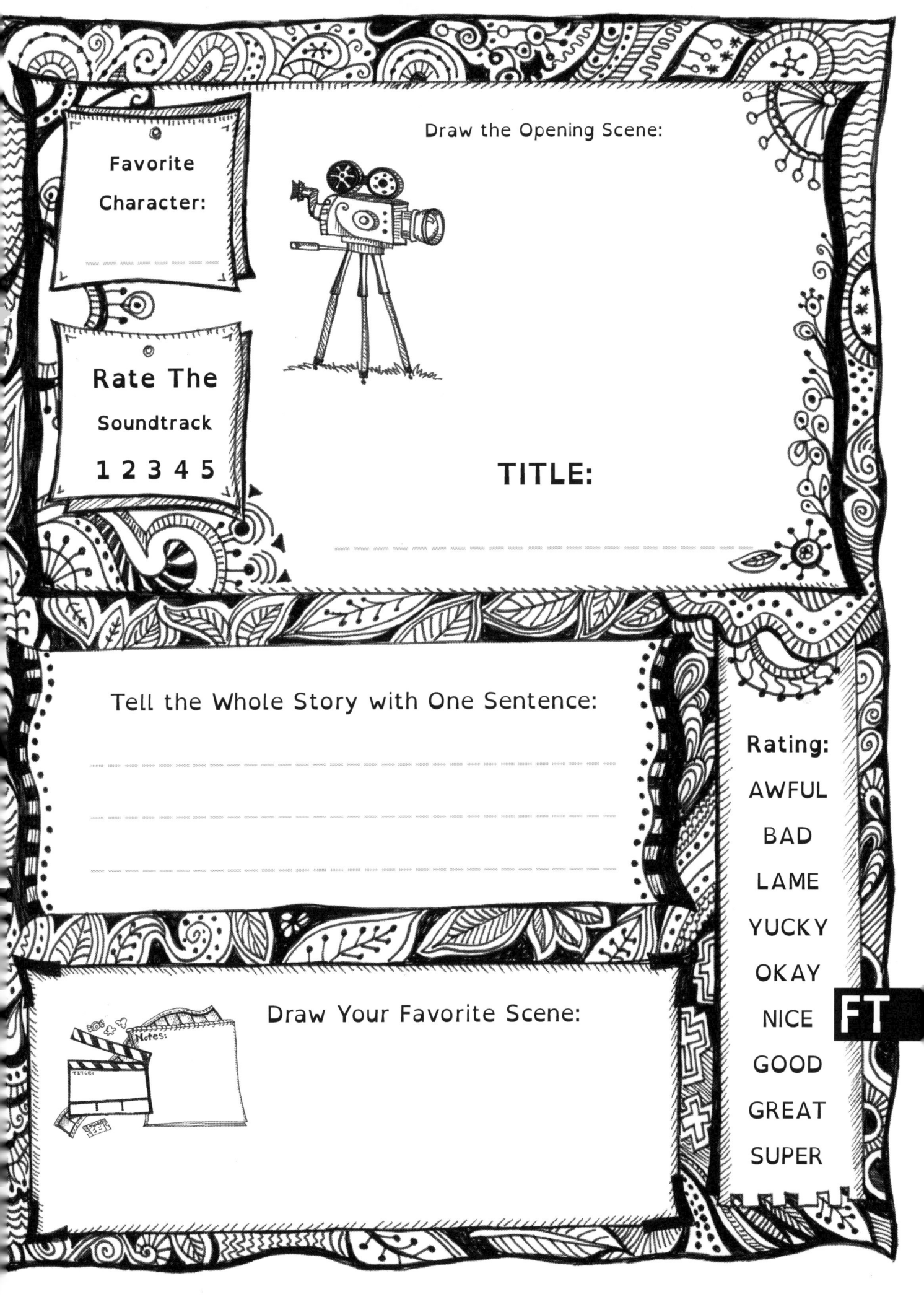

Rate The Soundtrack
1 2 3 4 5

Draw the Opening Scene:

TITLE:

Tell the Whole Story with One Sentence:

Draw Your Favorite Scene:

Rating:
AWFUL
BAD
LAME
YUCKY
OKAY
NICE
GOOD
GREAT
SUPER

FT

Favorite Character:

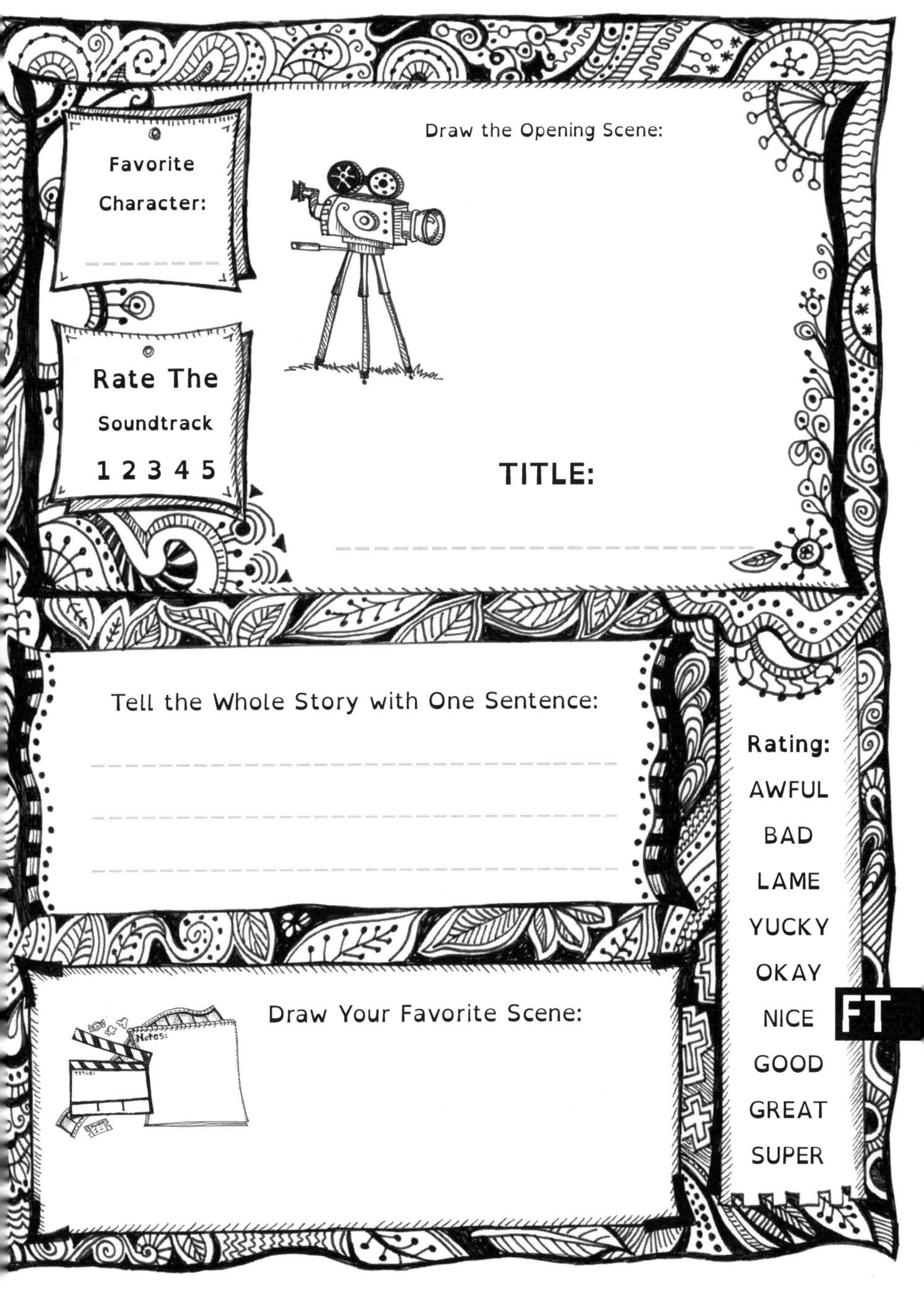

Rate The Soundtrack
1 2 3 4 5

Draw the Opening Scene:

TITLE:

Tell the Whole Story with One Sentence:

Rating:
AWFUL
BAD
LAME
YUCKY
OKAY
NICE
GOOD
GREAT
SUPER

Draw Your Favorite Scene:

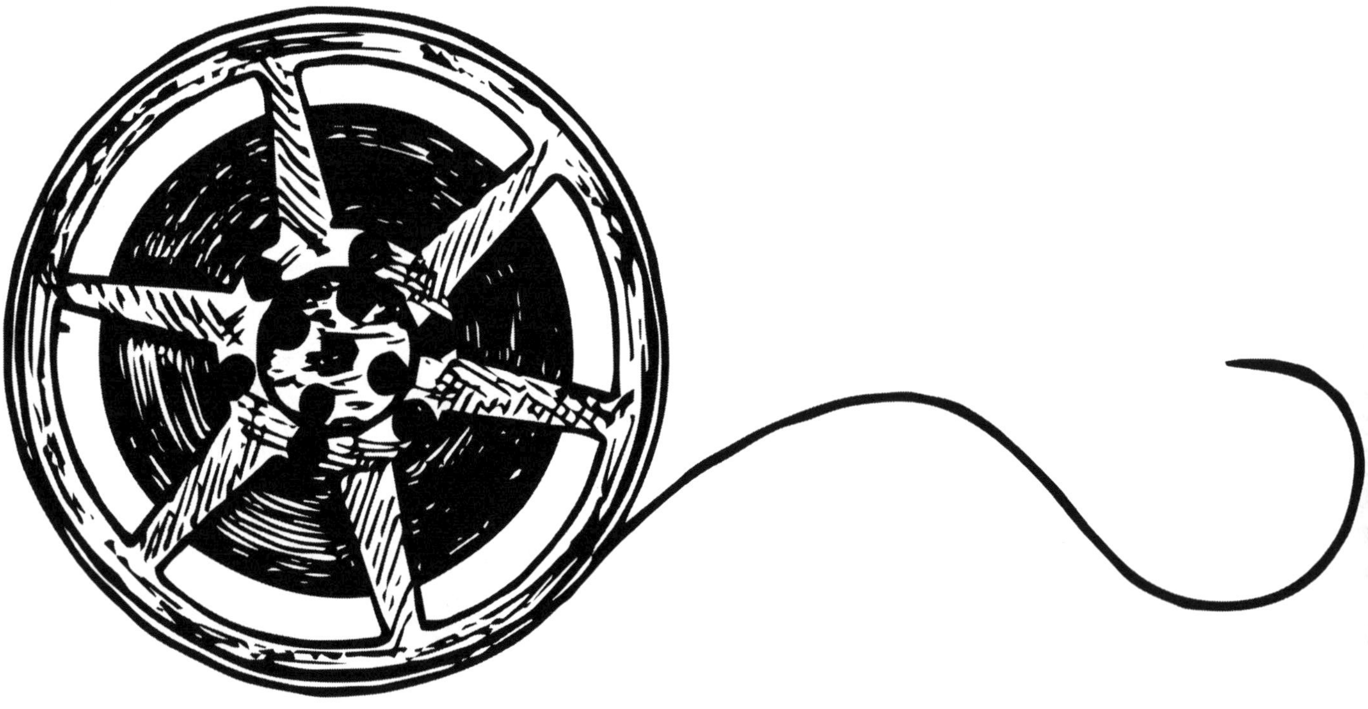

Favorite Character:

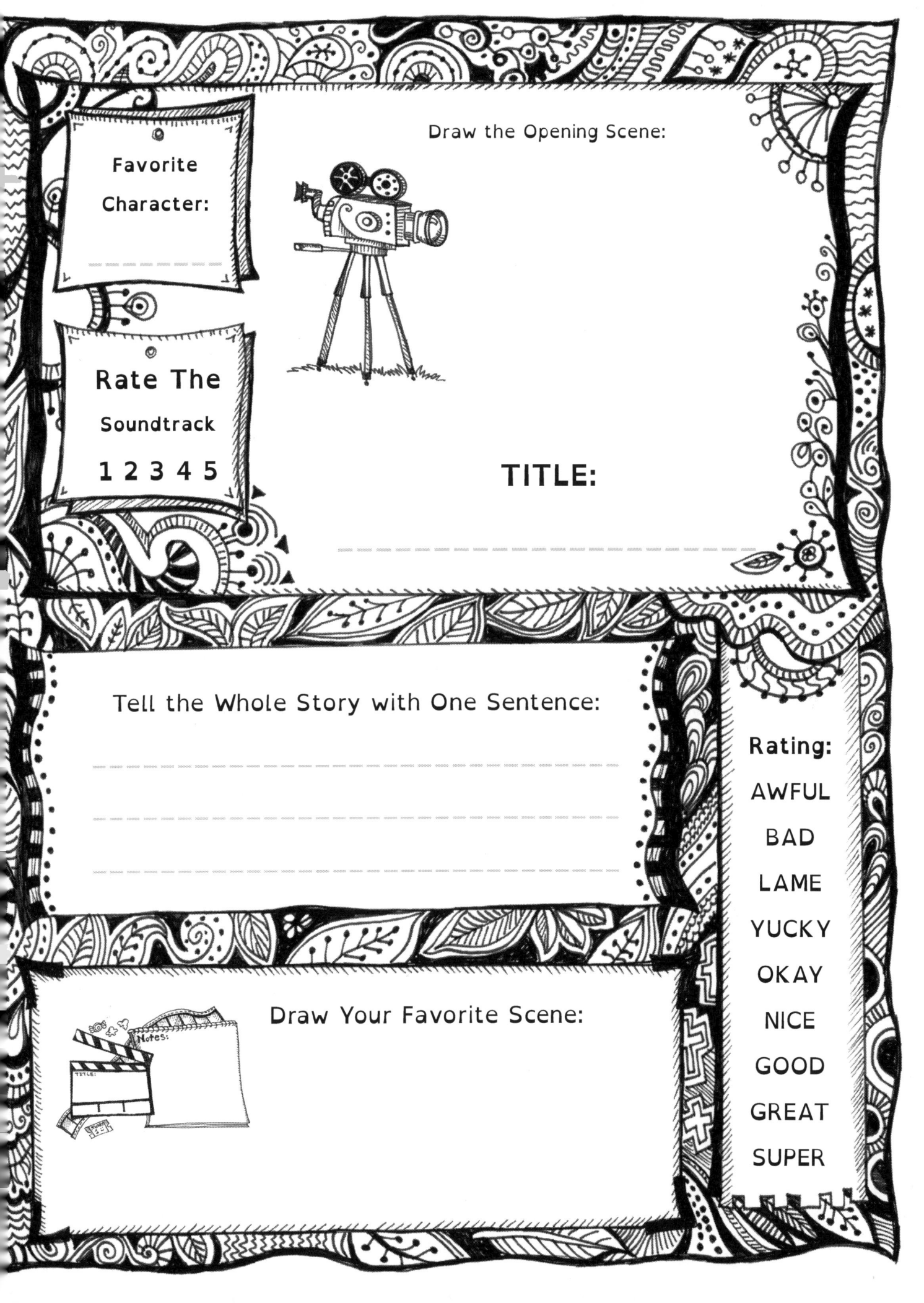

Rate The Soundtrack
1 2 3 4 5

Draw the Opening Scene:

TITLE:

Tell the Whole Story with One Sentence:

Draw Your Favorite Scene:

Rating:
AWFUL
BAD
LAME
YUCKY
OKAY
NICE
GOOD
GREAT
SUPER

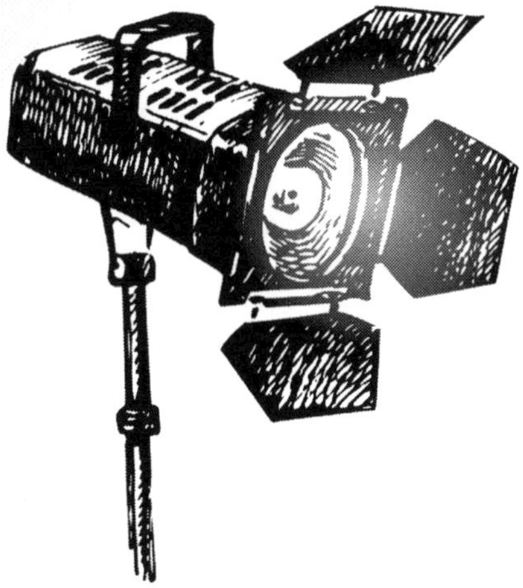

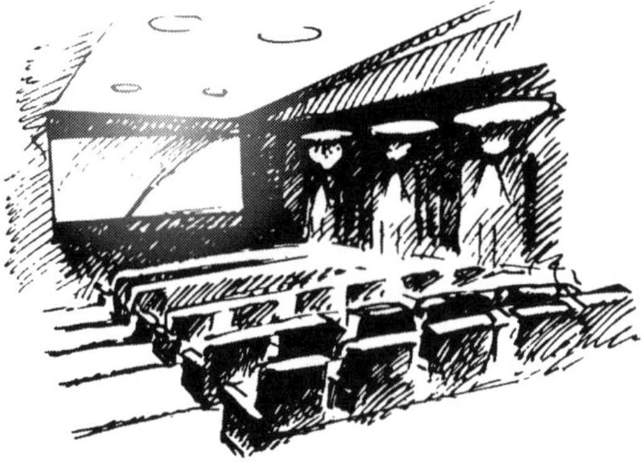

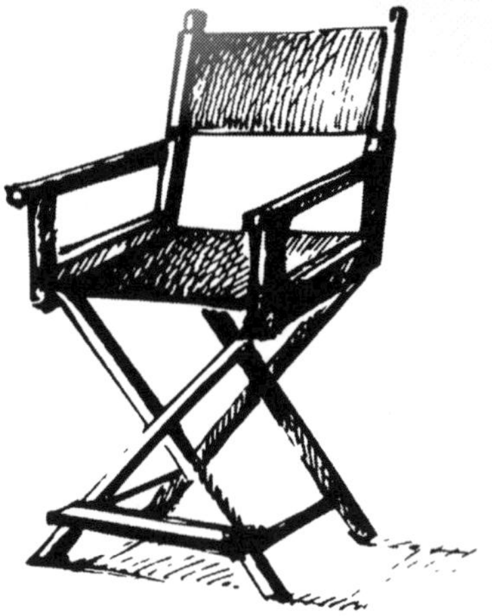

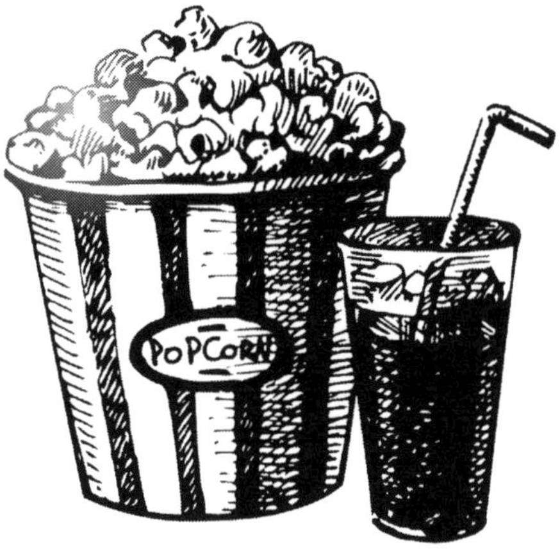
POPCORN

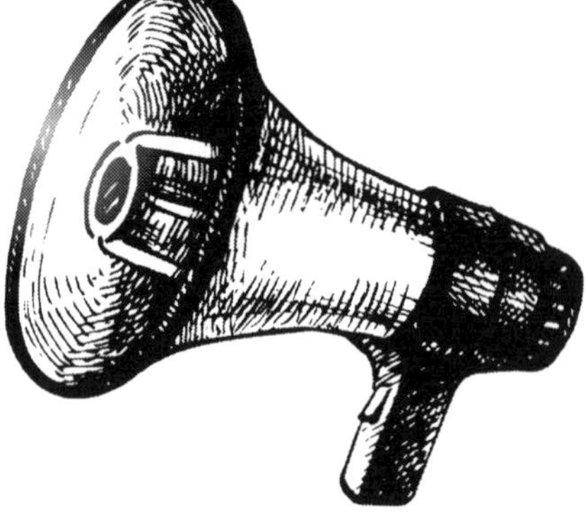

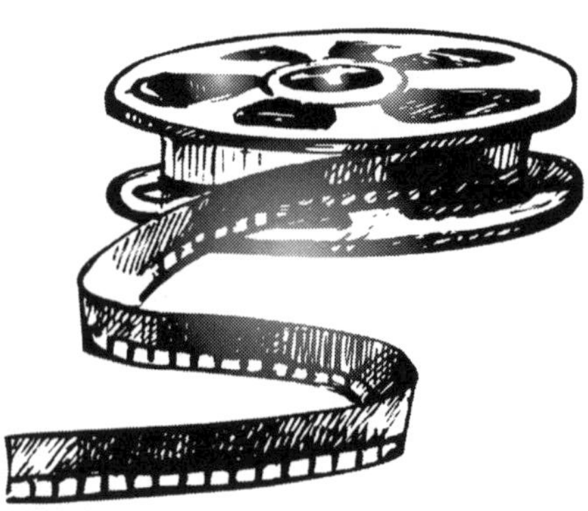

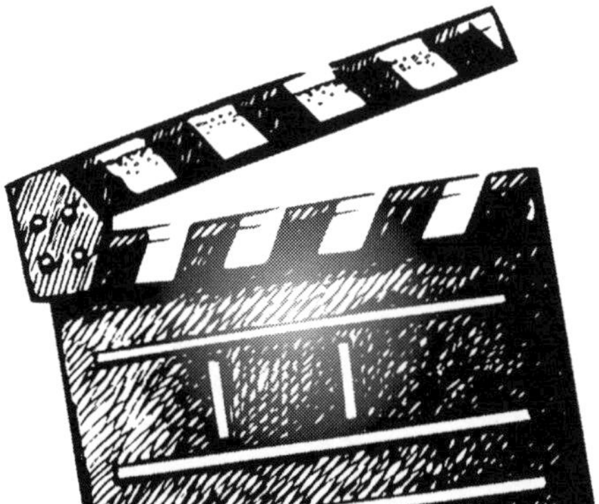

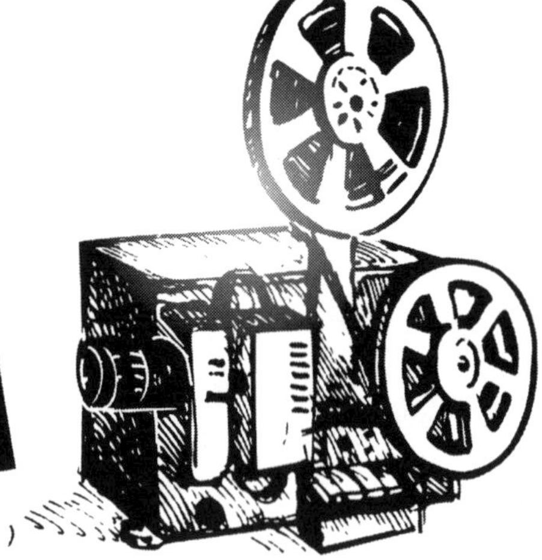

Favorite Character:

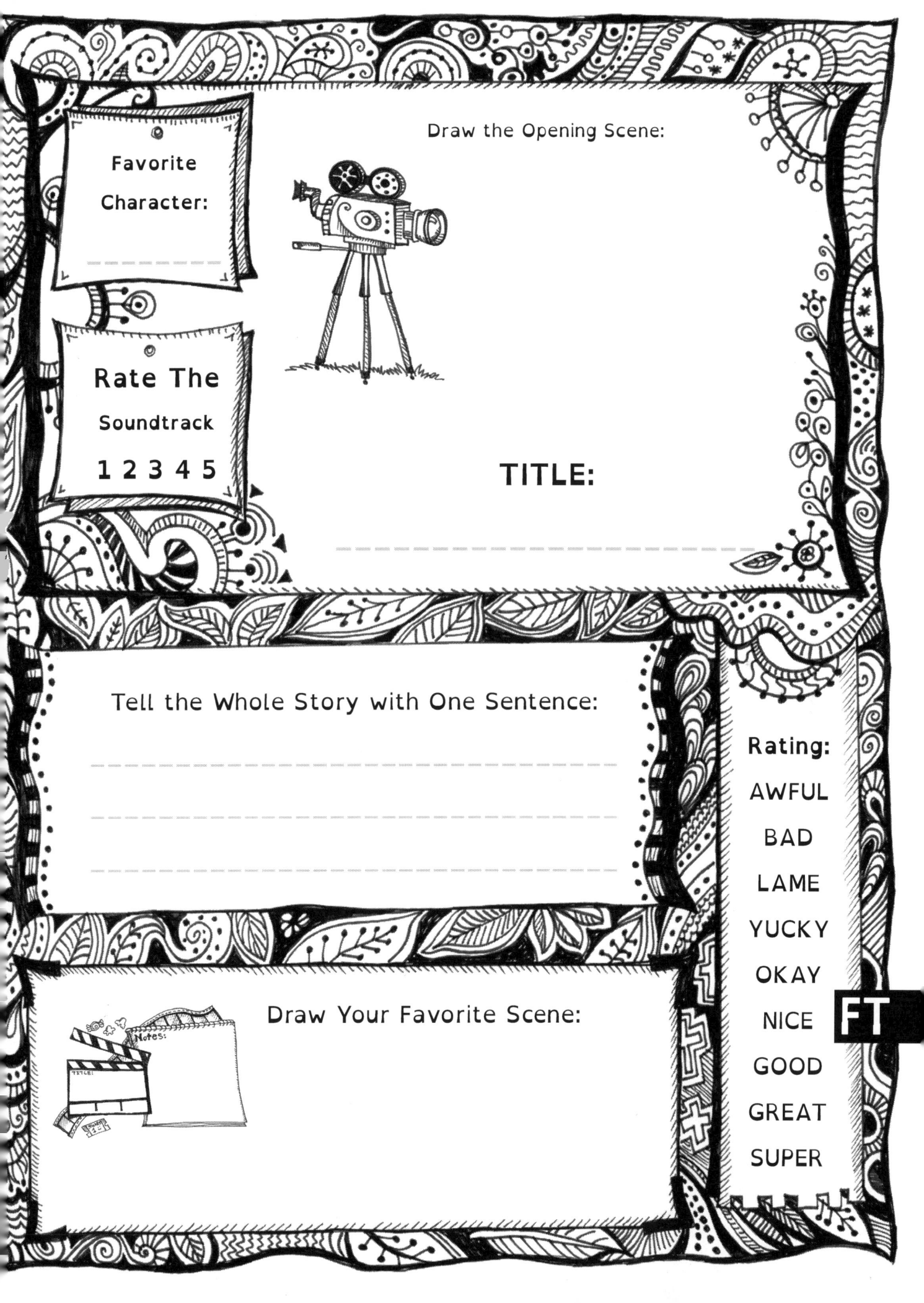

Rate The Soundtrack
1 2 3 4 5

Draw the Opening Scene:

TITLE:

Tell the Whole Story with One Sentence:

Draw Your Favorite Scene:

Rating:
AWFUL
BAD
LAME
YUCKY
OKAY
NICE
GOOD
GREAT
SUPER

Films & Tutorials

List all the Films, Tutorials & Documentaries
That you are using for your research and training:

DATE: _____TITLE: _____
TOPIC:_____
_____

DATE: _____TITLE: _____
TOPIC:_____
_____

DATE: _____TITLE: _____
TOPIC:_____
_____

DATE: _____TITLE: _____
TOPIC:_____
_____

DATE: _____TITLE: _____
TOPIC:_____
_____

DATE: _____TITLE: _____
TOPIC:_____
_____

Favorite Character:

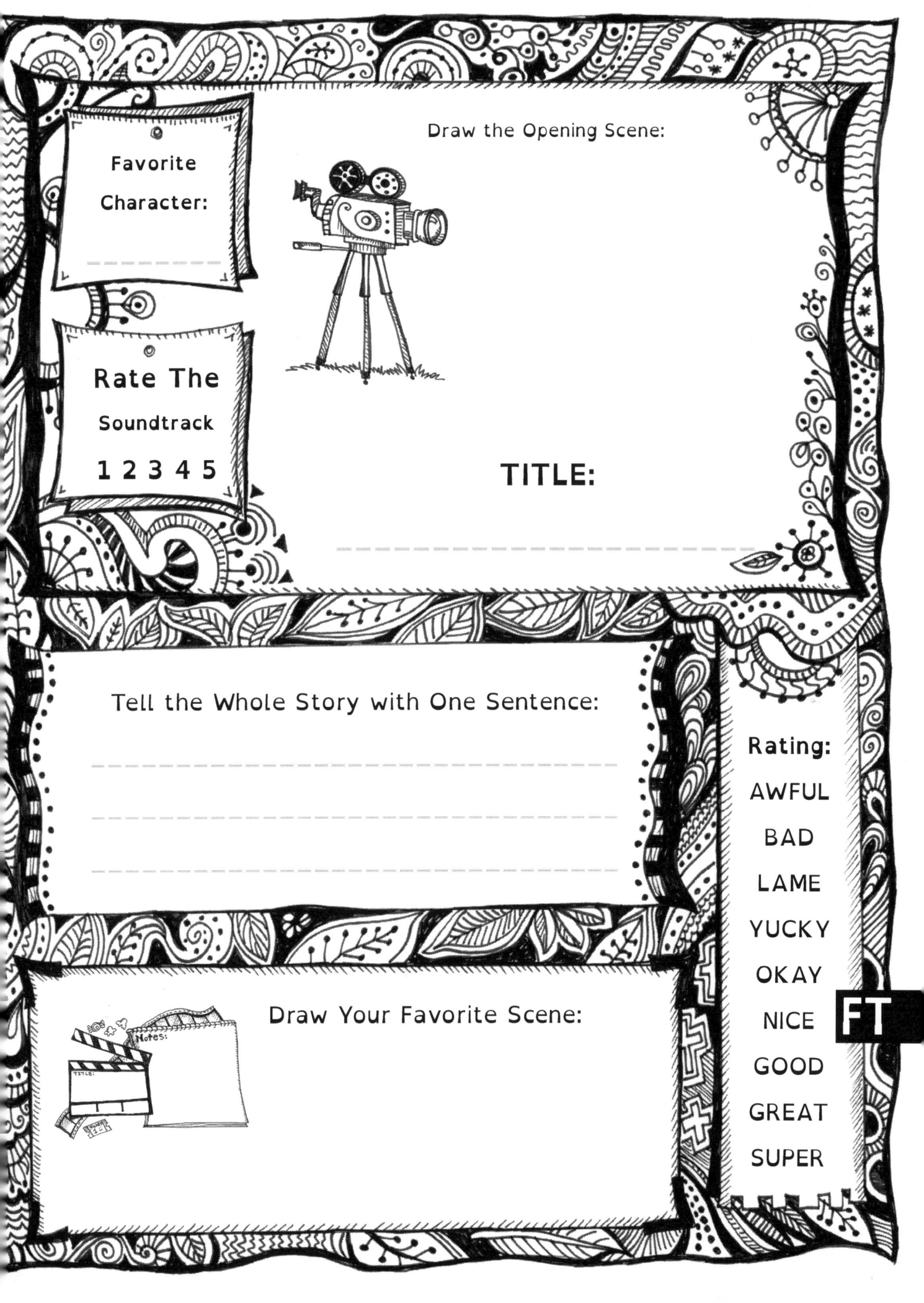

Rate The Soundtrack
1 2 3 4 5

Draw the Opening Scene:

TITLE:

Tell the Whole Story with One Sentence:

Rating:
AWFUL
BAD
LAME
YUCKY
OKAY
NICE
GOOD
GREAT
SUPER

Draw Your Favorite Scene:

Films & Tutorials

List all the Films, Tutorials & Documentaries
That you are using for your research and training:

DATE: _____TITLE: _____
TOPIC:_____
_____

DATE: _____TITLE: _____
TOPIC:_____
_____

DATE: _____TITLE: _____
TOPIC:_____
_____

DATE: _____TITLE: _____
TOPIC:_____
_____

DATE: _____TITLE: _____
TOPIC:_____
_____

DATE: _____TITLE: _____
TOPIC:_____
_____

Favorite Character:

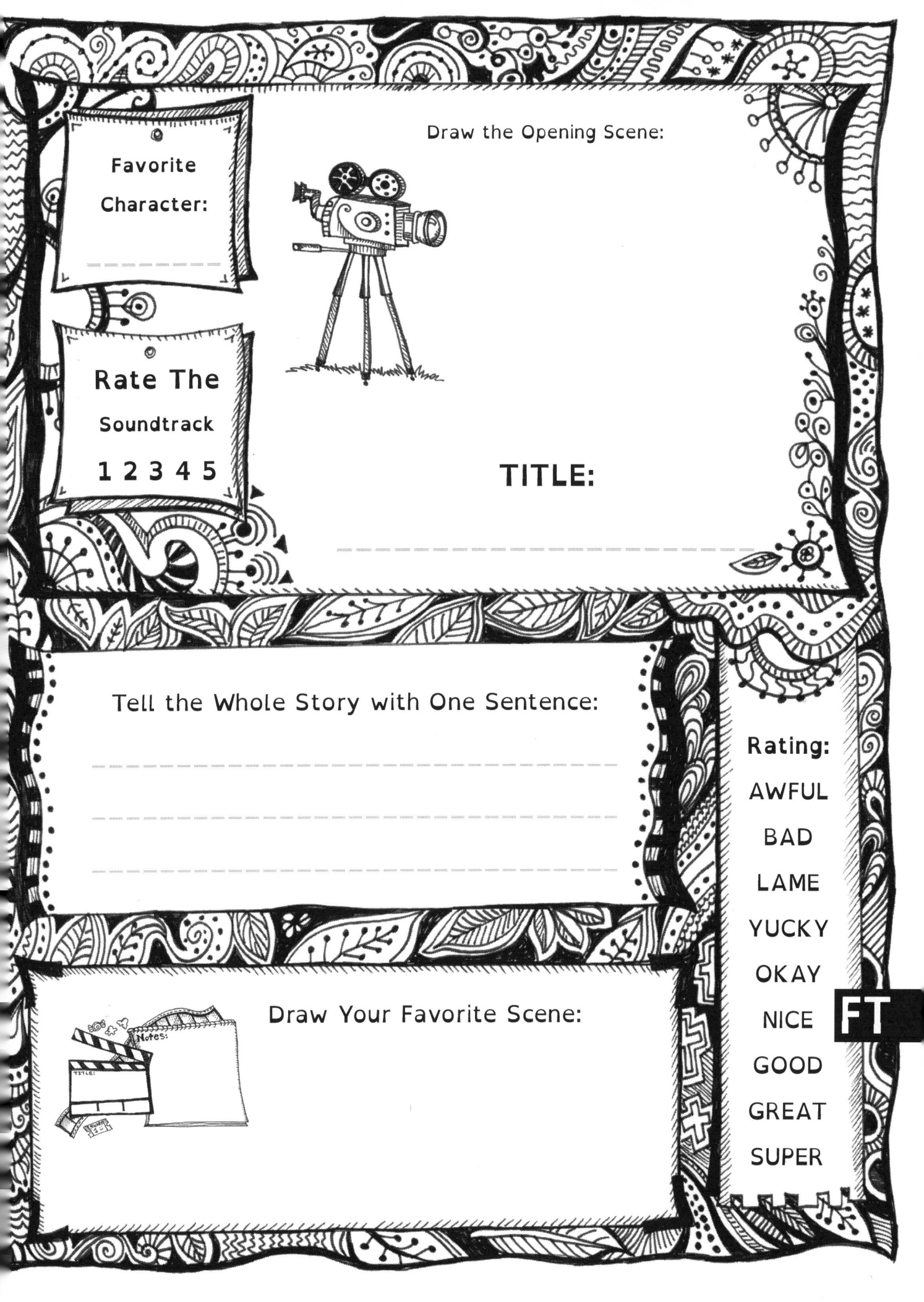

Rate The Soundtrack
1 2 3 4 5

Draw the Opening Scene:

TITLE:

Tell the Whole Story with One Sentence:

Rating:
AWFUL
BAD
LAME
YUCKY
OKAY
NICE
GOOD
GREAT
SUPER

Draw Your Favorite Scene:

FT

Films & Tutorials

List all the Films, Tutorials & Documentaries
That you are using for your research and training:

DATE: _____ TITLE: _____
TOPIC: _____
_____

DATE: _____ TITLE: _____
TOPIC: _____
_____

DATE: _____ TITLE: _____
TOPIC: _____
_____

DATE: _____ TITLE: _____
TOPIC: _____
_____

DATE: _____ TITLE: _____
TOPIC: _____
_____

DATE: _____ TITLE: _____
TOPIC: _____
_____

Favorite Character:

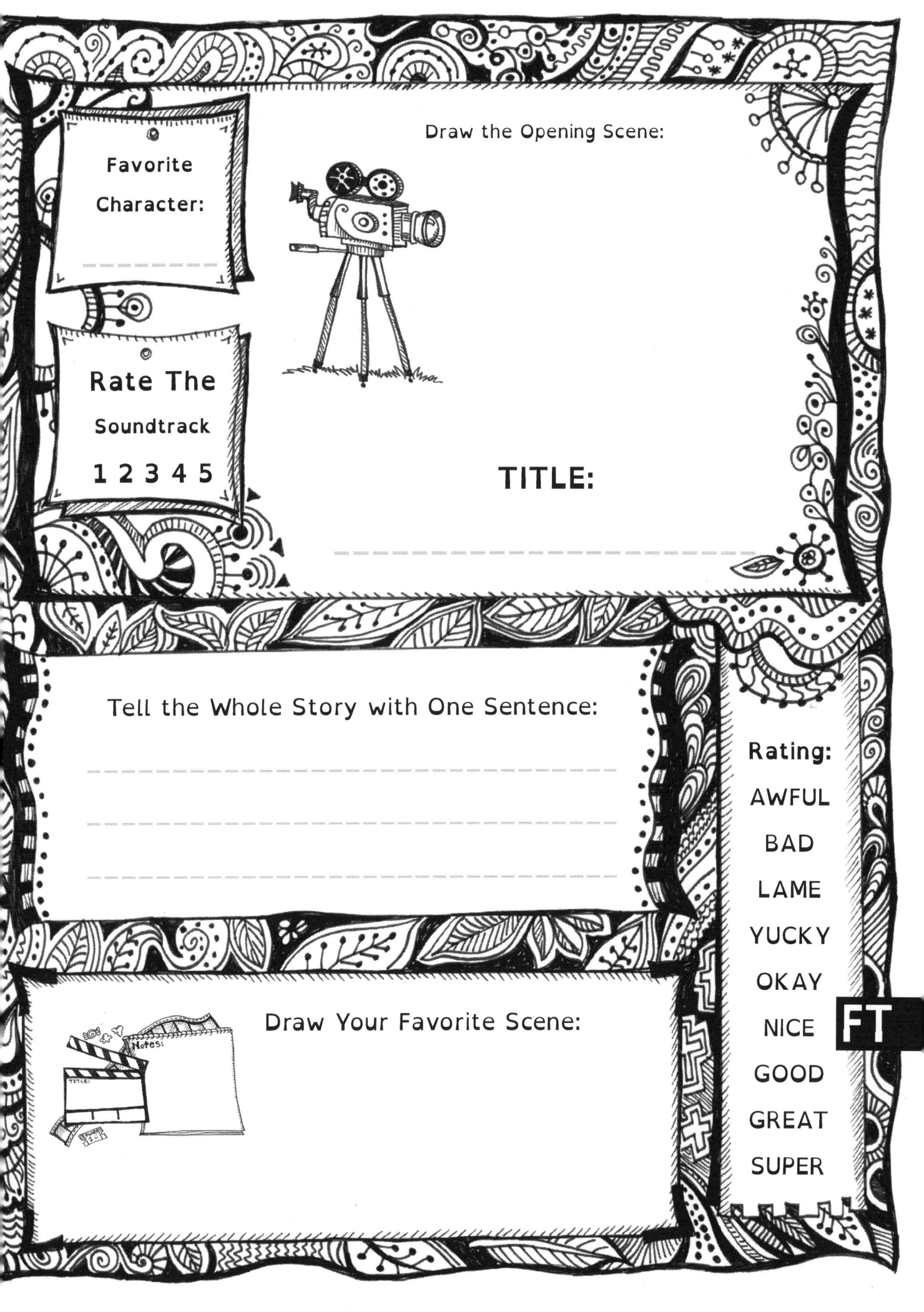

Rate The Soundtrack
1 2 3 4 5

Draw the Opening Scene:

TITLE:

Tell the Whole Story with One Sentence:

Draw Your Favorite Scene:

Rating:
AWFUL
BAD
LAME
YUCKY
OKAY
NICE
GOOD
GREAT
SUPER

FT

Films & Tutorials

List all the Films, Tutorials & Documentaries

That you are using for your research and training:

DATE: _____ TITLE: _____

TOPIC:_____

_____

DATE: _____ TITLE: _____

TOPIC:_____

_____

DATE: _____ TITLE: _____

TOPIC:_____

_____

DATE: _____ TITLE: _____

TOPIC:_____

_____

DATE: _____ TITLE: _____

TOPIC:_____

_____

DATE: _____ TITLE: _____

TOPIC:_____

_____

Favorite Character:

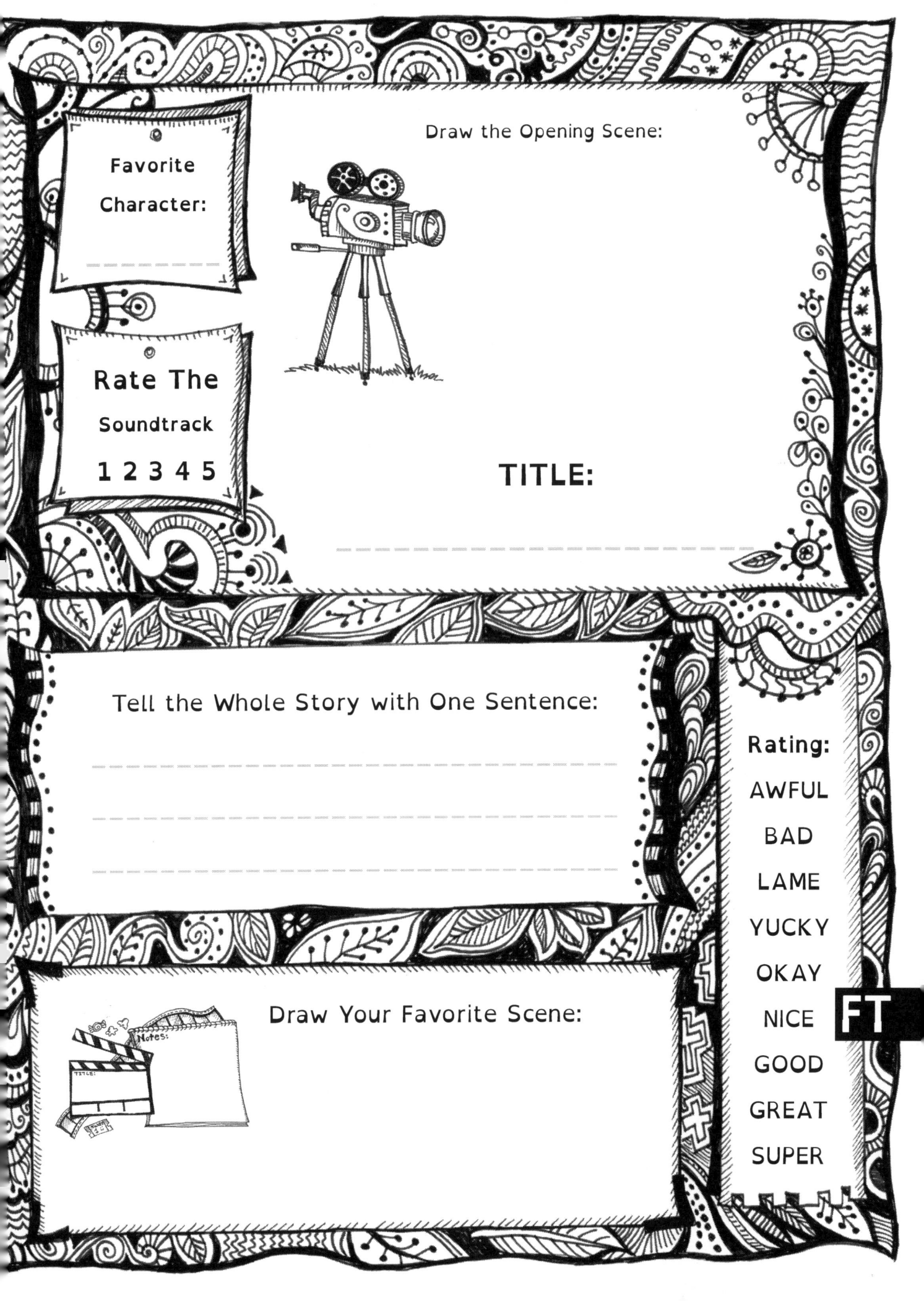

Rate The Soundtrack
1 2 3 4 5

Draw the Opening Scene:

TITLE:

Tell the Whole Story with One Sentence:

Rating:
AWFUL
BAD
LAME
YUCKY
OKAY
NICE
GOOD
GREAT
SUPER

Draw Your Favorite Scene:

Films & Tutorials

List all the Films, Tutorials & Documentaries

That you are using for your research and training:

DATE: _____ TITLE: _____
TOPIC:_____
_____

DATE: _____ TITLE: _____
TOPIC:_____
_____

DATE: _____ TITLE: _____
TOPIC:_____
_____

DATE: _____ TITLE: _____
TOPIC:_____
_____

DATE: _____ TITLE: _____
TOPIC:_____
_____

DATE: _____ TITLE: _____
TOPIC:_____
_____

Favorite Character:

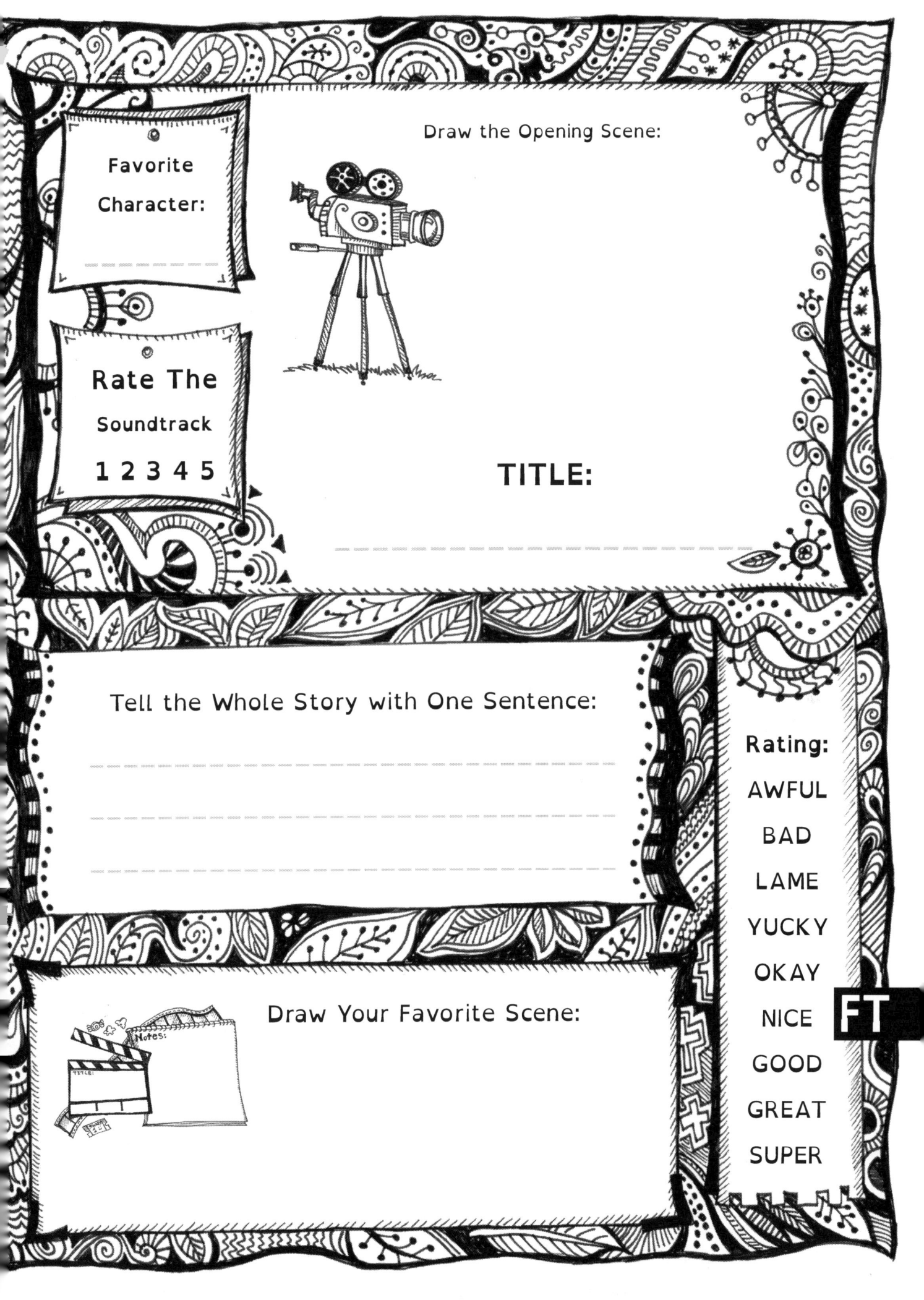

Rate The Soundtrack
1 2 3 4 5

Draw the Opening Scene:

TITLE:

Tell the Whole Story with One Sentence:

Draw Your Favorite Scene:

Rating:
AWFUL
BAD
LAME
YUCKY
OKAY
NICE
GOOD
GREAT
SUPER

Films & Tutorials

List all the Films, Tutorials & Documentaries

That you are using for your research and training:

DATE: _____TITLE: _____

TOPIC:_____

_____

DATE: _____TITLE: _____

TOPIC:_____

_____

DATE: _____TITLE: _____

TOPIC:_____

_____

DATE: _____TITLE: _____

TOPIC:_____

_____

DATE: _____TITLE: _____

TOPIC:_____

_____

DATE: _____TITLE: _____

TOPIC:_____

_____

Favorite Character:

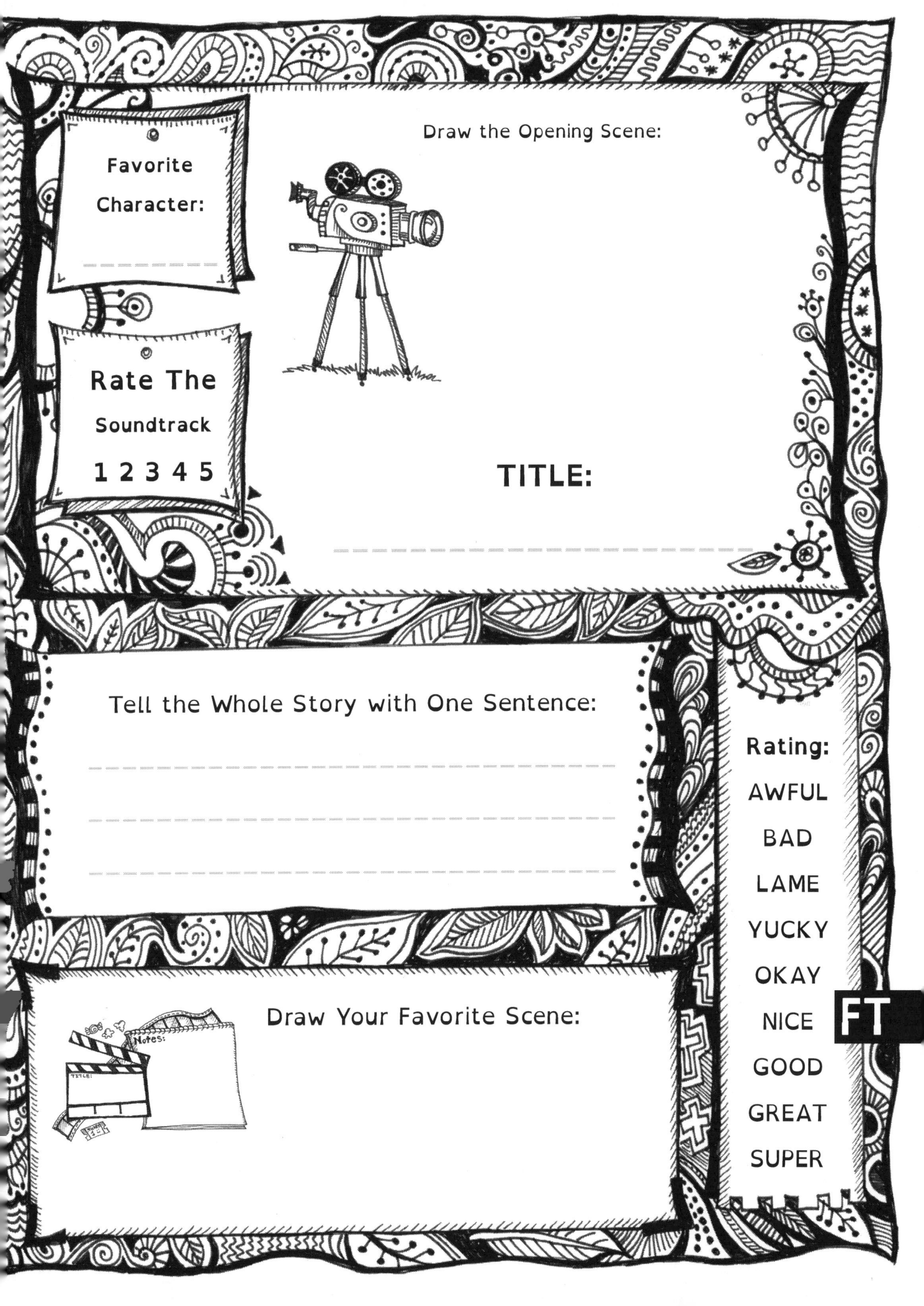

Rate The Soundtrack
1 2 3 4 5

Draw the Opening Scene:

TITLE:

Tell the Whole Story with One Sentence:

Rating:
AWFUL
BAD
LAME
YUCKY
OKAY
NICE
GOOD
GREAT
SUPER

Draw Your Favorite Scene:

Films & Tutorials

List all the Films, Tutorials & Documentaries
That you are using for your research and training:

DATE: _____ TITLE: _____
TOPIC:_____
_____

DATE: _____ TITLE: _____
TOPIC:_____
_____

DATE: _____ TITLE: _____
TOPIC:_____
_____

DATE: _____ TITLE: _____
TOPIC:_____
_____

DATE: _____ TITLE: _____
TOPIC:_____
_____

DATE: _____ TITLE: _____
TOPIC:_____
_____

Favorite Character:

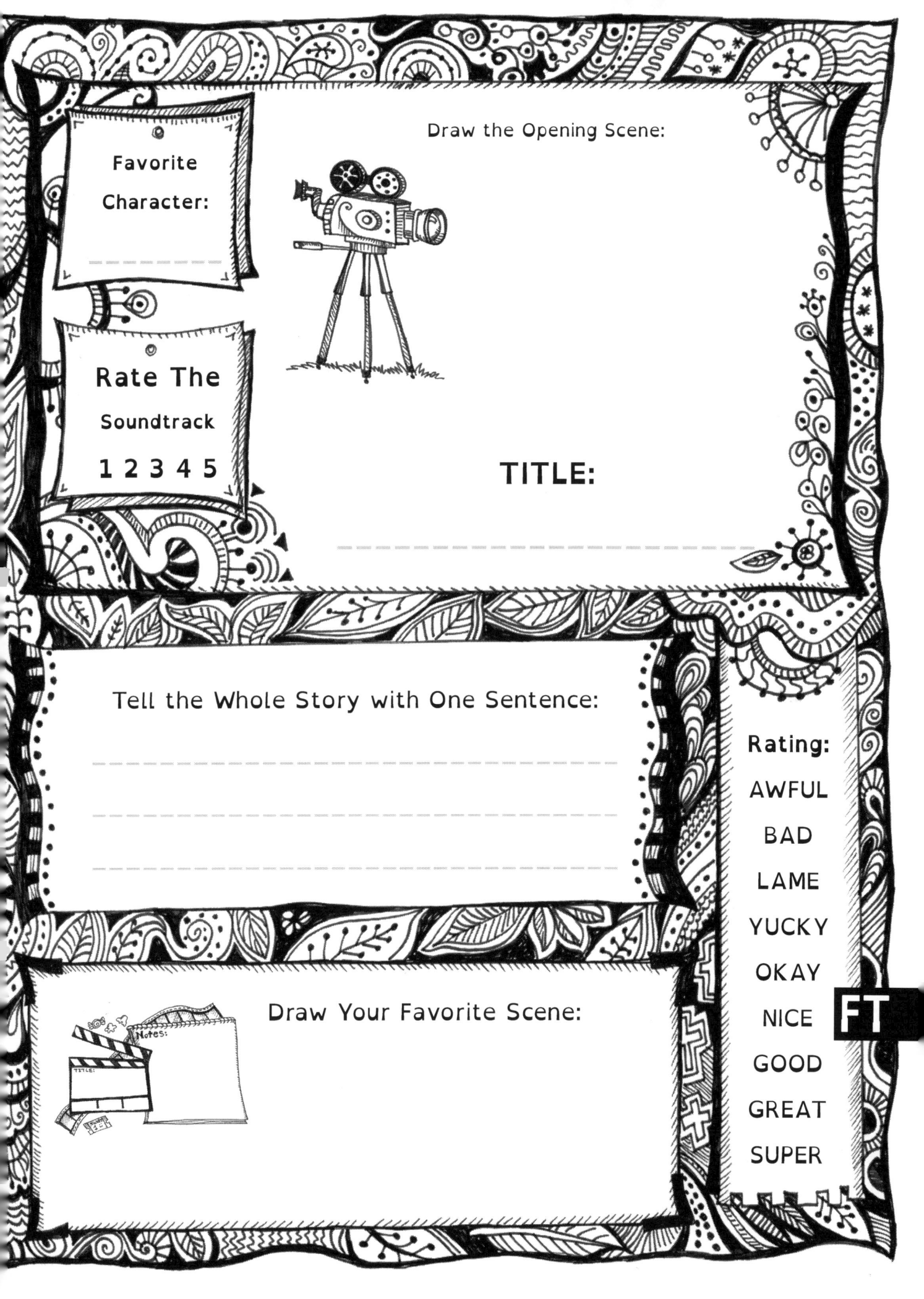

Rate The Soundtrack
1 2 3 4 5

Draw the Opening Scene:

TITLE:

Tell the Whole Story with One Sentence:

Rating:
AWFUL
BAD
LAME
YUCKY
OKAY
NICE
GOOD
GREAT
SUPER

Draw Your Favorite Scene:

Films & Tutorials

List all the Films, Tutorials & Documentaries

That you are using for your research and training:

DATE: _____ TITLE: _____
TOPIC: _____
_____

DATE: _____ TITLE: _____
TOPIC: _____
_____

DATE: _____ TITLE: _____
TOPIC: _____
_____

DATE: _____ TITLE: _____
TOPIC: _____
_____

DATE: _____ TITLE: _____
TOPIC: _____
_____

DATE: _____ TITLE: _____
TOPIC: _____
_____

Favorite Character:

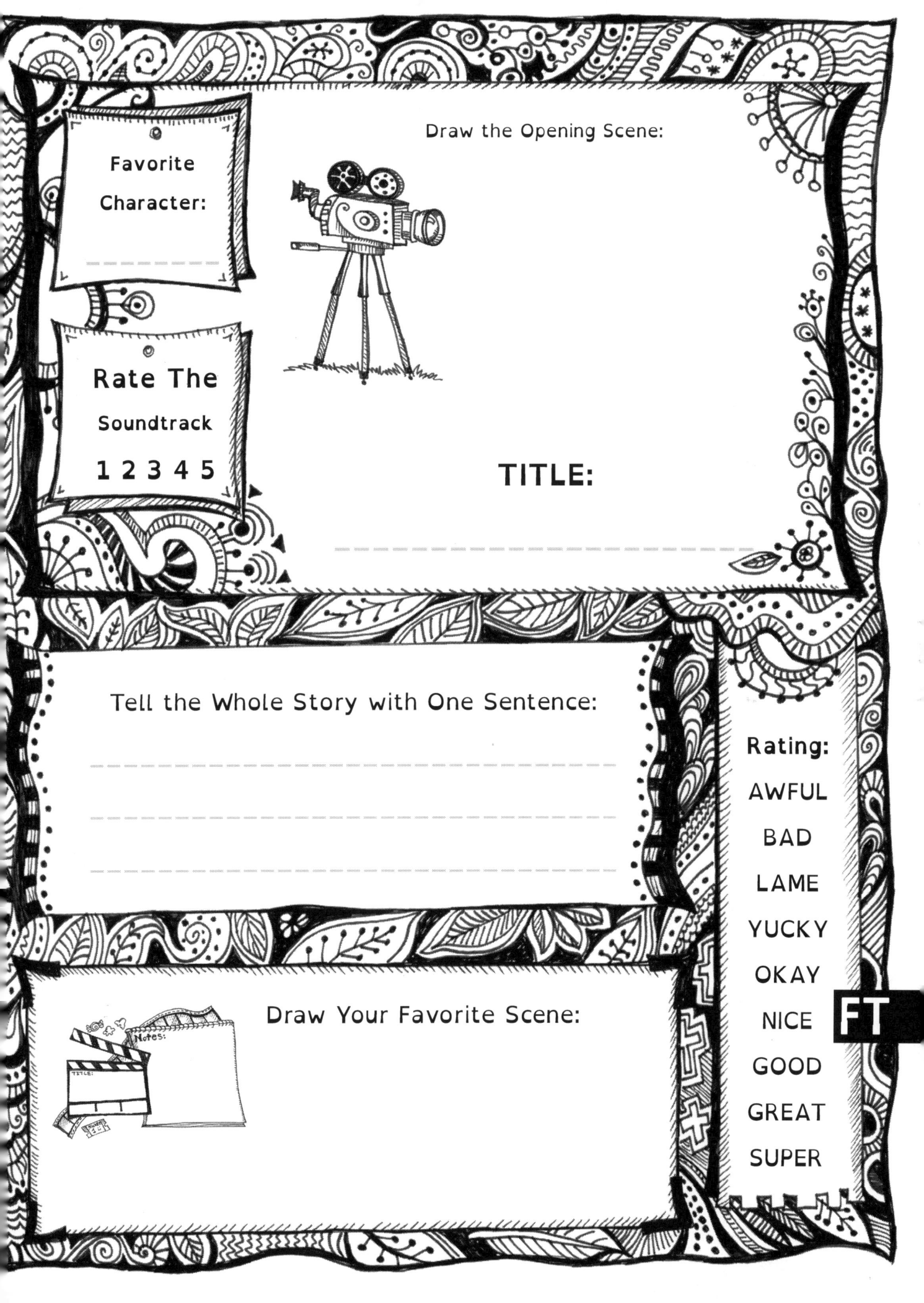

Rate The Soundtrack
1 2 3 4 5

Draw the Opening Scene:

TITLE:

Tell the Whole Story with One Sentence:

Rating:
AWFUL
BAD
LAME
YUCKY
OKAY
NICE
GOOD
GREAT
SUPER

Draw Your Favorite Scene:

Home Economics

What do you want to learn about managing a home, cooking, domestic skills, marriage, child care, shopping, and family life?

1.

2.

3.

4.

5.

Action Steps:

1. Go to the library or bookstore.

2. Bring home a stack of at least FOUR interesting books about home economics or cooking.

Choose some that have diagrams, instructions and illustrations.

Supplies Needed:

You will need pencils, black drawing pens, colored pencils, gel pens and markers.

List the Projects, Chores, and Activities
that You are Doing in Your Home Now:

_____

_____

_____

_____

_____

Choose FOUR Books About Home Economics To Use As School Books!

1. Write down the titles on each cover below.

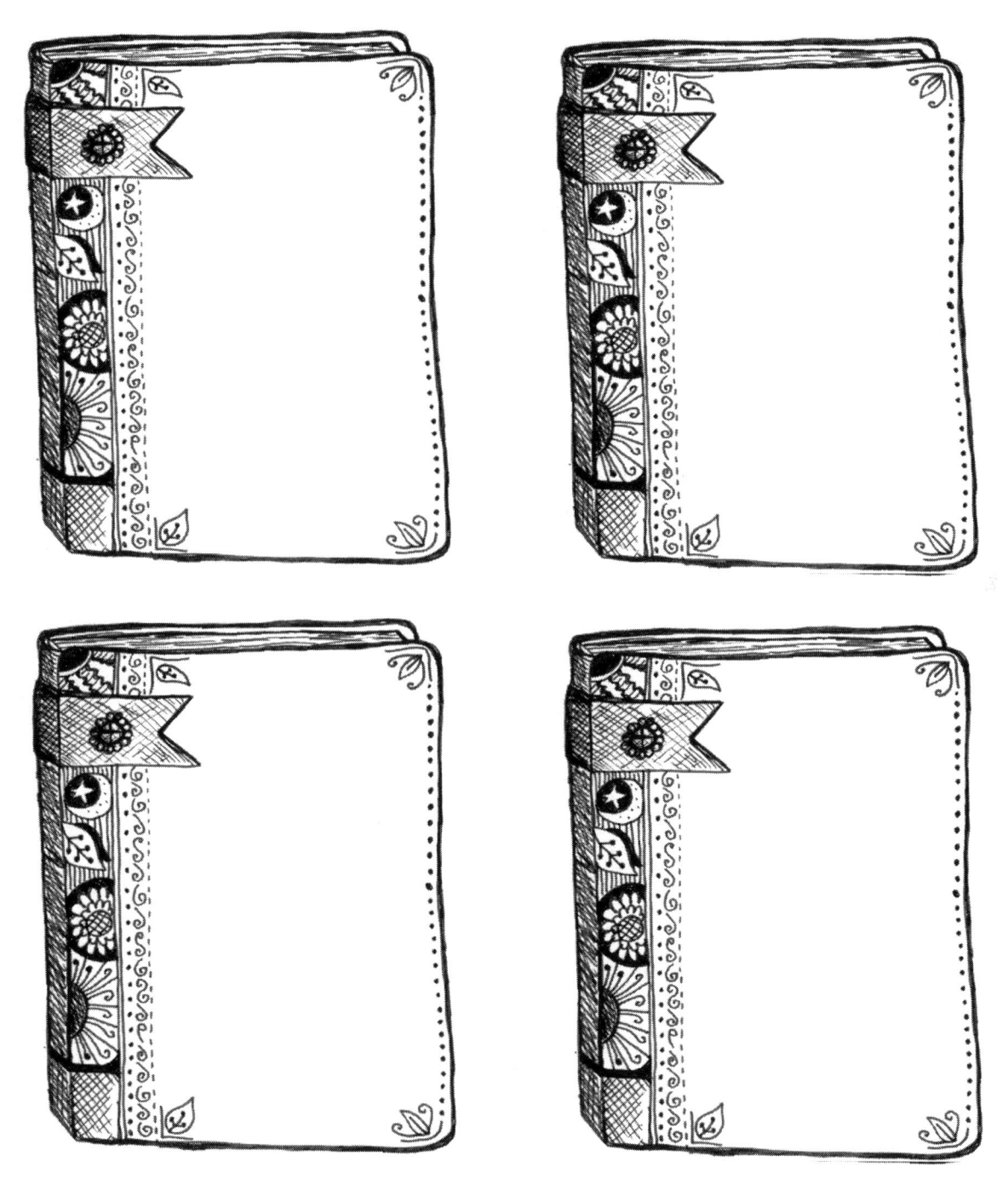

HE

Home Economics Illustrations:

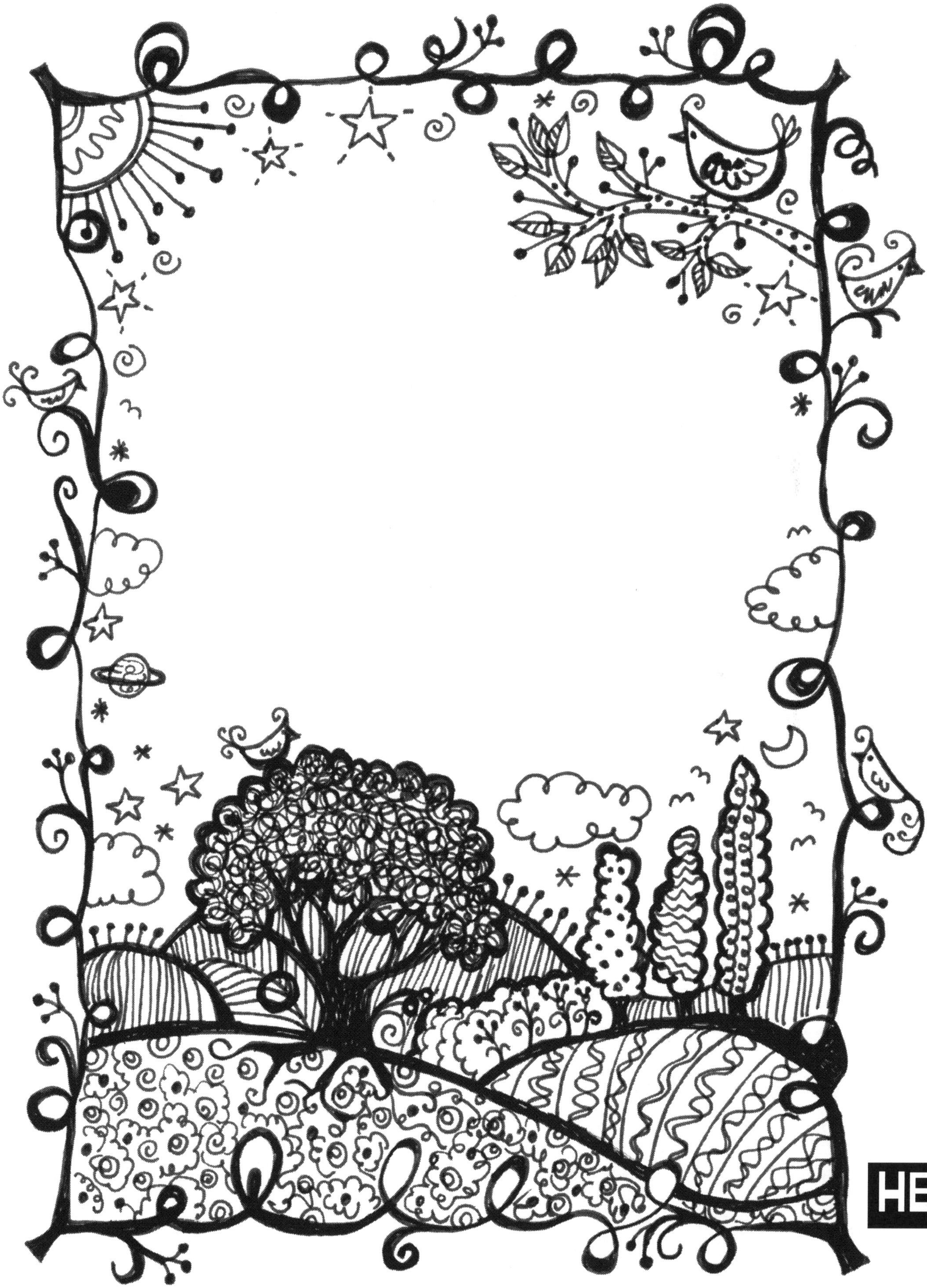

HE

Home Economics Journal

Date:____ Topic:_____

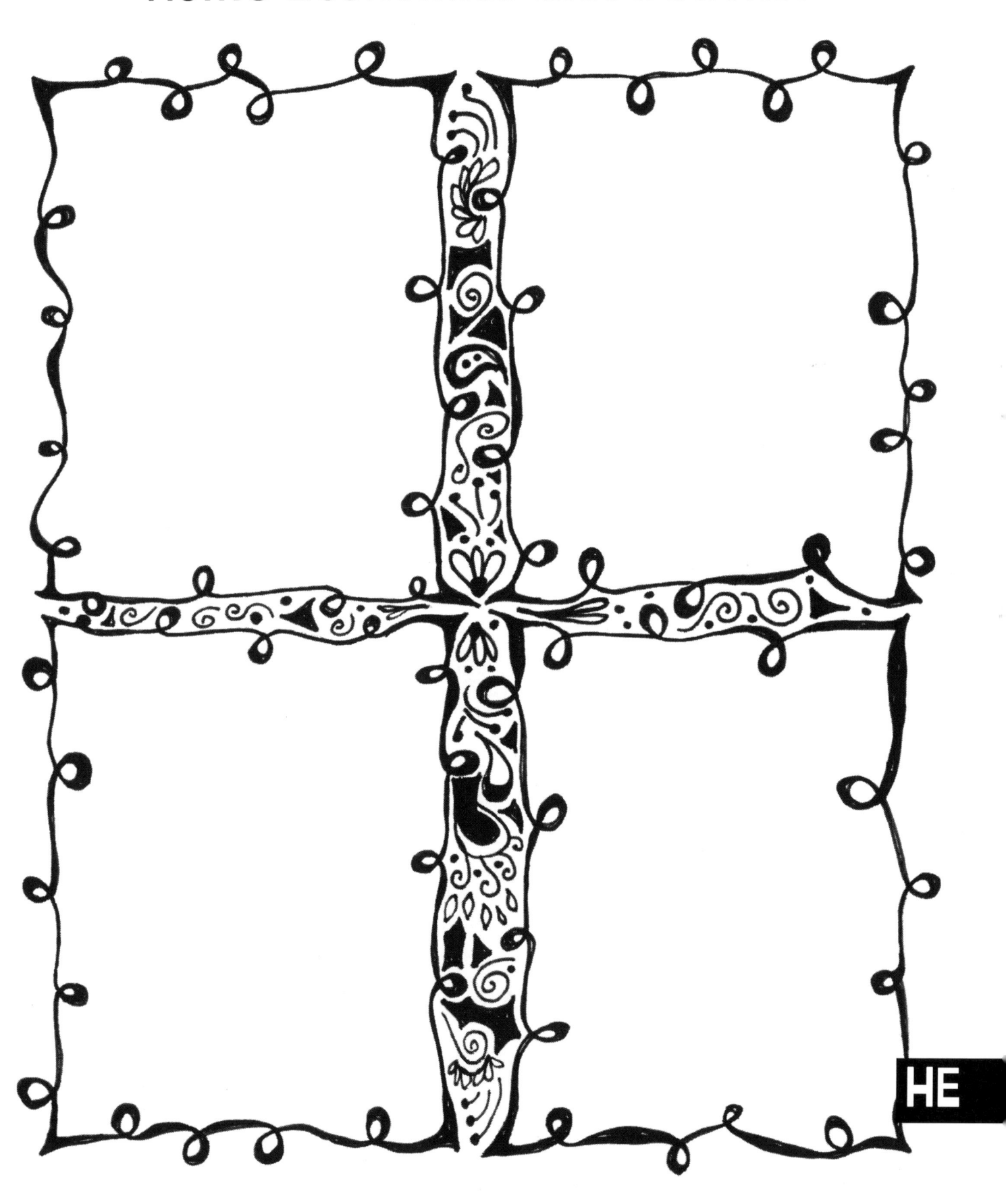

Home Economics Illustrations:

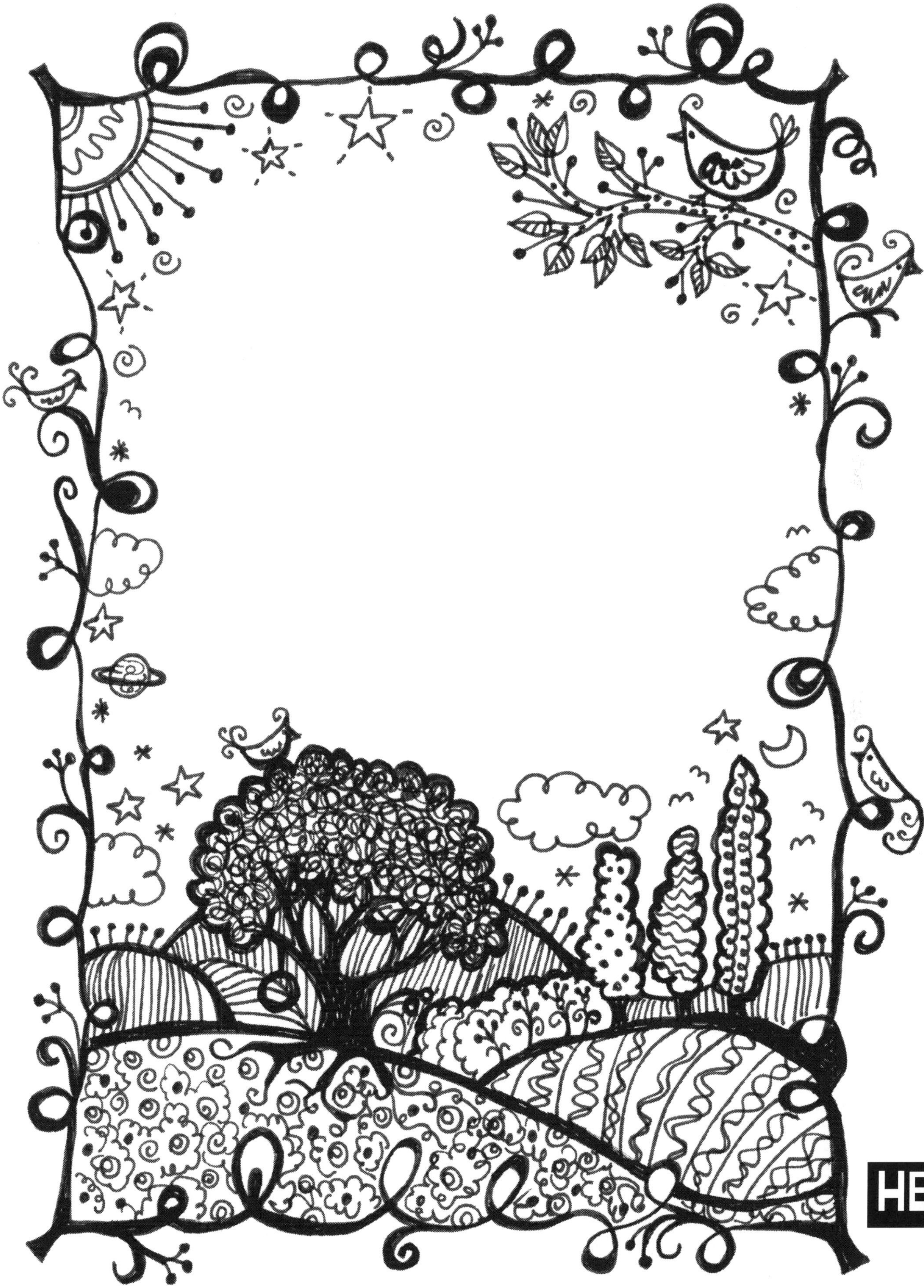

HE

Home Economics Journal

Date:____ Topic:_____

12:02
A B C
1 2 3

CLEAN

Home Economics Journal

Date:_____ Topic:_____

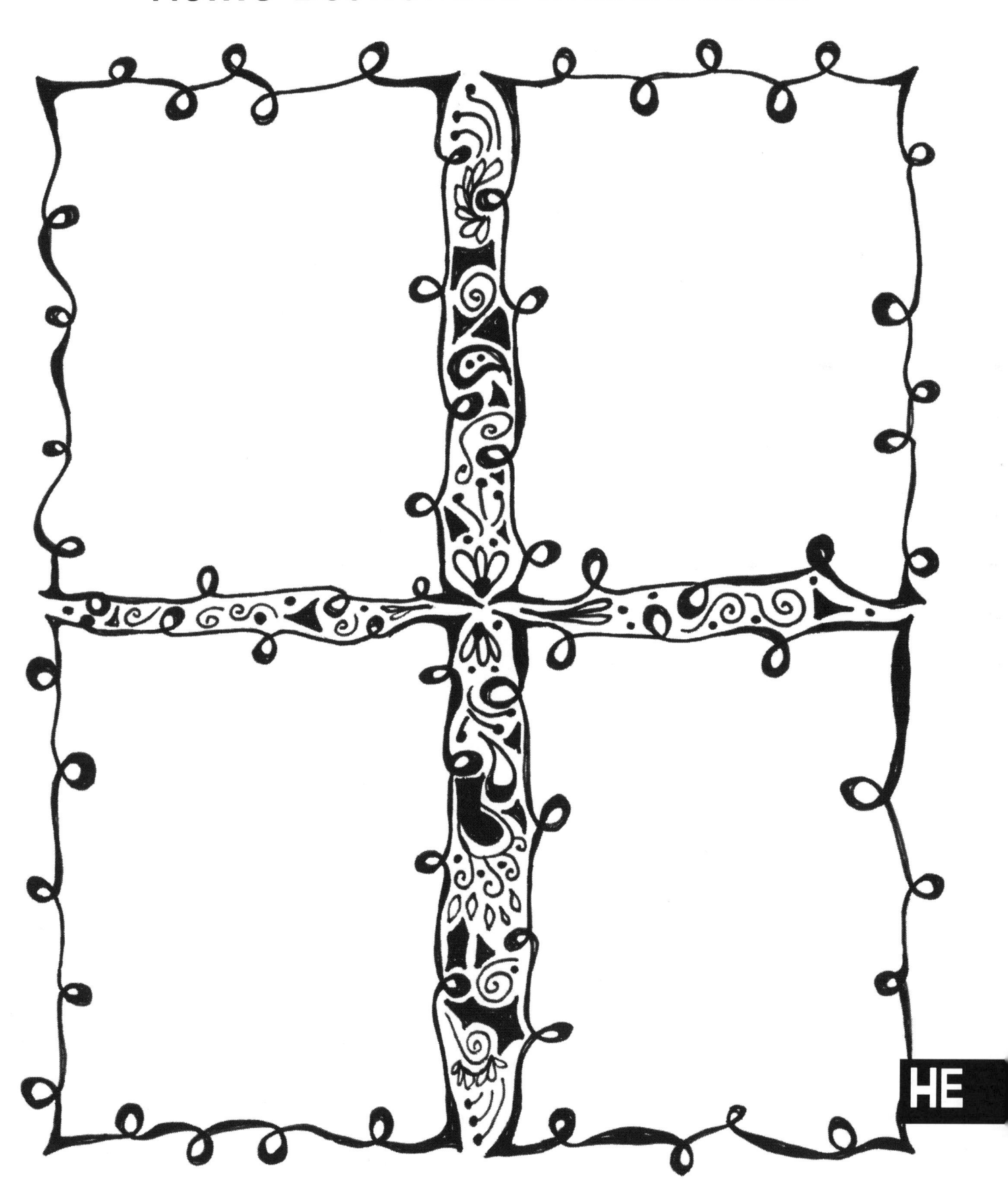

Home Economics Illustrations:

HE

Home Economics Journal

Date:____ Topic:_____

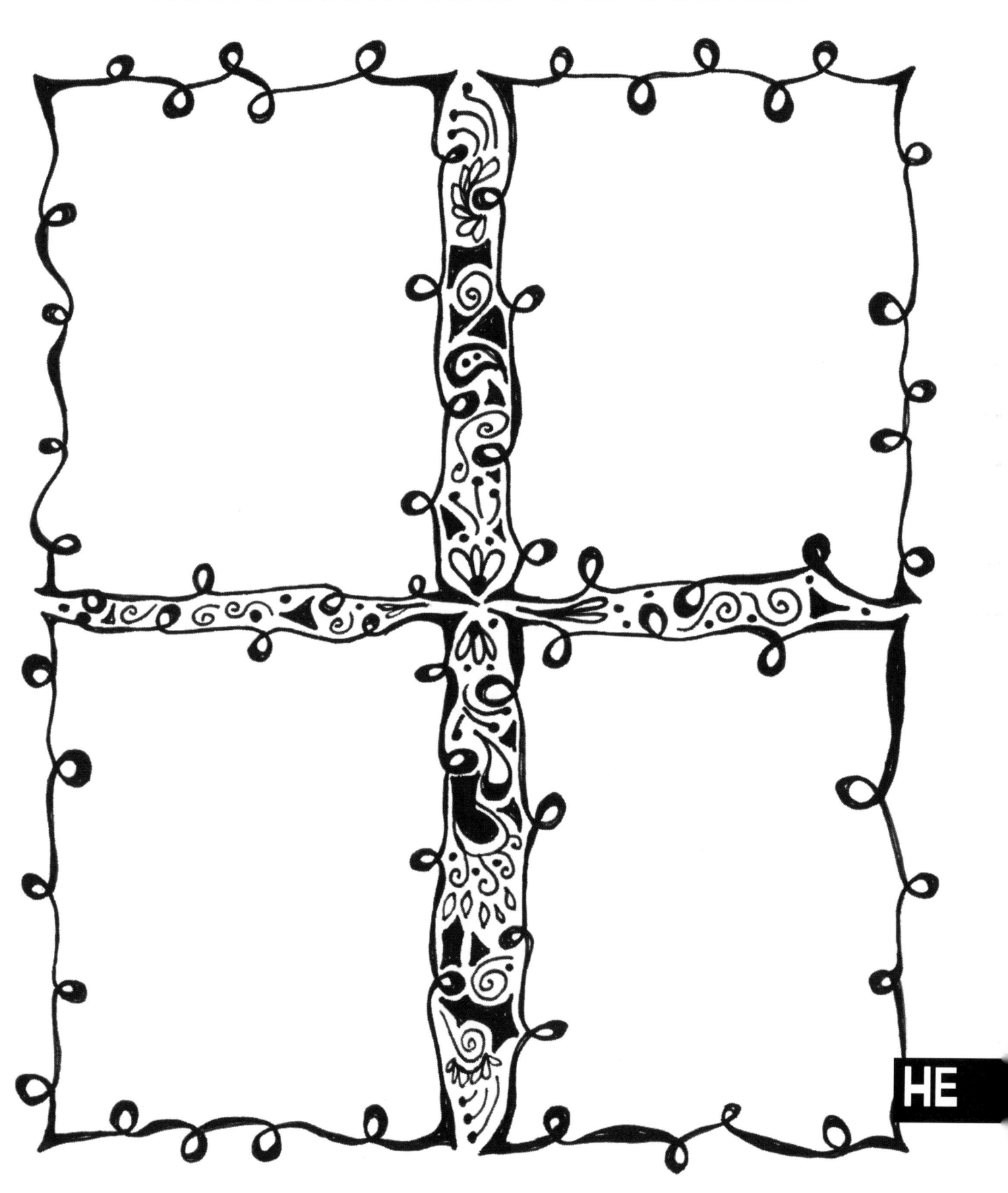

Home Economics Illustrations:

HE

Home Economics Journal

Date:____ Topic:_____

Home Economics Illustrations:

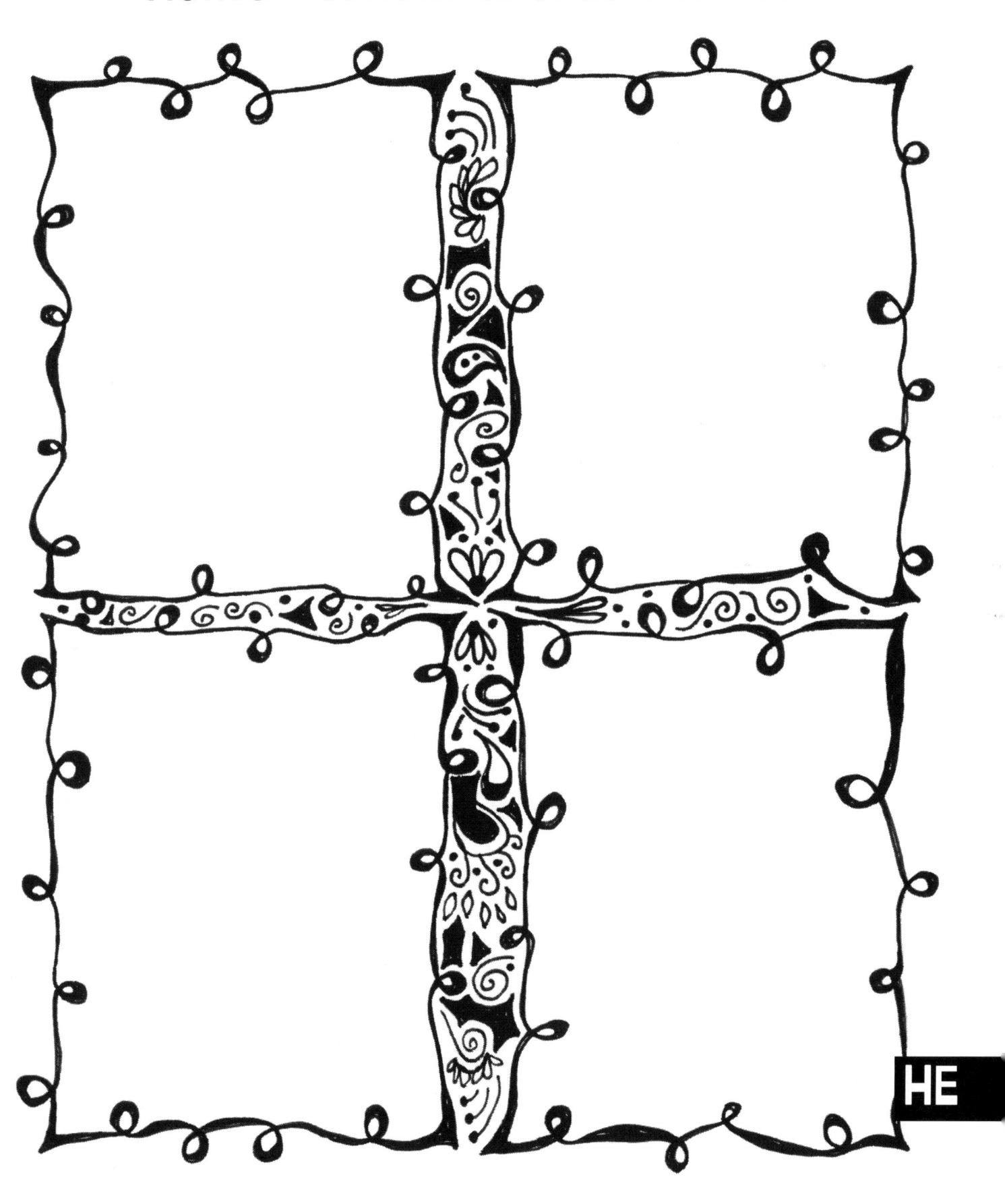

GARDEN

Complete 12 Projects

Make Something. Build Something. Invent Something. Cook Something. Investigate Something. Design Something. Plan Something. Do a Project.

Draw pictures of your projects or tape photos in this section.

List of Projects:

1 _____
_____
_____

2 _____
_____
_____

3 _____
_____
_____

4 _____
_____
_____

List of Projects:

6 _____
_____
_____

7 _____
_____
_____

8 _____
_____
_____

9 _____
_____
_____

10 _____
_____
_____

11 _____
_____
_____

P

Name of Project:

Date Started: _____ Date Complete: _____

Matherials: _____

_____

_____

Results: _____

_____

_____

Images:

Drawings, Photos & Images:

Name of Project:

Date Started: _____ Date Complete: _____

Matherials: _____

_____

_____

Results: _____

_____

_____

Images:

#2

Drawings, Photos & Images:

Name of Project:

#3

Date Started: _____ Date Complete: _____

Matherials: _____

_____

_____

Results: _____

_____

_____

Images:

Drawings, Photos & Images:

Name of Project:

#4

Date Started: _____ Date Complete: _____

Matherials: _____
_____
_____

Results: _____
_____
_____

Images:

Drawings, Photos & Images:

Name of Project:

_____

Date Started: _____ Date Complete: _____

Matherials:_____

_____

_____

Results:_____

_____

_____

Images:

#5

Drawings, Photos & Images:

Name of Project:

_____

#6

Date Started: _____ Date Complete:_____

Matherials:_____

_____

_____

Results:_____

_____

_____

Images:

Drawings, Photos & Images:

Name of Project:

_____

#7

Date Started: _____ Date Complete:_____

Matherials:_____

_____

_____

Results:_____

_____

_____

Images:

Drawings, Photos & Images:

Name of Project:

#8

_____

Date Started: _____ Date Complete: _____

Matherials: _____

_____

_____

Results: _____

_____

_____

Images:

Drawings, Photos & Images:

Name of Project:

_____

Date Started: _____ Date Complete: _____

Matherials:_____
_____
_____

Results:_____
_____
_____

Images:

\#9

Drawings, Photos & Images:

Name of Project:

#10

Date Started: _____ Date Complete: _____

Matherials:_____

_____

_____

Results:_____

_____

_____

Images:

Drawings, Photos & Images:

Name of Project:

#11

Date Started: _____ Date Complete: _____

Matherials:_____

_____

_____

Results:_____

_____

_____

Images:

Drawings, Photos & Images:

Name of Project:

#12

Date Started: _____ Date Complete: _____

Matherials:_____

_____

_____

Results:_____

_____

_____

Images:

Drawings, Photos & Images:

Date_____

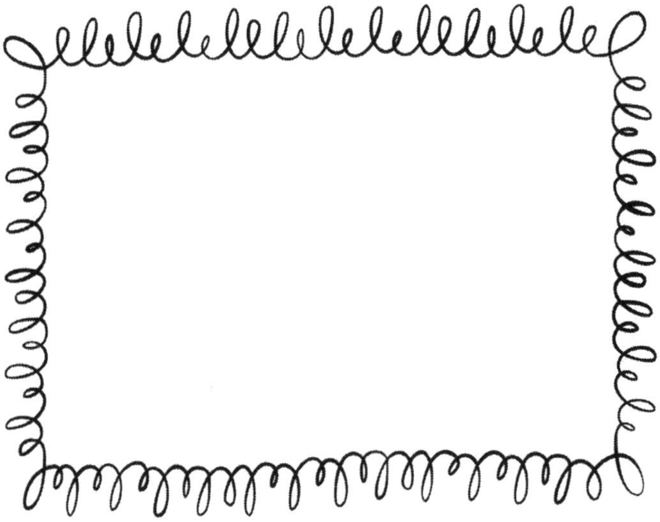

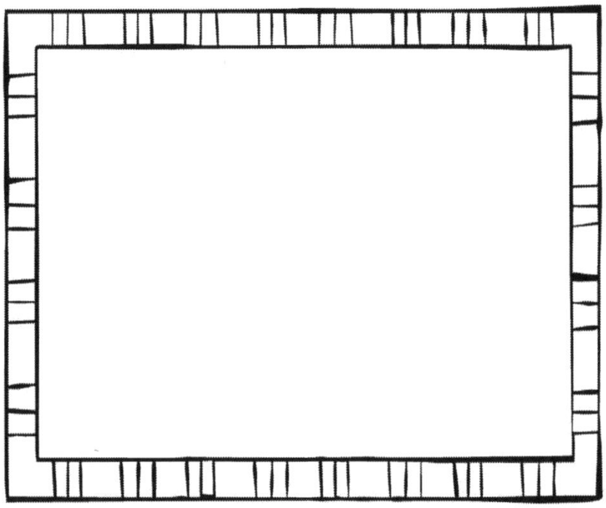
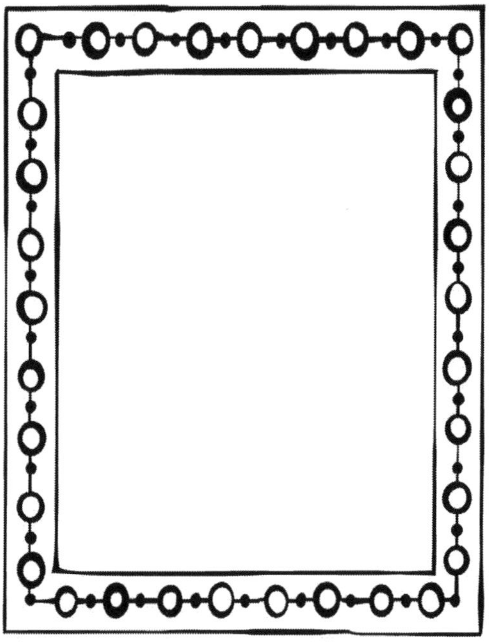

TITLE:_____

Date_____

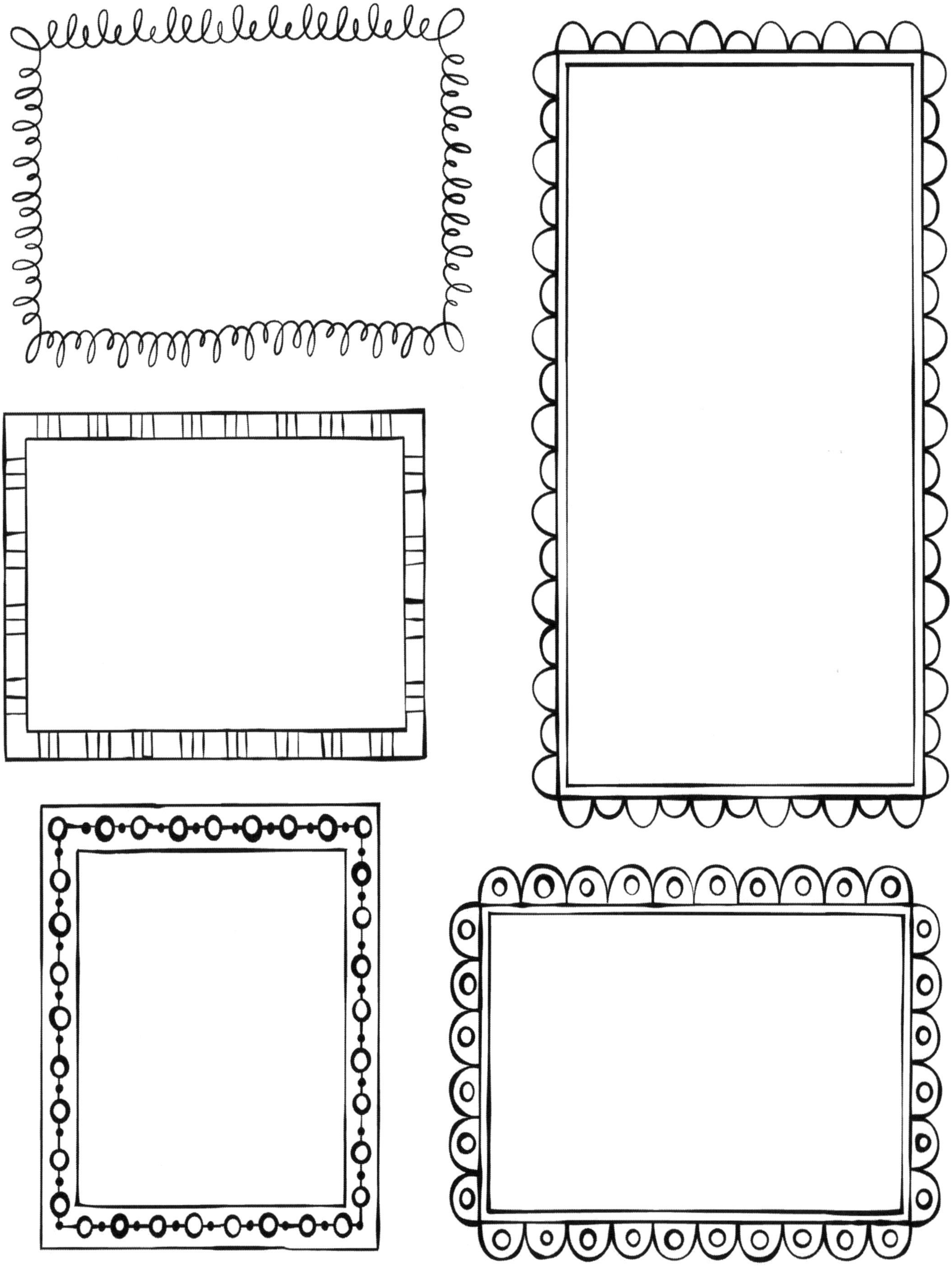

TITLE:_____

Date_____

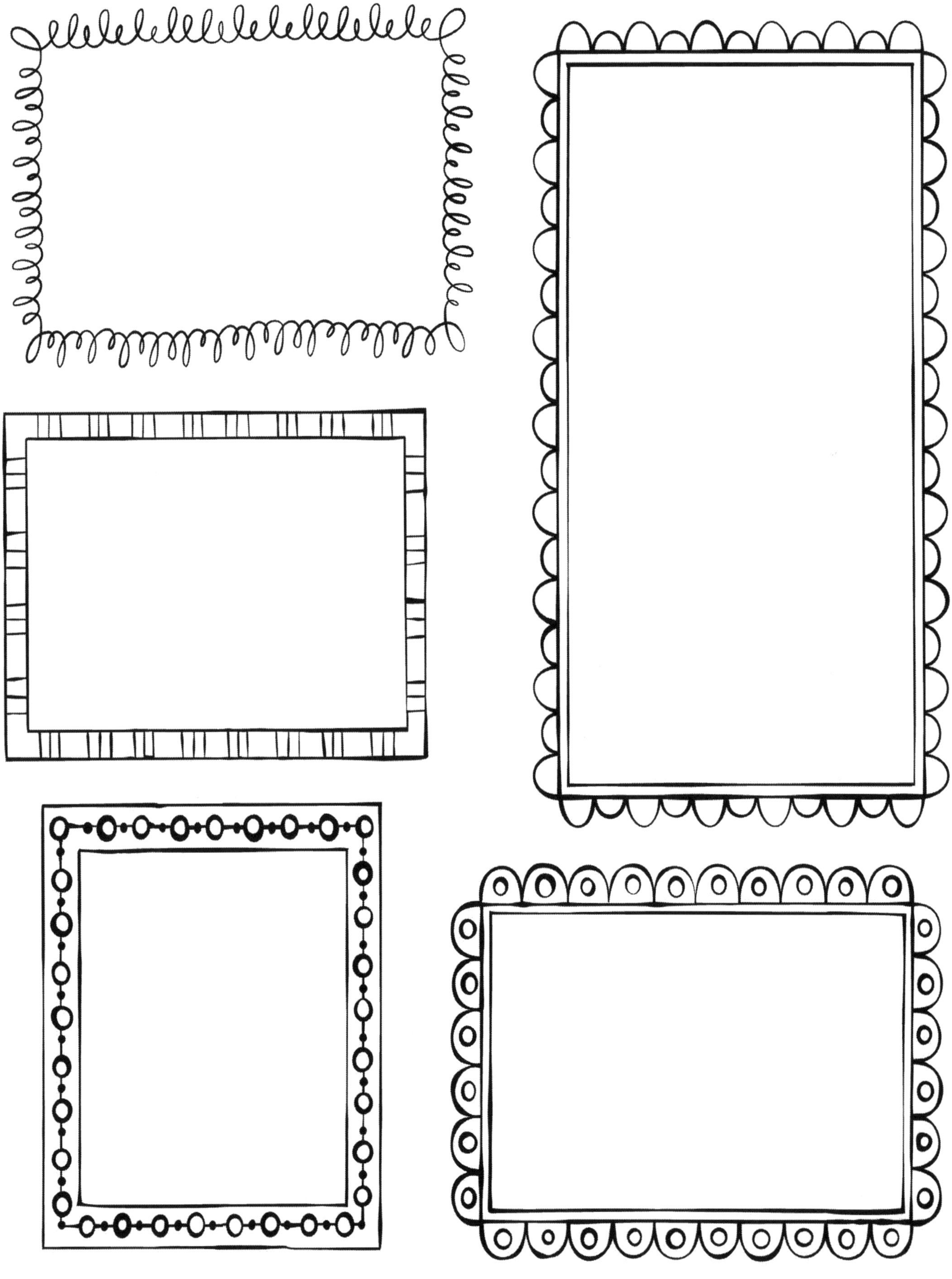

TITLE:_____

Date_____

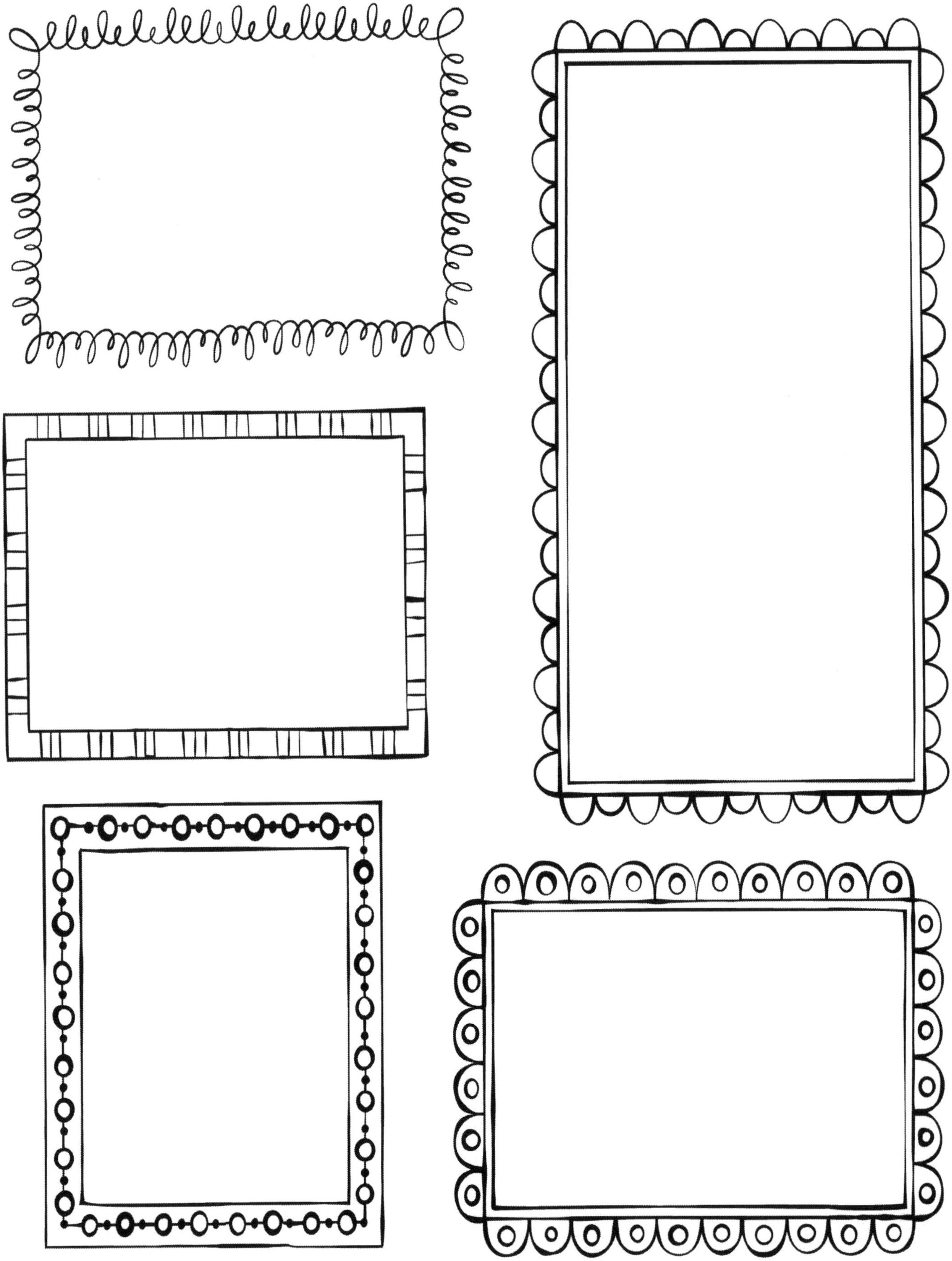

TITLE:_____

Date_____

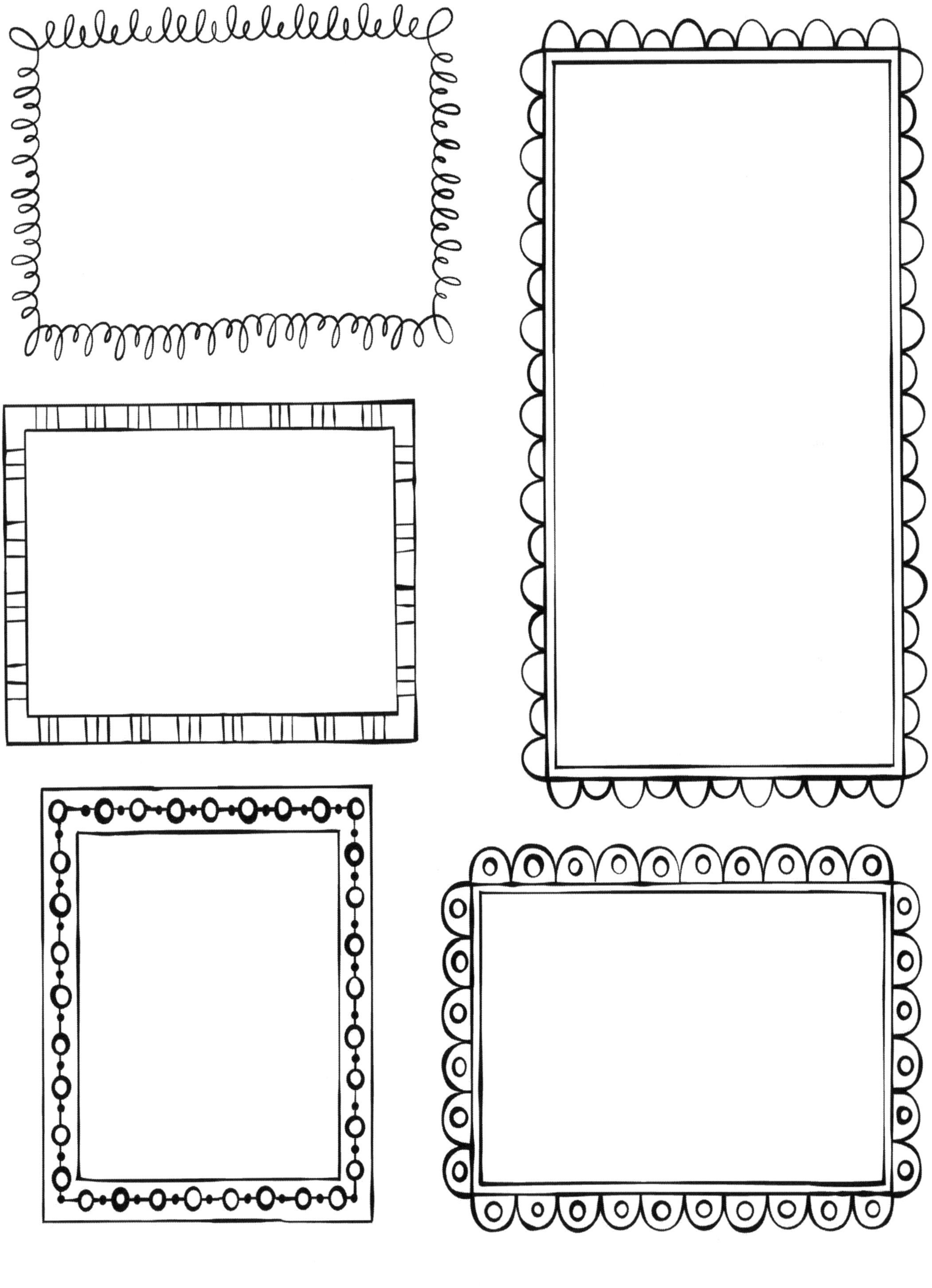

Do It Yourself Educational PORTFOLIOS

Copyright Information

Do It YOURSELF Homeschool Journal and Portfolios, and electronic printable downloads are for Home and Family use only. You may make copies of these materials for only the children in your household.

All other uses of this material must be permitted in writing by the Thinking Tree LLC. It is a violation of copyright law to distribute the electronic files or make copies for your friends, associates or students without our permission.

For information on using these materials for businesses, co-ops, summer camps, day camps, daycare, afterschool program, churches, or schools please contact us for licensing.

Contact Us:

The Thinking Tree LLC
617 N. Swope St. Greenfield, IN 46140. United States
317.622.8852 PHONE (Dial +1 outside of the USA) 267.712.7889 FAX
www.DyslexiaGames.com

jbrown@DyslexiaGames.com

Science

History

Geography & Travel

Mathematics

Business & Technology

Language Arts

Literature &

The Arts

Social Studies

Films & Tutorials

Home Economics

Projects

Made in the USA
Las Vegas, NV
19 July 2023